Forgotten Love

Inès de Warren

Forgotten Love

Preface by Chantal Delsol

Salvator
103 rue Notre-Dame des Champs
75006 Paris

Original title: *Cet amour que le monde oublie*

English edition

Yves Briend Éditeur S.A.
103 rue Notre-Dame-des-Champs
F-75006 Paris
www.editions-salvator.com
contact@editions-salvator.com

ISBN:
Cover with Christ: 978-2-7067-1296-8
Cover with a landscape: 978-2-7067-1297-5

"Write on a scroll what you see"
Revelation 1,11

Advertisement to Reader

This book does not claim to give an account of the call of the monastic Family of Bethlehem, of the Assumption of the Virgin and of Saint Bruno to live in the desert, nor to reveal the mystery of their life of silence, solitude and of liturgical and fraternal communion.

I am not an historian or a theologian, and I am even less a specialist of monastic life. I simply tried to respond to questions raised by the entry of my sister in the monastery five years ago.

The names of certain monastic sisters were changed out of respect for their hidden life. The names of others were also changed according to their wishes.

Inès de Warren

Preface

Letter to my niece, a monastic sister of Bethlehem

> The young girl – she is my soul – was introduced by the four winged demons into my bedroom, her arms bound. They were about to saw her wrists! She fainted. But Our Lord said: "Come here, for among the saints are many children that resemble you!"
>
> Max Jacob – in Defence of Tartuffe

Dear Sophie,

The question mark that you left will not easily be erased.

In our large family – there are in your generation some twenty-five first cousins who have on the whole remained quite close – the news of your departure was a startling and even for some a painful surprise. The various reactions it brought forth incite us to question our society –all families reflect, more or less, the society at large in which they live. Of course, some of us acknowledge your vocation as a plenitude, and consider it as a commitment of faith known to our religion. Others, without understanding, simply state that they are happy that you are happy, and would say the same if you had gone to the end of the world with a community of acrobats or of protectors of whales (so long as no harm to people, animals or to the earth would ensue). Finally, still others, who also do not understand, do not show the same tolerance and consider your departure as a kind of desertion, as forsaking your family and those who need you, as a voluntary semi-death: something unfortunate, discordant and disconcerting coming from a person as well-balanced as you are.

One might as well say that your choice leaves no one indifferent: is not this proper to truly significant choices?

It is a circumstance that reveals to us, under the impact of the event, the mentality of our contemporaries: that is, mainly, their abysmal atheism and their undeniable generosity.

For unbelievers – they are the great majority, including (even if a bit less) our family – Christians are strange people who should therefore remain strangers. There is of course no question of their professing their faith openly, lest they appear like fanatics or visionaries. If believers accept to live like everybody else, without saying anything or making trouble, one can easily forgive them their difference, allowing oneself just a condescending smile when they go to Mass. But should they break with their social milieu, then lightning flashes. By breaking with their social milieu I mean, for instance, having a large family or joining a contemplative community. In the first case, they will be considered either as half-wits who know nothing of the contraceptive pill, or as fanatics of the apocalypse who want to revive the Crusades. In the second case, they will be compared to followers of sects who, being under the spell of something they alone can see, choose as existence one of the many forms of death. Do you think that I am exaggerating? Not at all.

The reactions of part of our family with regards to your vocation and your choice lead me to reflect on this question: what does "entering the convent" mean in an unbelieving society like ours? How can we understand their misunderstandings?

We live – I have no need to spell it out for you – in societies where Heaven is closed. Heaven did not darken by itself. It was closed by decree, as Marie Balmary says. You only need to read the Preamble to the Universal Declaration of Human Rights of 1948: "The advent of a world where human beings will be free to speak and believe, delivered from terror and misery, has been proclaimed as the highest aspiration of man." The hope for an earthly world freed from oppression and hunger is thus given by proclamation as the highest aspiration of man! That is what it means to close Heaven by decree.

However, let us not consider, we Christians, ourselves as pure victims of a modern plot to eliminate transcendence. We ourselves have also been the zealous instruments of our own ruin. For the past two centuries (one could even start earlier with numerous references), a great number of Christians have reduced faith to a form of utility. That is what could be found in times past with Machiavelli and also in the first half of the nineteenth century with Tocqueville, and that is what we still find in our families in the twentieth century: "Religion, biblical history, the resurrection, all of that is probably false, but it is useful that good people should believe it in order to safeguard society; as for me, being the head of the family, I am of course more enlightened, I know that all of that is a vulgar farce; but I maintain at least a religious practice in my family, so that everybody will be well-behaved." The responsibility of "sociological religion" and of the spirit of Charles Maurras, has been decisive in the twentieth century for the collapse of religious faith. What is more, the whole of history clearly shows that reducing belief to mere utility is a deadly disease for religion – when two oracles cannot meet without a smile, as Plutarch says... Thus the devotion to Charles Maurras, so frequent in our circles, has opened the way to religion being replaced by ethics, as is the case today, in other words, to a form of orientalism of the West.

This is not the place to hold forth on all of that. But the result is the closing of heaven. The aspiration to eternity and to transcendence are now considered as pure fiction, unworthy of rational human beings, and monotheistic religion has become, as Borgès says, "a chapter belonging to the literature of the fantastic." Hence, for us, everything is meant to take place exclusively here below. Our life projects are therefore considerably transformed, compared to those of the former Christian society. What matters for us is to be happy, to be successful, to be honored here and now, for there is no other world, no other values that would be superior to these. In this frame of mind, the old saying "We have but one life" becomes particularly significant. Everything is accomplished and completed here below. Consequently, the wish to attribute exterior finalities to this unique and exclusive existence is considered as sacrificing what is real to mere imagination. Our era is so sure that any transcendence is but fiction and deceit that it is seen as a complete sham.

That being the case, "entering the convent" becomes something absolutely incongruous and unfortunate, an aberration in a world that is sure of its radical immanence. And it is necessary to say even more: in so far as the death of God is understood as a victory over the demons of clerical imposture and popular naivety, anything that seeks to regain this victory appears as a sickly and pathetic return to the abyss from which we so painfully managed to emerge. "Killing God" was a difficult and costly liberation: let us not descend the very steps that we have already climbed... Thus a believer who is not lukewarm not only is wrong, but also insults the progress that always goes in the direction of atheism. It will be admitted that someone might invoke the "Christian culture" to provide the landscape of their life; but a genuine fervor is deemed out of place.

One shall not for all of that underestimate our era to the point of believing that, because it does not need transcendence, it would have fallen into kind of nihilism. This point is very important for it explains to a large extent the contemporary mentality. Since the era of the French Revolution, which was truly the starting-point of modernity, the Christians among us have had the tendency to consider societies without God as societies on the edge of the abyss. This comes in fact as a rather natural conclusion: faith in God has been our horizon for two thousand years and has structured our whole social and historical existence, from politics to acts including parenthood and education. How then could we easily believe that the loss of God would not imply the loss of everything else? That is what Dostoevsky said when he affirmed, "if God does not exist, everything is possible," implying that ethics disappear together with God. Nietzsche also suggested that when he wrote: "Who gave us a sponge to entirely blot out the horizon?" thus affirming that with the death of God the sense of life and its finalities are also blotted out.

Yet I believe that it is not so. Even if it would be in a way more satisfying for Christians to think: "Either the hills or us will fall." Our era is not deprived of ethics. On the contrary, it has partly replaced the zeal of faith by zeal for the good. That is why I said that our atheists are generous. How did that happen?

Today, most people think that professing one's faith equals not living it. Why is that? Because the previous era was used to giving contrary testimony. For a long time, people lived as though faith were merely a matter of speech. How often did we meet people whose spirit was fervent for dogma but slow to feel compassion; so attentive to God and deprived of attentiveness towards beings of flesh and blood, when they indeed made claims to love; ready for all far-away crusades and yet so indifferent to the crusades of the heart that flourished beneath their windows. We even began to think that those strange believers brandished their faith to dissimulate less noble motives... For it is indeed written: "If you have no Love, you are but a clashing cymbal." And finally, the more recent modernity, our own time, has put an end to the grief and incoherence of those times without love. We have taught our children thoughtfulness and compassion. The former world has been completely crushed, as a sign of a barbarous past never to return. Yet that love was displayed under the form of sickly sentimentality and quite often of weakness. A good balance is always impossible to achieve. Yet a curse that seemed definitive has been eradicated. Our children do not have faith, because they think that they have to choose between faith and love. It is a shame that they are reduced to such an alternative. It is for us now to put things straight, by showing that both terms are, on the contrary, very much bound together. It will take us a very long time and much patience, for what is quickly destroyed takes ages to be rebuilt.

Of course, one could criticize the kind of *sui generis* "good" with which present day ethics nourishes itself. One might also mention, and rightly so, that these ethics have no stable foundation, at least compared with those of two thousand years of Christianity. That is the fact. People of our time value exclusively thoughtfulness toward others – I mean genuine thoughtfulness, not speeches about it. That is why many people close to you would have perfectly understood if you had committed yourself to an order that is socially active: that you give your life to educating children in the street or to helping people who live in slums near or far. There is no need of a religious vocation to give oneself to this type of action, since many people commit themselves, temporarily or not, to what is called "humanitarian aid." Seen from this perspective, your religious vocation, viewed as an ethical vocation, would have sounded more familiar and, if I dare say, more reassuring…

In the end, the purpose of our era is to save ethics from the grip of religion and to enthrone ethics as a goddess while destroying religion. Saving the Good from the grip of faith, which is supposed to bring it to nought. Which is finally an ironical way of setting before their truth those defenders of the "useful" or sociological religion of which I have just spoken. A way of replying to them would be: since you use faith as an instrument to preserve good morals, you might as well throw faith away all together, it would be less hypocritical.

Thus entering a monastery in order to give one's whole existence in praying for the world appears as a gloomy tale. Providing free meals for the homeless, yes, a thousand times yes; but the communion of saints, behold an extravagance that is ludicrous, and which, besides, seems to be a good pretext to avoid taking care of others.

Moral exigency has become so imposing today that an ideal exterior to it, which would be liable to rob part of its daily duties, is suspected of having obscure intentions by this very fact. In *Existentialism is a humanism,* Sartre's hero asks the question: "Should I go to war to defend my homeland or stay here to take care of my sick and lonely mother?" Faced with such a question, our present time no longer hesitates, it does not bother to defend the homeland or any other finality or value beyond the intimate circle. That is why it has become impossible to admit that religious should be exempt from caring for their kin on the grounds of their religious vocation. In a general way, our contemporaries no longer accept that one's family be sacrificed for one's homeland or religion.

There is still more, for the misunderstanding exists on several levels. Western societies are at present haunted by the consequences of two totalitarianisms. They have perceived that the essential crime of totalitarianism is to impose its dominion on people's conscience; in other words, to forbid Antigone to exist. What they, of course, have not perceived is that modern atheism is directly responsible for totalitarianisms because it erases natural law (i.e., Antigone is possible) so as to leave room only for the positive law (i.e., the State is always in the right). Contemporary societies have only seen this one thing: that there is a link, as though genealogically speaking, between the Church's perversions and totalitarianisms or, to put it another way, between the Great Inquisitor of Seville and Moscow's trials. They have realized that what made the Nazi horror possible was the fact that personal conscience was erased (the executioners obeyed their superiors and their obedience served as their conscience). And so the International Penal Court was established to judge those who forgot their personal conscience and the leitmotiv of the I.P.C. could be: "No more Abraham! Why Abraham?" Because Abraham, an Old Testament hero who has become a European hero, was ready to commit a heinous crime in allegiance to God, in other words, without referring to his personal conscience to judge the order received.

What is the link between the story of totalitarianisms, of I.P.C. and of Abraham, and of entering a monastery? A close link indeed: western contemporary societies can no longer bear the allegiance of an individual to an authority liable to dictate to him his moral and existential choices. Therefore the main thing is that I decide what I want for myself, free from any constraint, above all not disguised or underhanded. Thus for instance, eugenics, which is considered a racist horror when it comes from Hitler, becomes acceptable when it is the parents who decide for their children. And so also, sadomasochism goes unpunished when the victim is willing. In other words, what is inacceptable is no longer such or such behaviour or world vision (we no longer have any objective criteria to judge them), but rather the fact that consciences be seduced or be under dominion. We now come to the point that most troubles our contemporaries concerning entering the convent: they do not really differentiate between a convent and a sect. Let us be a bit more precise.

Of course, we are no longer in the age when, in ancient Spanish Peru, families would have their twelve-year-old daughters enter the monastery of Arequipa, and leave them there their whole lifelong, without bothering to inquire about their vocation. We know perfectly well that people like you do not enter a monastery under anyone's pressure. But there remains a real difficulty today to differentiate between religious communities and movements akin to sects, in which followers do not really choose to be there of their own free will. Finally, what differentiates those two types of communities? Of course, I do not speak of the crazy sects that organize collective suicides, but of the groups which are simply a bit odd, that open the mail, forbid their followers to share about their inner life outside the community, that allow their followers to go out only two by two, or other inventions of that kind that simply show that they exercise a slight control or surveillance without giving orders. How in fact are monastic practices different from them? One should understand that suspicion toward sectarian movements is grounded on the fear that exterior pressures can subvert our spirits, and that such pressures can be exercised just as well in the name of a religion as of anything else. Our contemporaries have the impression that personal conscience, which is indeed precious, is taken hostage, and that is no longer acceptable – even if today personal conscience is insidiously taken hostage by the "politically correct" mentality and by a whole ideology of emancipation that stifles it.

Let us add that, in our societies, a long-term commitment is no longer legitimate. That requires further clarification with regards to the moral exigency, which I spoke about: our contemporaries are generous and thoughtful toward the other so long as that is thought to contribute to their common happiness. Hence, a promise of eternal fidelity strikes them with amazement, whether regarding marriage or religious life. For, "we have but one life"... (And what should be done with that life, so precious as it is? I must say that I do not see the point of living an existence without a long-term commitment. And I cannot even conceive that happiness is an essential value of short-term committments. But I do not want to make more trouble). Here there would be much to say, for this lack of understanding of long-term fidelity proceeds from the undoing of the person as a unified substance – here again a far-eastern influence comes into play, but that would lead us too far from our subject.

The consequence of all of that is that we are more or less irreducible to the society in which we were born. This is certainly due to a large extent to the errors we have committed – let us say that we pay for the errors of preceding generations and it's perfectly normal: one does not accept a castle without the debts! Authoritarianism and cynicism that have caused us to be detested as Christians now relegate us to a marginal situation; we are compelled to a keep a low profile and to bear witness rather than to boast. I rejoice over this new necessity. We shall come out of it better, even if we are not at the point of conquering the world – but I do not think that the Lord asks it of us, especially at the heavy cost that was paid in general... Let us strive to act upon what we say and to be the subjects of our own discourse. That would be very new and important indeed.

Dear Sophie, I wrote this letter to you in my own name and of course I did not involve anyone else in it. For my part, I believe that our era is a rather dark one for the faith. At bottom, what is our task? We need to keep vigil over this glimmer of faith.

Chantal Delsol
Paris, February 28th 2012

Dear Chantal,

Thank you very much for your letter, which I received with great joy. You have an objective gaze upon our era. When I finished reading your letter I thought: how could one respond otherwise except by love? I could have restricted myself by recommending that you read the magnificent prologue to the Song of Songs by André Chouraqui. But if one strongly advocates love in act, why not simply respond by concretely recounting how God one day came into my life and how He then asked me to leave everything for Him? For me, there is no greater love. One can always suspect that "in fact I am not truly and completely happy" and that "there is something not quite right in this hidden life." Of course... But he whose heart seeks with ardour and who does not understand, let him come! Without doubt he will not understand any better, but at least he will have seen. Since he will have gone from the idea to the reality, from self-reasoning to relationship, his heart will without fail be touched. No one leaves here unscathed.

While waiting, my dear Chantal, let us together beg the grace to be living and true witnesses of the One in whom we believe. And let us keep vigil over the glimmer of faith, which is attacked from all sides, but will never go out because the victory is already won!

I send you and your loved ones my love and I do not forget any one of you in my prayers.

Sophie
Monastic sister of Bethlehem

FOREWORD

To love that carries you away, do not ask where…

Chantal Delsol's niece "entered the convent" at the same time as my sister. The same monastery. We met and shared our questions and our experience of their entrance into religious life. It is relatively easy to think about consecrated life as a philosopher, as in the case of Chantal Delsol, or in my case, as a journalist. But it is another thing to be hit right in the heart when a member of one's family makes that decision.

For me, it all began with a gaze…a gaze from elsewhere. It was an elsewhere that I thought I knew: I had been taken there in my childhood and dragged there during my adolescence, without being able to say a word. I had come to accept it as a promenade on Sunday mornings. For me, it was a very boring elsewhere. God, who looked like a scolding father, reigned there. It was an inaccessible God whom I ended up fearing.

It was twenty-five years ago, but that gaze has never left me: a blue gaze that penetrated my eyes like two arrows of fire. I was at the monastery of Currière-en-Chartreuse, accompanied by another journalist. We were going to meet Sister Marie, the prioress of the monastic sisters of Bethlehem, for an interview, though nothing was certain. We had arrived from another monastery where the sisters had kindly explained: "Our life is hidden with Christ in God. If you don't understand our silence, you won't understand our words." It was a bad start for a radio program!

I still remember when she entered the room: I had in my head the image of a severe Mother Superior with large black veils as is seen in certain movies. Sister Marie was nothing like that. She was a woman of real beauty, and she too was from elsewhere...a woman of the desert. I saw in her face a humanity that does not hide anything of the exigencies of life. I was impressed, unable to say a word or to ask questions. All I could do was to start my tape recorder. After the usual introductions, my journalist friend, apparently less moved, asked a lot of questions. But the future would reveal that she had been deeply touched: five years later, she entered a monastery!

Fully satisfied, we left with a tape of the interview. I forgot everything, except that she had spoken about silence, the desert and contemplation. But I did not forget this little sentence which stunned me: "Bethlehem is a promenade in the impossible."

For me, what seemed impossible was this life of silence and solitude, hidden in prayer, far away from the world. But I was safe...two months later I got married!

I never forgot Sister Marie's gaze, and it is only now that I can understand what it meant for me.

A mystery was hidden in her gaze. Just a little bit, she had lifted the veil of the mystery of her life, the mystery of a love that was her life and that had been revealed to me even though I had not perceived its depth. This God of Love was to replace the image of my childhood of a scolding father and one day carry away my own sister. I never could have guessed that.

To write this book, I looked for the cassette with our interview, and in listening to it I found the answer to my question: "It seems that the whole of human life has an orientation that is not always known by man. How can one explain the immense proliferation of life thousands of years ago on this small planet if not for the accomplishment of a plan, of a huge project which we cannot conceive and don't think much about?"

That is God's way. He waits, He lets us seek Him, and it is said that He may even cry when we refuse this game of hide-and-seek. A monastic sister recounted this little story to me: "A rabbi was watching two children who were playing hide-and-seek. One of them, his grandson, had found a good place to hide and the other one got tired of looking for him. He finally left and joined the adults. The grandson waited a long time in his hiding place. Finally he left and went to his grandfather.

He started to cry and said: "It's no fun, my friend doesn't want to look for me anymore." His grandfather also began to cry and told him: "My child, it's the same for God. God also cries because He is hidden and we don't bother to look for Him."

Could that be possible? Does God really cry, waiting for his plan of Love to be fulfilled in each one of us? The only way to know is by carefully reading the writings of his closest friends: "For the Lord, a day is like a thousand years, and a thousand years are like a day. The Lord is not being slow in carrying out his promises, as some people think He is; rather He is being patient with you, wanting nobody to be lost."[1]

And if this were true? Our indifference towards Him, a relative interest for Him at our convenience, recourse to Him in the midst of hardships, or an outright rejection of Him, these are the many ways in which we make God wait. God is always present for gamblers, those who believe and those who don't.

My sister made Him wait before giving her life to Him. She was the youngest child in our family. Since her childhood, the family knew that she had a great secret which she never revealed to anyone except our mother. Our parents died...with the secret.

She graduated from the Beaux-Arts High School: she had her own art workshop. She loved the sea and gardens, movies and champagne. She preferred nights to days. Whatever she did, it was according to her own schedule. She didn't take life lightly, but she remained silent on the important issues of her life. Silence...one day she decided to leave and seek true silence in the desert. I remember the quotation by Henri Lubac which she had taped on her fridge a long time ago: "Why always complain about the gravity of the elements, the aridity of the desert? Why not rather admire the fertility of the oasis, the straight growth of the blade of grass? Is the grass too rare and the desert too vast? But isn't it precisely what should fill us with admiration? Life is always the triumph of the improbable, the unexpected miracle. Don't we know that there is nothing to expect from him? And suddenly, nevertheless, the miracle occurs. In the middle of this oppressive and rocky land, on this

1. 2 Pet 3 :8

small spot over there, water springs forth and grass grows. On one side there is only the law, far too natural, and on the other side, the exception…so wonderful. And if we watch carefully, the exception multiplies. Everywhere throughout the desert, the oases turn green."

She had signed up for an adventure in the Sahara, but the day before her departure she was stuck in bed with a horrible sore throat and a high fever and she had to renounce her plans. Once she felt better she left…somewhere else…without telling anyone. For three days.

She was different when she came back. Almost transformed. She looked better; her face had changed. There was something in her gaze: a new radiance in her green eyes. Her smile was different. Had she gone on her own? Had she met someone? Had "the unexpected miracle" happened?

Within a few weeks her life completely changed. During dinner, she announced to us that she was going to join the sisters of Bethlehem! She was like a young *fiancée*, but we were so stunned that we couldn't understand. At the time, we thought that this kind of thing only happened to others. How can I describe the emotion, the confusion, the fear that this announcement provoked. The memory of Sister Marie's gaze returned…I knew this monastic Family, but that didn't keep me from bombarding her with questions. She was disarmed…she blushed as she spoke about love. There was nothing to explain…

Can love be explained? "The secrets of God belong only to God and to those whom they concern." Was that the great secret of her childhood? God had whispered his desire to her: "I am going to lead you into the desert and speak to your heart."[1] He had ceaselessly repeated his desire; she resisted and questioned Him. And finally, one day, it became incredibly clear: To love that carries you away, do not ask where…

It all went very fast: she emptied her apartment and gave away her clothes, her cowboy boots, her jewelry, her sun glasses, books, CDs, DVDs, her collection of stones, of sea shells, match boxes, postcards…She was a collector and she

1. Hos 2 :16

kept everything. She had even kept her teeth: her baby teeth and her wisdom teeth!

She arranged all her art materials. The paper of different sizes, colors and textures. Paint, felt tip pens, colored pencils, pastels. Notebooks, drawing pads, sketch pads. She gave everything to the primary school in the area where she lived.

In Paris, she visited one last time the places that she loved: museums, art galleries… She went for mint tea at the Grande Mosquée, for a glass of champagne in a nearby café. She took a drive in Normandie and in the Basque country to enjoy the sea and to swim in it. She took a quick visit to the countryside that she loved: her sister-in-law's apricot trees near Chartres, the renowned cathedral where, as a child, she may have told her secret to our Lady of the Pillar.

On the eve of her departure, we spent the evening together, with our brothers, sisters, nephews and nieces. We all knew that she was leaving for a long time, probably forever, but nobody wanted to believe it. We behaved as if nothing were wrong. It was so nice to be together. We kissed and hugged each other before leaving. We were laughing with a kind of fake laugh, but still, we were laughing. Except Matthew, her godchild, he didn't laugh. He was seven years old and he knew his godmother very well: he had understood that she was leaving for good. He cried a lot.

She was leaving for the Holy Land, to enter the monastery of Bet Gemal. Very early in the morning, we drove her to the airport. After she had left, we found her cell phone on the rear seat of the car.

Several months later, I went to visit her. It had been a long ten months of questioning and mourning. I had passed through the valley of tears. I had bought every single book on monastic life and I had desperately searched on Google for something about the sisters…Nothing.[1]

Then I met Sonia, Olivier the florist who gives flowers to the monastery in Paris, Eric a young waiter in a café, Laurence the head of a kindergarten school…the local shopkeepers, the people of her neighborhood who were accustomed to seeing

1. Today there is a website : http://english.bethleem.org

her. They all asked me: "Where has she gone, your sister, the little one with brown hair?" First surprise: had she imagined that her disappearance wouldn't be noticed? My eyes full of tears, I answered: "she entered a monastery." Another surprise: there was no indifference, and no mockery, but a lot of questions. And also tears sometimes.

They all wanted to know and to understand what life is like in a monastery, and most of all, they wanted to know what happens in the heart of a young woman who leaves the world to consecrate her life to God.

The monastic sisters of Bethlehem, of the Assumption of the Virgin and of Saint Bruno are women who have been drawn by the Holy Spirit to worship and praise God Most High. This definition was not enough for me…

I decided to go and meet with them "in the desert," not unlike the Little Prince. Just to see. With my unanswered questions. The Little Prince gave me a key: "What makes the desert beautiful is that somewhere a well is hidden."

Like him, I visited as many planets as monasteries. I wanted to understand everything and to know everything. I wanted to know about the death of Sister Marie, of course, but I also wanted to know the entire history of this family of Bethlehem. My sister was now part of this family…a "family-in-law" hidden under the mantle of the Virgin Mary and the hood of Saint Bruno. The *Orientale Lumen* had shone upon the beginnings of this new order like the star over the manger in Bethlehem.

Sixty years later, life continues there just as one might imagine in Heaven, but it is not Heaven. Not yet. The monastic sisters of Bethlehem live in the desert, in silence, solitude and prayer. They come from the four corners of the earth and have various stories, sometimes incredible. They left everything for this life. It's a high risk life, but a life where love is worth more than what it costs.

Visiting these oases where "one is continually digging a deep well, from which one can draw 'living water' to quench one's deepest thirst"[1], I met monastic sisters, women who thirst for

1. Benedict XVI

God in the desert. In the guest area of the monasteries, I met others who also thirst, people who were different from those the Little Prince encountered. I didn't meet a proud king, a self-important person, a geographer or a lamplighter, but I met a Bedouin, a cardinal, some men from the French Public Assistance, those who build monasteries, a young woman with tattooed hands, a Palestinian sheikh, a Swedish pastor, sons and daughters of Israel, a former fashion model, a Mexican business man and many others...They had all found the well. We don't share the same faith, but we all have the same Father.

I

A PLAN OF LOVE

1

Return to Currière

> To remain absolutely faithful to the
> absolute of love and, in a mad
> contemplation, to go to the end of madness.
> André Chouraqui

For it concerns madness, and that is why the shock is so big.

The shock of the encounter for the one who lives it.

The shock for the family and for those who are near and dear.

The shock in our competitive modern world that these lives be given to contemplation and to the accomplishment of a mad love.

The very personal shock of a transition that my sister made me go through in giving her life: she made me pass from the existence of God to the love of God. Until then, it didn't seem to me to be very complicated to believe in the existence of God…much less than to love Him to that point! And this God to whom she, like others, gave her life, was it necessary that He be living? Can one love one who is dead and give one's life for him?

The shock of faith: to understand my sister, it was necessary that I believe in the living God. It was necessary that I believe in the Resurrection. Truly.

It is Father Daniel Ange, whom I met at the monastery in Paris, who gave me no other alternative. With his typical ardor, he swept away all my journalistic questions about monastic life, its utility and its meaning…in order to ask me one single question: "Would you give your life to a skeleton? That's the real question. If Jesus died two thousand years ago, and if he's a skeleton buried in a tomb, I don't see how someone could give his entire life for him, for a skeleton! It's one or the other. Can one consecrate one's life to a great man in history whose skeleton lies buried somewhere? Often as a proof of Jesus' Resurrection, I give the example of martyrs (one cannot give one's life in love, forgiveness and joy except for someone who is alive) and of monks and monastic sisters who have no exterior activity. The only explanation for their life is the living Jesus: there's no other explanation for their existence. Otherwise, they would need to be locked up in a psychiatric hospital. In a human gaze without faith, the consecrated life of monastic sisters is a wasted and useless life. Even if one cannot understand that, it raises a question; it's a shock and the shock is necessary. Seen from the outside, it is completely crazy and the fact that it is a shock is prophetic. It's a shock. But that awakens what is spiritual in us and it's an evangelisation in itself which is stronger than everything else.

"When I'm in a classroom and I speak to young unbelievers, I say to them: how do you explain that a radiant young girl who has everything to be happy in this world leaves everything and closes herself between four walls until the end of her days? That doesn't raise any questions for you?

"Their life bears witness to God, and that's what evangelizes people. It's perhaps the most powerful evangelisation: the martyrs who bear witness to God and the monks and monastic sisters who bear witness to God. Other consecrated persons, priests for example, of course what they do is for Jesus, but it's less striking, it's less apparent. Their work is passionate; there is a visible fecundity, which can also explain their joy in giving themselves to others and in devoting themselves to a parish. There are human explanations; it's not as sharply defined.

"Life in the desert is vital: it's the respiration of the Church. Remember what John Paul II said at Lourdes: 'Women are the sentinels of the invisible.' Monastic sisters are, par excellence, the sentinels of the invisible; they live as if they already see the Invisible, as the epistle to the Hebrews says.[1] They do everything as if they already see what we don't see yet.

1. He 11 :27

"With the Comforter and in the Comforter, they console humanity: in weeping for their sins and the sins of the world, they dry the tears of a multitude. The gift of tears is very dear to monks and monastic sisters; their tears are 'tears for humanity,' as John Paul II says, and they are a participation in the tears of God, the tears of Jesus for Jerusalem. It's like parks in a city: if there were no trees or parks, we would suffocate. They are parks where humanity can breathe; the little sisters are better than trees, but we need trees too, of course."

Somewhat under shock after the formidable affirmation of Father Daniel Ange, but even more determined, I went to visit the "parks." "Some go to monks as one goes looking for mushrooms" : I liked this well-turned phrase of Didier Decoin in his *Sentinels of Light*...and yet, whenever I go looking for mushrooms, I always come back empty-handed; however, after my long trips to the monasteries, I brought back a basket full of answers to my questions! I had questions on two subjects: why her? and why Bethlehem? My thoughts returned to all the questions that arose among us when my sister left. Could we doubt her decision? Was she a mystic? Had she been disappointed in love? How did she make her decision? Why the sisters of Bethlehem? And there were all the questions about religious life. Would she be cloistered? Would she have the right to leave? Would we be able to see her? Would we be able to communicate with her? And if things didn't work out? And if she became sick? And who are these sisters of Bethlehem? Where are their monasteries? For how long have they been in existence? Are they hermits? Carthusians? Contemplatives?

My other sister, Hedwige, and I went for our first visit of reconnaissance to the monastery of Montsvoirons to take a look, to approach the sisters and to ask our questions...They welcomed us with immense kindness. They were attentive to our questions and our sadness, but they were also a bit surprised. I remember Hedwige's slip of the tongue when she questioned them about the various stages of monastic life: "Before her clothing, will she receive the handcuffs (*menottes* in French)?" Surprised, the sisters replied, "You mean the *mélote*?" The *mélote* is a navy blue tunic with a hood which the future sisters wear before being clothed with the white habit.

That was our mentality, and it is widespread: the monastery or prison ...it's the same system!

I needed to find answers to all these questions and many others... I have to admit that the answers exceeded my expectations. I didn't imagine that in landing on planet Bethlehem I would discover an undreamt-of world above reproach and I that I would draw near to the Love forgotten by the world...

I wanted to return quickly to the monastery of Currière-en-Chartreuse. That's where it all began. That's where I encountered Sister Marie, the first and only time. I knew only the year of her death, nothing more. In waiting to meet with some of the sisters, I went to her tomb: there was a simple black cross, planted in the soil, and there were two others on either side of it. There was no tombstone, just a little mound of earth. The Carthusian tradition is that one is buried in the earth without a casket. There is only one deviation from this tradition: Sister Marie's name is inscribed on the cross. For the other sisters who have also left this world, their names are inscribed only in the heart of God: the curious cannot know who lies there. Like their life, their death is hidden in God.

My heart melted when I saw Sister P. enter: she is short, but the gentleness of her gaze and wisdom of her words make her a "big" sister, an elder. She has been in the monastery for fifty years, and for many long years she accompanied Sister Marie. I asked her to tell me about her death.

"It was in 1999. She had given a very beautiful evangelical month.[1] At the time, the tree of Bethlehem, rooted in France, had already extended its branches: there were already some small branches: in Poland, in Lithuania, in Argentina. We were between 400 and 500.

"The evangelical month was at the monastery of Montsvoirons, and when she returned to Currière, she was exhausted. She went to see a doctor who diagnosed her with cancer, and she needed an operation immediately. The operation went well; it was an infection that caused her death. She had accomplished her mission and had put something very powerful in our hearts.

1. The evangelical month is a discernment retreat for young men and women.

She died a little too soon, but it was God's plan. All the sisters were, of course, very sad because they loved her very much. There was sorrow in our hearts, but there were no dramas.

"For forty-nine years she was the 'delegate'[1] of the Holy Virgin, charged with caring for this tree and, as it is said in the Gospel, she did everything so that this vine would bear fruit."

"Delegate" of the Holy Virgin?!

"Yes, this term might be surprising, but I truly believe that Sister Marie had received a grace of communion, of union with the Virgin Mary, which was very powerful and which she imprinted upon and transmitted to our monastic Family. She always insisted that the foundation of our Family was not her initiative, but a grace received from the Virgin Mary. After her death, it was as if we had seen that grace, and its continuation was certain. We were sure of it. Something beautiful happened. Sister Marie had collaborated a lot with Sister Isabelle in our Council and also as her assistant. She sent her for the foundation of a monastery in the Holy Land.

"Just a little bit before her death, she went to the Holy Land and I still haven't forgotten what she said to me when she returned: 'You know, it's wonderful. I went to the monastery of Bet Gemal, I saw the sisters. There's something ultimate about this monastery.' Her visit to the monastery in Israel was one of her final joys.

"After having laid her body in the ground at Currière, we continued our path in peace, following Christ and listening to the Holy Spirit with the Virgin Mary.

"We were a living body which breathed with a good pair of lungs. Reunited in chapter, in the unity of hearts and in love, Sister Isabelle was elected as prioress of Bethlehem.

"There was a marvelous continuity for us: Sister Isabelle succeeded Sister Marie and became, like her, the 'delegate' of

1. In the decree of pontifical erection of the Family of Bethlehem, it is written : "In receiving their vocation, the members of this new community have, from the beginning, reserved the title and function of prioress and foundress of their monastic Family to the Virgin Mary." For this reason, the general prioress of Bethlehem is the delegate of the Holy Virgin.

the Virgin to guide our Family. Instead of being torn apart by her death, we found ourselves strengthened by the presence of Sister Isabelle, who had received Bethlehem's charism in plenitude, with the ultimate dimension of a monastery in the Holy Land, the land of Jesus."

I couldn't help but ask the same question of Sister E., who is seventy-five years old and is Bethlehem's finance manager: for fifty years it is she who has been responsable for the financial accounts for the entire community! It's not the most amusing of tasks, but it would take much more to change Sister E.'s joy. Her bursts of laughter punctuated our conversation, except when she spoke about Sister Marie's death.

"Before the evangelical month, she led a retreat for the lay people of Bethlehem in July 1999, and I can still see her seated in an old carseat, her eyes closed, the micro in her hand. She was speaking about the wound of sin and the wound of death: "We make a lot of fuss about death. We make things darker than they are, when it's very simple...one day you learn that you have a little cancer. Perhaps it will take time, perhaps it will go quickly. You tell some of your friends, and one day they receive the death notice: it's over. The person has gone to be with God. Why make such a fuss?" In hearing that, I sensed that she had an intuition about something. Perhaps it was her way of preparing us. She left us in the month of September. Now it's Sister Isabelle. There was no discontinuity, and one thing that was powerful for us is that, like Sister Marie, she has the boldness to listen to the Holy Spirit and to be creative within the the charism received from the Church. It is important not to be immobilised in the past. What interests us is the thought of God. Today."

2

The first sister of Bethlehem

I knew enough about Sister Marie's death, but almost nothing about her life, except for a few tidbits from the conversation that I had with her twenty-five years ago. Father Daniel Ange recalled his first encounter with her at Montsvoirons: "Sister Marie was entirely present to every person she met. She was very free. It's the freedom of love. She had a mixture of seriousness and joyful spontaneity. She had the heart of a child – everyone could see that – a heart that marveled at the beauty of the world and of people."

I wanted to know more about her, especially her biological family before entering the Family of Bethlehem. In the sisters' library at Currière, I consulted a book by Father Bernard Peyrous, from the Community of Emmanuel, *Saints of the 20th Century*, which speaks about the first sister of Bethlehem: "Odile Dupont-Caillard was born in Havre, in a Christian family connected to the Dominican order. Called to religious life in 1946, she entered the convent of the Dominicans of Tourelles, in Montpellier, which was then a remarkable convent for studies. But she felt that she was destined to lead an eremetical life, and, with the consent of her superiors, she spent one year in solitude at Perthus, in the Pyrenees, in 1949-1950. On November 1st, 1950, she had already returned to Tourelles, and Pope Pius XII proclaimed the dogma of the Assumption of the Virgin Mary. A group of pilgrims from Havre was at Saint Peter's Square, including Odile's parents. Seven among them, without consulting one another, received in their hearts a deep understanding of the meaning of the dogma and a call to accomplish the 'project of the Virgin,' which was to found a new religious community extended throughout the world in honor of this mystery: 'All men and women of good will of all generations should remain, with Jesus and Mary, in the Father's presence, holy and immaculate in love, on earth as in heaven for eternity.'

"Sister Marie also welcomed this request of the Virgin, and she understood that her experiences had prepared her to respond to it. Only twelve weeks later, in the beginning of 1951, in the village of Chamvres in the diocese of Sens, Sister Marie and a companion began the new community which would soon be recognized as a 'pious union.' It was the beginning of an adventure of discovering God's will. Little by little, things fell into place, not without the difficulties and hesitations that are inherent to every foundation.

"During the first years, in deep poverty, the first members of the community tried above all else to place themselves in the school of Jesus, to gaze upon Him, to ceaselessly meditate his Word in their hearts and to celebrate the Word in solitude and in community life. The organization, the liturgy and canonical status fell into place, with the discovery of the eastern Church and the western tradition of solitude which progressively led the community to the grace of Saint Bruno. The presence of Mary, who lives in her body in the heart of the Trinity in joy and praise, accompanied the community. God blessed the work. Vocations arrived and formation was necessary. Foundations quickly followed one after another, first in France, beginning in 1967, then, beginning in 1981, throughout the world. In 1976 the branch of monks began. In 1986, Monseigneur Matagrin, bishop of Grenoble, recognized the monastic sisters of Bethlehem as a religious community of diocesan right. In 1998, the monastic Family of Bethlehem, of the Assumption of the Virgin and of Saint Bruno was recognized by Rome by pontifical right in the two branches of monks and monastic sisters.

"Sister Marie had contacts with hundreds of people. Innumerable young people, who were seeking God, opened themselves to her and she knew some of the most remarkable relgious personalities of her era. But she lived a hidden life: she was enveloped in deep silence, the silence of solitude which she so appreciated and with which she wanted to impregnate her sisters. She did not want to give importance to herself, but she was certainly one of the great foundresses of her time. The vitality of her work bears witness to her fidelity to the call which she received and to which she responded without ever yielding to discouragement, pressure or criticism. Her devotion to the Lord was intense and she led the good fight, like Saint Paul, *unto the end*, for the Church and so that love might reign in the hearts of men."

After reading this text, I wanted, of course, to listen to Sister Isabelle. I wanted her also to speak about Sister Marie, whom she had succeeded. I was struck by my encounter with the general prioress: I had imagined that one day I would have a long discussion with her, perhaps in her office...I had prepared a long series of precise questions by theme...It was because I didn't know this woman, who does nothing without God and the Virgin, and who does everything according to their time. By way of a "conversation," we had informal exchanges which were unexpected and unforseen. She didn't hide from me the fact that she would have prefered to remain silent throughout my work on this book. Her intention was to avoid arousing a fascination for secrets and mysteries, and, above all, not to interfere with my work. With her sisters, she had decided to open wide the doors of their monasteries and of their hearts too so that I could seek and find answers to my questions. Attentive to my questioning and to my doubts, she accepted to reply with wisdom and with this certitude : "For me, living is Christ and dying is gain.[1] My only glory is in the Cross of Christ." I will not give a portrait of Sister Isabelle. She is a sister of Bethlehem, of the Assumption of the Virgin and of Saint Bruno. Her gaze is of one who has made a choice: the choice of God. Her first reply concerning Sister Marie surprised me. I was expecting her to confide in me on a human level about her person and her real-life experiences, as we say in the world...There was nothing of that: "When someone has led you by the hand of your freedom, with all that is cumbersome in you, in the breath of the Spirit, you fear to speak for fear of spoiling love. That is

1. Ph 1 :21

why, by way of an answer, allow me, Inès, to let the song of the Trisagion spring forth from my soul, and, with Sister Marie, to sing it in all its solemnity:

Holy, Holy, Holy,
Holy the absolute of love
Holy the burning Fire of the communion of the Father, the Son and the
Holy Spirit,
Holy for the poor sinners that we are.
Holy God, Holy mighty One, Holy Immortal One, have mercy on us.

And you, Sister Marie, I believe and hope, that you are hidden in the silence of the divine simplicity,
in the silence of eternity, it is you whom we should ask if you have a message for us.
Today, are you not telling us anew the secret of the beauty that took hold of your poverty
to the point of ravishing the heart of your Beloved?
The Woman clothed with the Sun of the unfathomable Trinity had already chosen you with predilection long ago
to flee with her to the desert
of the ultimate maternity.
She led you there by the sweet bonds of a mad obedience.
Saint Bruno nourished you there with his wisdom,
and the lonely expanses were repopulated.
But already I hear you reminding us
of the titles of our identity:
more miserable, there is not
more forgiven, there is not
more joyful, there is not.

Sister Marie, behold:
sons and daughters are coming from afar
from the north and from the south,
from the east and from the west.
Young prophets of the love of an open heart,
a new humanity born upon the wings of the burning Breath, elevated before time
in the presence of the forgotten Fatherhood which is waiting.
They come to abolish the successions and the distances

between earth and heaven,
time and eternity.
They come, you see better than I,
to tear the veils
so that Reality may finally appear:
Someone who is all in all,
Jesus, the Son of the Father, the Son of man,
He who is, who was and who is to come,
gift offered to their freedom
through theirs to ours
covered with dust.
That is why, in silence,
you say to those who wish to listen:
"Do not be afraid, you who have been chosen from eternity,
the Trinity is your Dwelling.
Offer yourselves as perpetual beggars
of his Light of Love beyond all.
Allow yourselves to be ceaselessly consumed
in Jesus' burning Heart,
in Mary's burning Heart.
To love who carries you away, do not ask where.
Always try to begin again to say yes to the true Life.
Say "I'm sorry," say "thank you"
a thousand times per day, breathe in the Spirit,
without forgetting the night.
Be the Bride who says with Him:
Come.
Hear the voice of the Bridegroom who says to you,
today:
Yes, I am coming.

"Inès, Sister Marie didn't like idols and I would be infinitely sad if I were to make a little idol of her by inapt words. I don't want to rob her of what she was and what – I hope – he is now for eternity: hidden with Christ in God."

3

The Project of the Virgin

All the elder sisters whom I met afterwards during my visits to the monasteries repeatedly insisted that Sister Mary wasn't the "foundress" and that she never pursued a personal project. She had even, in a certain way, renounced her own desires in order to listen to the Virgin and to "her project," as she explains in one of the numerous texts that she wrote:

"I was guided and led from the exterior of my ideas by another idea, by another force, which I besought ceaselessly in my prayer. The result was that I was very light and joyful and I had a mad desire to be faithful to what Mary wanted, knowing that it could not be anything other than a continual life of prayer, of listening with her to the Gospel, and of very great attentiveness to events and people in the greatest possible love. Progressively, my search for a life of silence, illuminated by the life of the Divine Persons, took flesh in the hearts of the first sisters. We felt that we were too little to invent our own wisdom of life. We had to receive it."

It was thus that during the course of many years, the charism was received, new sisters arrived and monasteries were established. "Charism" is a word that often returned in the different discussions that I had, and I wanted an explanation of this word. I was in the library of Currière, busily consulting their archives, when I discovered a little brochure which, in a few words, gave me an explanation of the Bethlehem charism and also of the origin of the community's name. "In this time, when the Church is ardently awaiting the return of Christ, the Spirit draws to the desert men and women of all nations, races, peoples and languages to adore and praise God Most

High. Following the holy monks who, in the early years of the Church, left for the deserts of Egypt and Palestine with the Gospel in their heart, the monks and monastic sisters of the monastic Family of Bethlehem, of the Assumption of the Virgin and of Saint Bruno choose to lose everything in order to gain Christ. Their life in the desert is, above all, the contemplation of Christ's Face and of the invisible and hidden Father, drawn from the pure spring of the Gospel, in the school of the Virgin Mary, and ceaselessly renewed in the breath of the Holy Spirit. That is why their life is caracterized by silence, solitude, fraternal communion, continual prayer, liturgical celebrations and manual labor, which reflects the beauty of the Creator.

"This life in the desert is also a life of interior struggle against oneself and against evil: the monks and monastic sisters who embrace this life, which is entirely dedicated to God, experience their weaknesses, their faults and their human and spiritual limitations. They learn, day after day, to rely in faith on the Goodness and the love of God.

"The Family of Bethlehem, of the Assumption of the Virgin and of Saint Bruno was founded on November 1st, 1950, at Saint Peter's Square in Rome when Pope Pius XII proclaimed the dogma of the Assumption of the Virgin, which confirms that Mary was raised from the earth to Heaven in her body and soul.

"Several French pilgrims received the call to do everything possible in order that new communities could be born in the Church. Their vocation would be to share in the life of the Mother of God, present in the heart of the Trinity, in a life of adoration of the Father in Spirit and in Truth. And thus, in 1951, in a little village in France, a community of consecrated women began to live this 'Project of the Virgin' in hiddenness.

"A stable, reminiscent of the grotto where the Son of God was a little child, was converted into a chapel for the first sisters. There, following the example of the Virgin Mary, the monastic sisters adored Jesus in the Eucharist. That is why the newborn community spontaneouly received the name of 'Bethlehem.'

"The community also received the name of 'the Assumption of the Virgin,' which reminds the monks and monastic sisters that the glorified Virgin is the model and archetype of their vocation and that they have not received any other responsability from the Church than to anticipate on earth the life of loving contemplation of the Virgin Mary who dwells in the Most Holy Trinity.

"This vocation is also rooted in the tradition and wisdom of life of the lauras of the deserts of the East in the 4th century, following the manner in which Saint Bruno, a monk of German origin, received them in the 11th century in the West. That is why the monks and monastic sisters received the name of 'the monastic Family of Bethlehem, of the Assumption of the Virgin and of Saint Bruno.'

"The monastic Family of Bethlehem has approximately seven hundred members in 35 monasteries spread throughout Europe (France, Italy, Austria, Spain, Germany, Lithuania, Poland, Belgium, Portugal), North Africa (Algeria), North America (USA, Canada), South America (Argentina, Chili, Mexico), the Near East (Israel, Jordan, Cyprus): there are thirty-one monasteries of monastic sisters and three of monks."

4

Saint Bruno, man with a deep heart

"Bruno received the grace to introduce into the Church a life similar to that which the Virgin leads in the Holy of Holies of the Three Divine Persons. Today, in this vocation of an earthly life transfigured by celestial life, he begets innumerable children who cannot be healed except by immediately beginning to live in their human life what awaits them in Heaven.

"In fact, God desires that all of them resemble the Virgin Mary ever more closely, just as children resemble their mother. And Mary, who dwells permanently in the beatitude of love, awaits them as the Woman in the desert who gives birth. She awaits them in the same solitude of love, in the immeasurable communion of love.

"And so it is from Saint Bruno that today they receive the better part on earth, the wisdom of the solitude of love and of light which keeps them in continual dependance to the life of Mary in heaven.

"It is from Bruno that they receive a balanced life, concrete and realistic, which the Spirit taught him and his sons and daughters.

"Yes, Bruno is a true prophet of holiness, the holiness of love which the Virgin wishes for her children of the new millenium so that the Church of the end times might be built upon the absolute truth, in the absolute light of love, in the absolute silence of love and of uninterrupted adoration, and that they make of that a secret structure of their person and of every human being invited to the eternal feast of the solitary and universal Father."

Sister Marie

Before leaving Currière, I understood, in gazing upon the steep cliffs which overhang the monastery, why Saint Bruno came to hide himself with his brothers in the inaccessible depths of the massif of Chartreuse. Everything here leads to Heaven, in the verticality and gentleness which emanate from the rocks and from hearts.

In order to understand why and how the paternity of Saint Bruno is exercised over the Family of Bethlehem, it is first of all necessary to remember an event which, at the time, had aroused a lot of emotion. It was in 1970: where the massif of Chartreuse begins, in the town of Saint-Laurent-du-Pont, a terrible fire in a nightclub killed forty-six people, mostly young people. Afterwards, the firemen's security council redoubled their vigilance and decided to close a summer camp which was in an empty Carthusian charterhouse. The Carthusians began a restoration project, and then they sought several solutions in order to avoid leaving the buildings abandoned. They finally decided to invite the sisters of Bethlehem to come. Why the sisters of Bethlehlem? One of the sisters of Bethlehem had a brother who was a Carthusian and, once per year, she visited her brother, accompanied by Sister Marie. Naturally, bonds of friendship developped between the two communities. The sisters of Bethlehem accepted the charterhouse of Currière. Several months later, on December 24, 1973, Sister Marie met with the general prior of the Carthusians and here she recounts the message that he addressed to her:

"In the Church of today, Saint Bruno extends an invitation to you. You will not be members of the Carthusian family since you have received the influence of the first monks of the East, but you can fully receive Saint Bruno's spiritual paternity and his wisdom of life. At a time when one can ask if Saint Bruno himself didn't receive the charism of the monks of the East during the last years of his life when he was at Calabria, it would seem desirable that from now on there exist in the Church, one the one hand, the disciples of Saint Bruno who faithfully live and and pray according to the Latin rite, and, on the other hand, the disciples of Saint Bruno who receive the influence of the monks of the East.

"If we took the trouble to restore the charterhouse of Currière-en-Chartreuse, it is so that in this place of silence and solitude a community might live and pray according to the wisdom of life of Saint Bruno, in the spirit and tradition of the 'upper house.' The guest cells are situated in a place that could become the 'lower house.' There, guests from all over who wish to pray in solitude could be welcomed.

"You may extend to all your monasteries this same experience of prayer and solitude of the two houses."

In reading this text, I understood just how much I still needed to discover about this monastic Family, and, above all, about Saint Bruno, for I knew almost nothing about him.

Born in Cologne around 1035, Bruno left Germany in his youth to begin his studies at the Cathedral School of Reims where he became the school master. When he was forty-nine years old, he decided to leave everything for "the one thing needful." Upon the advice of one of his former students at Reims, the holy bishop Hughes of Grenoble, he settled in the remote solitude of the massif of Chartreuse with six companions. They began their life in the desert on the solemnity of John the Baptist on June 24, 1084.

In the monastic horizon of the West, marked by the Rule of Saint Benedict, Bruno introduced the monastic solitary life of the lauras of the first years of Christianity in the East. Dom Jacques, prior of the charterhouse of Calabria, expressed this to Patriarch Bartholomeos of Constantinople in March of 2001:

"We, the sons of Saint Bruno, humbly consider ourselves as a graft of the big tree of ancient monasticism. In fact, Saint Bruno, our Father, followed the *Orientale Lumen*, the light of the East, that is to say, that of Anthony, of Macarius of Egypt, of Sisoes, and so many other monks who, burning with love in the remembrance of the Blood that the Lord shed, populated the deserts to dedicate themselves to solitary life and poverty of spirit."

Unexpectedly, in 1090, Pope Urban II, also a former student of Bruno at Reims, asked him to come without delay to advise him. He received the summons from the pope as coming from God Himself. It was asked of him to sacrifice what was most dear to him: his intimate life with the Father for whom he had left everything and his brothers "whom he loved more than all else in the world after God."

After one year with Pope Urban II, the pope allowed Bruno to return to his life of solitude.

During the final years of his earthly pilgrimage, Bruno, the Latin monk, was asked, in obedience to the Church, not to return to Chartreuse, but to live in Calabria where there were numerous communities of monks of the East. Nine years later, Bruno died in the monastery of Holy Mary of the Tower on October 6, 1101.

I then better understood the light of the East to which the general prior of the Carthusians had made reference when he spoke to Sister Marie. I also understood that Saint Bruno is a saint who goes beyond the Carthusian Order, and that he could, nine centuries after the foundation of their order, extend his paternity, different but real, to the sisters and brothers of Bethlehem. The Carthusian order doesn't exercise any authority or paternity over the Family of Bethlehem, even if there is a fraternal relationship and a friendship in Christ between the two families.

What is the situation today? How do the sisters live this paternity of Saint Bruno? One sister, whom I met with at Currière, explained this to me: "Saint Bruno introduced solitary life in the West when it no longer existed. He wanted that this life of solitude be evangelical, that is to say, that it be lived in deep spiritual friendship with his brothers. It's the same for us: we aren't hermits who live near one another. We live in solitude, a solitude which is lived in a 'body,' in a community. I like this phrase that Saint Bruno wrote in a letter to one of his brothers: 'My brothers whom I love more than all else in the world after God.' We didn't choose our sisters, and they didn't choose us, and yet...there is a friendship between us, but a friendship which cannot be explained except by the paternity of Saint Bruno and also, of course, by the maternity of the Virgin Mary. Saint Bruno truly gives what is concrete, the form, the paternal exigency of what the Virgin Mary gives us interiorly in our hearts."

O great and blessed Chartreuse,
harsh desert suitable for the call of the Only One,
lush Sinai where the thick forests of Dauphiné
hide as many secrets as the deserts of Egypt.

Chartreuse, snow-covered Sinai,
burning like the height where God, in the Fire, had spoken.
From now on, a single burning Bush blazes from east to west.
Like Anthony, Amoun, Macarius and so many others in former times,
Bruno set ablaze the vast wilderness of Europe
with the burning light of the East,
with the *Orientale Lumen,* which in former times fascinated
and still fascinates so many sons of the East.
O Saint Bruno, our Father, man with a deep heart,
our Father, profound as the infinities of the desert,
how can we give thanks to the Lord for you?
O Bruno, you who came to introduce the reign of gratuitousness
in our barbarian hearts.
In the Christian West, too-well organized,
influenced by a well-intentioned spiritual efficacity,
you came in the Breath of the Spirit, He of whom it is said:
we don't know from whence He comes or where He goes.
You came to prophesy the usefulness of loving the Good,
which is God alone,
in pure gratuitousness.
Today, O Bruno, we celebrate your memorial
in ceaseless praise of the God of Goodness,
and with you, we cry: "O Bonitas!"
You who thirsted for Christ,
you who sought to please Christ,
you who were consecrated to Christ,
you who were attached to Christ,
you who remained in the presence of Christ,
you, the soldier of Christ,
you who walked with Christ,
you who bore the Cross of Christ,
you who sacrificed yourself for Christ,
you who were united to Christ,
you who, with the blessed, aspired to accomplish the Royalty of Christ,
sublime words of the Funeral titles for Saint Bruno,
the man of Christ.
O Saint Bruno, our Father,
obtain for us the grace to remain with you in the vision of God,

drawn to the desert by the Woman in the hollow of a refuge,
where only the voice of an absolute silence can be heard,
the voice of the Spirit, the Breath of the voice of the divine Bridegroom.

Sister Isabelle

5

The Spirit pulled harder

When I returned to Paris, I had the good fortune to meet a man, a companion from the beginning of Bethlehem, who, for forty-seven years has been an unfailing friend of the community. After having been a precious assistant to Sister Marie, he now helps Sister Isabelle. He is warm and precise and he is at home in the world. Hughes is married, the father of a family. None of his children entered Bethlehem. His intense professional life did not prevent him from accepting to be president of the Association of Bethlehem. "There was perhaps also a gaze upon me," he explained to me, "she immediately imposed herself upon me when I was visiting one of our friends who was in a difficult situation and had taken refuge with the sisters at Méry-sur-Oise." Hughes spoke of a sort of call, a strong attraction to silence and solitude: "I always tried to practice these two virtues. In a certain way, they are part of my constitution, but they haven't found expression in a spiritual or ecclesiastical dimension…"

What followed was a marathon of fifteen years with Sister Marie, during which time Hughes was her chauffeur, and, later, an advisor. "During those fifteen years we founded one monastery per year. It was a real race. I have a reputation for driving fast, and she is the only person who said 'faster !' We never went fast enough. That expresses the intensity of the call that she received. She knew that she was always behind in her response and God knows what personal capacities she had. The Spirit pulled harder and she had to follow: she needed a cane to help her walk. It was impossible not to follow her! That's the definition that I would give of Sister Marie, I sensed that she was carried by Another. It wasn't her own will. She had a mission to accomplish, and from the moment when one encountered her, either one turned one's back on her and left like the young rich man, or one followed her, and one followed as she did, that is to say, unconditionally. She was completely given, completely given.

"Sister Marie and her sisters were always aware that Providence guided Bethlehem, it wasn't their human will. They were 'instruments' who, without being perfect, but with all their heart, tried to respond with their human capacities and their human limitations. The Virgin was truly their prioress.

"If I hadn't been touched by the charism of Bethlehem, our friendship wouldn't have lasted all those years and with all the different people. There was a sort of permanent transparency and simplicity. There was never a problem. To tell the truth, I don't think that I received more than a simple reflection of Bethlehem's charism, but that was sufficient to give light to my life and to give meaning to the taste that I have for silence and solitude."

How would you define Bethlehem's charism?

"It is to be found in the two commandments, in the Gospel, in what is essential in religion: I created you, I chose you, I ask you to love others as I have loved them, and I ask you to do this in a charism of prayer and of intercession, in an offering of your humanity, and not in a charism of apostolic action. That's what I tried to understand. In Bethlehem, in the final analysis, one is chosen, whether a man or a woman, to be nothing in the city of men: it's not very easy to swallow. When we accept to be nothing, Christ can live in us and it's the condition for expressing and responding to the call that has been addressed to us. That's why I can understand that a brother or sister can live for fifty years without going to the end of his or her response to the call. It's both a perpetual purification and an acceptance of going beyond oneself. It's not easy: Sister Marie often used the words concavity and convexity. You can't use one without the other. We are concave in receiving the call that has been addressed to us and we are convex when we express it to the world."

Was it difficult to continue after Sister Marie passed away?

"Her death was difficult for me, but when Sister Isabelle asked me to continue, I had the confirmation of my initial intuition that the mystery or the miracle of Bethlehem is timeless with regards to those who bear the mystery. I accepted. There was Sister Marie and then the next morning all continued as before except now, with Sister Isabelle, but Sister Marie remains very present in my life as she does, I think, for all those who knew her. It's beyond time, because their vocation is beyond time and the love of Christ is, of course, beyond time. With Sister Isabelle, there was a change of regime, but we remained on the foundation of what had been created: one refers to the first chapter when writing the second one."

Hughes concluded our discussion with a paradox. That of slowness. Although he had insisted on the urgency that drove Sister Marie to always go faster, he spoke of one of the life lessons that Sister Marie had received: "Nothing is done without slowness. There is a real slowness in Bethlehem, which is in the Church. We aren't in a hurry, and the notion of time is intrinsic to the vocation of Bethlehem, of Saint Bruno, of solitude, of silence. We aren't doers, as Sister E. says. We aren't here to construct a house, or the house that we are constructing is of a different nature."

6

The Kingdom isn't very far away

Cardinal Barbarin, Archbishop of Lyon, is the fifth in a family of eleven children: four of them are consecrated to God, and two of the four are sisters of Bethlehem.

At the monastery of Poligny, fifty kilometers from Paris, near Nemours, I had an appointment with him. Our meeting was scheduled to be at the end of the day, and I arrived in the morning to have the time to prepare myself and to visit the monastery. The Cardinal was "tasting" a desert day, something which he tries to make time for whenever he can. It is also an opportunity for him to visit one of his sisters.

It was a radiant day and I discovered in an immense moor encircled by sand dunes and rocks. Surrounded by heather, the "lower house" is a house of hospitality for young people, families and priests who wish to retreat into silence and solitude.

Higher up, on a solitary plateau, there are hermitages-refurbished garden sheds-which shelter the sisters and constitute the "upper house." To go to the "upper house," there is a sand path that crosses a clearing where a cemetery is hidden in the shade of big pine trees. Six crosses. No tombstones, but mounds of earth covered with gravel and mushrooms. Accompanied by the prioress, I drew near. There were two crosses without a name: they are monastic sisters. There was also a cross for someone who was close to Bethlehem, "brother" René, who had formerly been homeless. Another for a priest, Father Quinquet, who had been the chaplain of the community for many years. He had been "an older brother and a father full of tenderness for the numerous people who came to seek consolation from him at Poligny." A very beautiful book, with a preface by Cardinal

Barbarin and a postscript by Father Guy Gilbert, is dedicated to him. Also buried there are a lay woman of Bethlehem and a child, Gregory, whose family is close to the community. A cemetery of the Family of Bethlehem…a Family that is on earth and in heaven. The bells began to ring: it was time for Mass.

From the tribune of the chapel, I saw the sisters hidden behind their hoods and the Cardinal who celebrated Mass. It was November 21st, the day when the Church celebrates the Presentation of the Virgin Mary in the Temple. It is a feast for consecrated persons whose lives are also presented and offered to the Lord. In his short homily, the Cardinal explained the meaning of this presentation, of the Presence, that of Mary who "treasured all these words and pondered them in her heart,"[1] before questioning our small assembly. "Do you respond to his Presence by your presence? What is our presence to this Presence? A good question…"

I took a stroll in the sun, walking on the sand which is unimaginable so near to Paris, and then had a short time of adoration in the big sanctuary before the hour of our appointment arrived. I still knew almost nothing about Bethlehem's charism, but I had found a "professor" who had his "doctorate" in charisms.

Father, you know the monastic sisters of Bethlehem very well. Would you kindly speak about their charism and what makes it unique?

"I don't like the word 'unique.' It's not a question of understanding what is unique in a community's charism, but above all of defining it and of understanding it. What does God give to us and ask of us? For what specific mission, in the world and at the heart of the Church, did He create our community today? And if the congregation has been in existence for a long time, does its charism need to be reinterpreted in today's world?

"In Christianity, there is an identification between the charism and the mission: if I don't give what I have received, it's

1. Lk 2:19

lost. Saint Basil makes a very beautiful comparison between the material goods which we lose in giving them, and the spiritual goods which we lose if we don't give them. Conversely, when we share them with others, we see that they increase even more in us. Before speaking about Bethlehem's charism, I would like to offer a preliminary remark, of a theological and spiritual order. There's a correspondance between grace, the mission and sin. We are always more vulnerable in what is best in what we have received, and since the devil is clever, it's there where he attacks! It is necessary to be well-informed in order to avoid being ruined by pride. A certain number of communities have fallen into this trap by thinking that they are 'unique in the world,' specially sent by God to 'save the Church,' or, simply by thinking that they are better than others.

"That's why the sisters of Bethlehem shouldn't seek to be unique. The question that they should ask themselves is rather: Lord, who are we? How do you express your love for us? With this charism, what place exactly do you give us in the big body of the Church? They know that what they have received was not given to them for their personal spiritual profit. On the contrary, what they have received never leaves them idle. It's a gift for the Church, a mission to accomplish among men, a gift that God gives to the world. It's a grace! They also know that they won't be happy unless they are receptive to their charism and completely engaged in the mission which is entrusted to them.

"In the course of its history, Bethlehem's charism received the influence from different Christian traditions of the East and West. Born under the auspices of the Dominican family, the sisters were dazzled by the discovery of the spiritual and theological riches of the Byzantine world. Their encounter with the Carthusians revealed to them their deep identity as children of Saint Bruno, who oriented them towards the early monasticism of the deserts of the East. It is from there, and more specifically from the laura of Saint-Sabbas, which is near Bethlehem in the desert of Judah, that they received the structure of their liturgical offices, their rhythm of life in the solitude of their hermitages and the elements of their fraternal life. Since the sisters and brothers are well-established in the

Holy Land, they have taken the pains to better understand and deepen our Jewish roots. All of that is harmonized little by little in the wisdom of life of Saint Bruno who, himself, received it from the East. The Carthusian prior doesn't have authority over Bethlehem, but he knows and loves this new monastic family. He watches over it with paternal attentiveness and kindness.

"That didn't happen in just a few years, and one senses that the interior work of the Holy Spirit isn't yet complete. There is, for example, the question of welcoming guests. In general, it's an important element in monastic life, but it's clear that today, at the Chartreuse, little attention is given to the guest house, even if it was different in other eras. What is Bethlehem's position on this subject? One has the impression now that it's not yet clear, and that one monastery will favor one aspect and another monastery another aspect. Here at Poligny, for example, there are two chapels. The sisters have Mass in the chapel of the 'upper house.' In the 'lower house' there is a chapel and there are hermitages for the guests. They are very much appreciated, especially by the numerous priests who come for a time of solitude.

"From the point of view of the liturgy, the work isn't quite finished either. Their openness to the richness of the texts and melodies of other Christian liturgies (Melkite, Copte, Chaldean, Syrian, etc.) might give the impression of a succession of fascinations or maybe of a kind of roaming about among different traditions, and then Hebrew and Arabic are also added, being the traditional languages of the Holy Land. The time has come for stability, for even if the liturgy always remains living praise, it needs to find harmony and unity in each new monastic family.

"A charism matures slowly. Now, Bethlehem is clearly part of the Family of Saint Bruno with an openness to the world, to those who come with their differences and sometimes their contradictions. And we see all of that as a grace, as a beautiful gift from the Lord."

You know Sister Isabelle. You knew Sister Marie. Have you noticed a change in Bethlehem since she passed away?

"With Sister Isabelle, one sees that the ecclesiastic roots are deepening, and that the sense of the 'catholicity' of the Church, its universal dimension, is blooming. What touches me is that everything was received from Sister Marie, and gratitude towards her is immense, but she hasn't, however, become a myth in the community; she isn't like the statue of a commander! She died twelve years ago, and the sisters are respectfully silent about her. Sister Marie was Sister Marie. Today it's Sister Isabelle who is the general prioress. And Bethlehem is alive and well. It's an important point of maturity because, in certain other congregations, when the founder or foundress dies, there is a period, sometimes long and painful, of instability or conflict. In the fire of the beginning, there is always dross that needs to be discovered, recognized and even named, in order that one be freed of it. It seems to me that what needed to be purified was purified. We see that the sisters advance and that things are in place. And, thanks be to God, nothing of the enthusiasm that they had at the beginning has been lost: the liturgy is still impressive, the sisters have remained fervent, the beauty, the attention to details and the intuitive and respectful quality of their welcome are still part of their life…"

A beauty which some might consider dangerous because it is seductive?

"Many new communities have an aspect of seduction, but one shouldn't be overly offended by that. Jeremiah says: 'O Lord, you have seduced me, and I was seduced.'[1] However, it is necessary to be careful because there is something deceitful in seduction. Beauty attracts…even seduces…yes, but it shouldn't deceive. It's perhaps inevitable in foundations. Some people left the congregation feeling as though they had been deceived. They have wounds that aren't easy to heal, and one understands that it isn't easy for them to forgive. That happens in a lot of foundations and new communities where there was a lack of prudence and errors in discernement."

1. Jr 20 :7

What aspect of the life of monks and monastic sisters do you think is prophetic? Eschatological? And, to begin with, could you explain to me the difference between prophetic and eschatological?

"Prophetic means 'to speak in the name of God.' The prophet is, in the midst of us, 'a mouth for God,' if one can say that. His words and gestures are captivating. A prophet is one who speaks a word of hope to those who are despondent or in a bourgeouis slumber. He awakens everyone, like a peal of thunder. That's the case for Jeremiah, for example. A prophet says something clear and powerful in the name of the Lord, he comforts or shocks according to the situation and, and, above all, he opens hearts to new horizons. One can say that that is prophetic. John Paul II had an incredible prophetic charism. He began his pontificat by saying: 'Do not be afraid! Open wide the doors of your life to Christ.' He repeated this simple phrase during the course of twenty-five years in every way imaginable and in a variety of circumstances…and many say that this phrase definately contributed to the fall of the Berlin wall in 1989, eleven years after his election!"

And for the sisters?

"The people who come to the monastery say that there is love and silence here…That's the prophetic aspect of their life. It's a manner of living, an openness of the spirit, a quality of welcoming others that 'speaks ' to hearts.

"For the eschatological dimension, it is necessary to listen to the Credo in light of the final phrase: 'I believe in the resurrection of the dead and life everlasting.' This phrase sheds light on all that comes before it, and this eschatalogical dimension should shed light on our daily life. The witness and the life of the sisters give us this gift. When we are in one of their monasteries, when we see how they live, and when we hear them sing, we immediately take account of what is ephemeral in our existence. We understand that another dwelling awaits us: Jesus went 'to prepare a place'[1] for us. Eschatology enlightens

1. Jn 14 :3

our faith and says to us: 'Don't worry, the last day isn't far away!' Newman draws attention to the presence of the Eternal in our daily lives in an admirable way: 'In the sacraments, the last day comes within a hair's breadth of each one of our days.'

"When you arrive at one of the monasteries of the monks or monastic sisters, you perceive that instinctively. Especially in Bethlehem, you see that the *Pantocrator*[1] awaits you and understands you, in interior peace and silence, and that one day you will find yourself before Him, face to face.

"The presence of the sisters among us makes me think of the invitation of the Song of Songs: 'Arise, my love, my dove, my fair one, and come away; for behold, the winter is past...'[2]

"Their monasteries are an image of the garden where the Risen Christ calls to us. The sisters themselves have heard the call of the Bridegroom and they have gone out to meet Him. Their voice is a prolongation of his: 'Come,' they say, 'the Kingdom isn't very far away!' They help us to perceive the ultimate truth of what we already live in love and in tenderness in our family life and in our married life, in our search for justice and peace, in our professional and social lives... The presence of the sisters, and of contemplative monasteries in general, are like an oasis of silence and praise, in a world that is concerned first and foremost with efficacity and productivity. It's a huge gift which reminds us that the Kingdom of God is not only in the future and beyond death, but that it has come to us, it is here, present, in our midst."

Is it important to have contemplative monasteries in a diocese?

"Of course, and in the diocese of Lyon, we are very poor. We don't have a single monastery of monks. Since my arrival in Lyon, I have seen three contemplative monasteries close. Fortunately, the Benedictine abby of Pradines is still there, and the Carmelites of Fourvière and Yzeron are still there. During

1. Christ Pantocrator is a favorite representation in Byzantine art. He is usually represented as seated on a throne of glory holding the book of the Holy Scriptures in his left hand and his right hand traces the beginning of a blessing.
2. Song of Songs 2 :10-11

this year of the spiritual life which we are offering in Lyon to prepare for the fiftieth anniversary of the opening of Vatican II, I asked that we pray for the foundation of a new contemplative monastery in our diocese."

What is lacking when there aren't any contemplative monasteries?

"It's a spiritual lung, a respiration of prayer. The Carmelites promised me that they will never leave Fourvière. I am grateful to them, because it's very important for all of Lyon. But we don't have any Benedictines, Trappists, Carthusians, contemplative Dominicans, Visitandines…blessed poverty!

"I would also like to mention their nocturnal rising, because it's a treasure. Monks rise during the night to pray. They ask God for light and consolation for those who are in darkness, in the ordeal of prison, sickness, suffering, drugs or despair… When one is in a monastery of Bethlehem and when one sees the sisters rise at 3 :30 AM to pray and to implore the presence and mercy of God for all those who suffer, one understands that it is truly a treasure."

And now what would you say to the parents who are grief-stricken when their child announces that he is going to enter a monastery?

"It's important that the parents feel that they are heard and loved, even if the question of their child's vocation creates an antagonistic situation. I would wish for them that they might recognize our gratitude, for it is they who brought their child into the world and took care of him with great love and devotion for twenty years or longer.

"I always encourage the parents to speak about what is in their hearts when one of their children announces to them that he has a vocation. The parents are at the same time blind and lucid: they know their children very well since their birth, and they can warn them of certain things by bringing their attention to certain defects and weaknesses that the children themselves and those who are responsible for the discernment of their vocation might not see. They should speak, even if they take the risk of hurting their child, because they can help him advance on the path of truth. If the parents are closed in their anger and refusal, and if they don't say anything, they fail in their duty of state.

"If the children were well-educated, one hopes that they will be capable of listening to their parents' objections and of taking them into consideration, all the while remaining free as to their final choice.

"Let us not forget that the parents also have their limitations and that they are 'poor sinners' like everyone else. Often they have their own plans, and frankly, sometimes they are possessive. One must not fear to remind them that they don't have any rights over their child, and that God is the source of the child's life and not them. We have one Father[1], He who alone is the Creator, and one calls the parents 'procreators.' They have a marvellous mission, but it is first of all a service which must be lived in a spirit of poverty. That should be in place from the birth of their child, but it is tested and verified when the birds fly away from the family nest. What's beautiful is that even when their children leave for the most secluded and cloistered vocation, they always remain their children. And experience shows that there are relationships, both beautiful and completely changed on the spiritual level, between the parents and the child who is consecrated in contemplative life or who goes to the other end of the world as a missionary."

If it isn't indiscreet, how did your parents react to the religious vocations of four of their children?

"It was different for each one of us. Four out of twelve heard a call. For Geneviève, my mother was very surprised, I think, and she shed some tears...But my parents welcomed the event as a grace from Heaven. As for me, they were very happy to have son who would be a priest, but they didn't hide from me their concern because, in the years that followed 1968, there was a big uproar in the seminaries and in the Church as an institution.

1. Mt 23 :9

"Isabelle entered very young. It went well...We were psychologically prepared for her choice. There wasn't a shock.

"Anne...everyone loved her very much. She was the last child. We would have been happy if she had married. She consecrated herself to the Lord...no doubt with the heart of a bride! But it wasn't a big surprise either, since she had spoken of that when she was five or six years old, and you didn't have to be a soothsayer to sense that the idea was at work in her heart, in silence, when she was fifteen or twenty years old.

"Today, all of that seems to us to be a remarkable gift from Heaven, totally unmerited. We all know what we owe, with regards to this, to our parents whose love, energy, presence and rationality filled us with wonder. In the education that we received, it was always clear that health, studies, the choice of a profession, friendships, social commitments are very important for well-balanced lives, but that none of that rivals the only treasure that counts, that of faith. Perhaps I could say that for the eleven children in our family, the person of Jesus, and the faith and the love that bind us to Him, are the *milieu* where our choice of life took shape and where it finds all its fecundity, whether in married life or in consecration to God."

II

APOCALYPSE NOW

1

An eschatological weekend

I intentionally questioned Cardinal Barbarin about the eschatological question. The sisters had suggested that I join them in the middle of the summer for the weekend of the Parousia. I quickly searched Google…Parousia: "The presence or the second coming of Christ. The glorious return of Jesus Christ at the end of biblical times in order to definitively establish the Kingdom of God on earth!"

I accepted the sisters' invitation: I wanted, during those two days, to try to approach that which for me still had an air of mystery.

Before leaving on vacation, I had also questioned a specialist about the eschatological question. Father Patrick de Laubier, author of many books on the subject, close to the community of Bethlehem, is honorary professor of sociology at the University of Geneva, professor at the pedagogical University of Moscow and associate professor at the Latran University in Rome. With much *savoir-faire*, Father gave me a short course on eschatology for which I am extremely grateful!

"The Parousia is the Presence. In French, there is unfortunately only one word for time. In Greek, there are two: *chronos*, which is historical time and *kairos*, which is prophetic time. In the parable of St. Luke – look at the Greek text – the Lord entrusts the care of his house to his servants and then he leaves: there we have the word *chronos*. When he comes back unexpectedly, it is *kairos*. *Kairos* is prophetic time. *Chronos*, you are at the bottom of a valley and you see a caravan. You need to count the camels. Whereas the prophet is on the mountain top and sees all at once the whole caravan. He cannot fix it in time, but he sees it in its finality... That is *kairos*.

"In order to apply this distinction to eschatology, the problem is that we often remain in *chronos*: a story slowly unfolds. We can predict what will happen, more or less, less rather than more. And we forget *kairos*, that is to say, the sudden appearance of grace, of a miracle, that which we did not expect and which reveals God's plan.

"Applied to religious life, one can say that contemplatives cultivate *kairos*. They are waiting like the wise virgins. They are waiting for the Bridegroom who is to come, but they do not know when. We are all in the night and we are waiting for Him. *Chronos*: we do not wait. We can even sleep! *Kairos* is prophetic time, the time which arrives unexpectedly. Contemplatives await *kairos* while keeping watch. The eschatological witness of contemplative sisters puts God back at the center of everything.

"*Kairos*, we wait...even on earth: 'Your will be done on earth as it is in heaven.' We are not dreamers: even on earth we must await something. In the Gospel, it is when Jesus enters Jerusalem, the *Hosanna* of history. Contemplatives are a cry: 'Hosanna in the highest.' 'Son of David' indicates his humanity, and 'in the highest' indicates his divinity.

"Eschatology is not a third way: it is not a political economy, it is an ideal orientation. The political economy is at the service of the economy of salvation. This must be seen. The criterion is the human person."

In the middle of the summer, I left the beaches of Biarritz, my family, my friends and the "Nutella paninis" in order to go to the Holy Desert in Piquetière, a few kilometers from St. Laurent du Pont and the Great Chartreuse. The monastery is nestled in a forest of ascetic pine trees. The round and green hills of the Basque country seem very far away: the mountains are not very high and they are rocky. The environment was austere, but the weather was beautiful.

The great iron gate of the monastery was closed and there, it was as if I were in another world... so far away from the one I had just left. I was in an immense "village," hermitages as far as the eye can see, a long building where the sisters have their printing press, a chapel whose steeple I could see, a cloister which runs along the guest house and a crowd of sisters, faces which come from the four corners of the world. They surrounded the fifty or so young women from all nations and languages who were participating in the evangelical month. They were all going towards the chapel for the closing Mass of this discernment retreat. It was the day of the Transfiguration, the feast of God's "unconditional love," as the bishop later explained in his homily.

I had just the time to put my things in a small hermitage and I found myself propelled to the tribune of the chapel reserved for the guests. But there were so many sisters that some of them had to come up to the tribune: I, in my jeans and my sneakers, I felt a little strange in the midst of all those white hoods!

I was swept away by the hymns, and without being able to explain why, tears came to my eyes. I cried. I don't know how to express the feelings that overcame me at that moment, though I remember them very well. My sister. The wound of her departure was re-awakened as on the first day. I thought about the families of those who were present that day. How were they coping with their daughter's vocation? And the beauty. All was unbelievably beautiful in the chapel. The beauty of those lives given, or ready to be given, lives still so young for many of them. I cried, even though they all looked so happy. I saw that there was light, purity and a deep joy which was in contrast with the world that I come from. Perhaps that also was making me cry.

The bishop of Newark, Bishop Cruz, a Cuban American, celebrated the Mass. He gave the homily in French and Spanish and that made me smile again!

"A vocation is easy! If you wish to serve God, you have a vocation. It is easy. The hardest part is the 'ego'; the hardest work is to cast out the 'ego'! You have questions, fears, dreams...God is there and tells you: 'do not be afraid.' What is about to happen is not easy, but I am with you. St. John of the Cross says: 'The first language of God is not Spanish, English, or French, it is silence'...The Church needs you. The world needs you..."

At the end of the Mass, I joined a long procession which led us to a prairie. A big fire crackled and the sisters formed a circle around it. I drew near to one of the sisters, Sister S., who explained to me what was going to take place:

"Sister Marie liked to put the Apocalypse at the end of the retreat of the evangelical month. It was a little bit her prophetic side: she had us read the Book of Revelation together in order to experience what takes place in Heaven. The young people enter into it, for them it is very simple: they are on the same level as the elect in Heaven who acclaim the thrice Holy God saying: 'Holy, Holy, Holy, to You honor, glory and praise!' and they sing with all their heart…It is an anticipation of the heavenly Jerusalem where we will all be one day.

"The Word of God is made for the human heart: they hear the words of the Book of Revelation, the words of all the elect who cry to God Marana tha, 'Come Lord Jesus! Come!' The light of the heavenly Jerusalem is the Lamb, it is Christ. It is normal that you do not understand every thing right away. In the world of today, all the other lights are fading out and only one will remain: that of the Lamb, of love, of suffering, of the Gospel. There is only one light in our battered world, it is the light of Christ: 'I am the Way, the Truth and the Life – I am the light of the world.'"

In that magnificent setting, at the foot of the cliffs of the Chartreuse, was the last evening of the retreat of the evangelical month. Sister Isabelle addressed these words, almost like a cry, to all the sisters and young women gathered around the fire:

> Children of faith,
> stand up now,
> stand up, believe,
> believe that nothing is impossible for God
> and that God never fails.
> Stand up and believe that love is victorious,
> believe and burn,
> believe and adore,
> believe in Jesus Christ.
> Know Him deeply, children of Friendship,
> become Jesus, children with an open heart,

draw near to the Fire
and become an unconsumed burning bush.
Stand up, believe,
children with a clear gaze,
wounded innocence miraculously kept.
Stand up, love.
Stand up, burn.
Let the true light of love come forth from your hearts;
resplendant monstrances in the form of the Son of Man.

Who were those young women who had come to spend one month of their summer at the monastery? What did they come looking for, they whom we call *les voyageuses*? Touched by solitary monastic life, in many cases they had already been in contact with one of the monasteries and they were invited to the retreat in order to help them to discern their vocation.

During the retreat, the young women are always accompanied on their journey of reflection by one or two monastic sisters and also by priests. Twice a day, the community welcomes them in the church to sing the liturgy, which celebrates the mysteries of the Most-Holy Trinity and of Christ made known to them through daily catechesis. Each one listens to these conferences in her mother tongue in her cell. Audio-visual "biblical pilgrimages" illustrate and complete the catechesis. Eucharistic adoration and prayer workshops are also offered as well as deep and joyful gatherings.

At the evening gathering, I saw them close up and I listened to their testimonies. They came from France, Chili, Italy, Austria, Senegal, Togo, Poland, Lithuania, Czechoslovakia, Hungary, Germany, Spain, Portugal, Peru, Mexico and Canada. Their stories were all very different. One of them was blind; another had her hands completely tattooed; another one, who was passionate about flamenco, danced before passing the mike to one of her friends who, with her tam-tam, led the group in a joyful "alleluia…" At the end of the evening, Sister Isabelle called the sisters in Mexico and also those who went to Burkina Faso to live the retreat of the evangelical month with young Africans. The telephone was connected to a loud speaker: we clapped wildly hearing that they were united to us in our joy. We were one big family!

They never forget love

After the celebration, Sister Isabelle accompanied me back to "my" little hermitage. I took the opportunity to question her about the joyful and very international group.

"Having come from Peru, Korea, Mexico, Lithuania, France, the US, Africa and elsewhere, these young women, each one in a different and personal way, is responding to the call of the same Lord. The cultural differences are like the shimmer of a bridal gown. All of them, from the four corners of the world, are responding to the Bridegroom's call. Their cultural and ethnic differences mark their specific ways of answering God's call. They also demand of our communities the exigency of mutual listening, receptivity, and the thirst to get to know the other; it is an exigency that is illuminated and amplified not only by the reality of this multicolored universality, but also by the revelation of the mystery of a 'single culture'...which is much more than a culture: it is the spirit of the Gospel, the mystery of Christ Himself, of His Body and of His identity as Son of the Father who is able to bring to resemblance this variety sprung forth from the hands of the Creator.

"These young women come from the north and the south, from rich and poor countries -and even very poor countries. They were engaged in manual or intellectual work, humanitarian or medical professions, paramedical or social professions or else the arts. Some were atheists, others come from Christian traditions; some are marked by the ambient relativism of our culture, others come from other monotheist or non-monotheist religions. Some have been fascinated by Christ for a long time, others have only recently discovered Him. These young women, whoever they may be, have one characteristic in common which always makes me marvel: they never forget love.

"A little clarification is necessary: what is this love? It is a path that opens before them as before all of us. It is a progressive discovery of the face of their Source who, in His paternal hand, holds the universe and the billions of human beings who inhabit the earth: each one is unique in His eyes, just as he or she is. Yes, the face of the Father of light whom Jesus came to reveal.

"I repeat, this new humanity, marked by a spontaneity of the heart, by vulnerability, tolerance, compassion and also by suffering of all kinds, instability, fragility, already bears the wounds in which love will be victorious, an 'anthropological mutation'[1] which announces the New Man of the Parousia."

While listening to Sister Isabelle, I asked myself: how can this life be possible? I tried to put myself in the place of the young women who were in the process of choosing this life. All these young women arrived with their "fire" and their weaknesses: will they be able to persevere in this life of silence and solitude? They are not prepared for this life, and yet they are drawn and fascinated by it. It takes a long time to make a monk. The answer is perhaps in those who have had the experience of such a life, as St. Bruno says: "What benefits and divine exultation the silence and solitude of the desert hold in store for those who love it, only those who have experienced it can know." Before questioning one of the *voyageuses* and one of the novices, I wanted to question a sister who possesses the wisdom of many years, even if this long life in the desert reduces them to a silence which is more eloquent than their words. Sister S. is one of these sisters. She has been in the monastery for fifty years. I had a conversation with her, which was deliciously disconcerting!

God's fidelity

Sister S., if you had to do it all over again, would you?

"I don't ask myself that question."

1. According to the expression of Benedict XVI in a homily to the Carthusians of Calabria in 2011.

How did your story of love begin?

"I have never been able to answer that question."

How is it that you are still here?

"It's because of God's fidelity. God's call is forever, if we try to respond to it despite our failures, our misery, our darkness, if we continue to rely on God. Sometimes suffering places us before the reality of God."

Is this deep silence difficult in the long run?

"We leave it to the grace of God."

Fifty years… that never seemed long to you?

"Some years are easier than others. Each year is different."

Did you ever want to leave?

"Yes, I think so."

What does one do in such moments?

"One begins anew the next morning. We can have all sorts of struggles, but we learn to discern what comes from God and what comes from elsewhere. It is a long labor. At first, there is confusion and then, afterwards, we notice that what was very difficult twenty years ago is no longer difficult."

What is obedience?

"In fact, we are not free. Freedom is gained little by little. In the beginning we are not free: we are prisoners of many things."

Is freedom is gained through obedience?

"Yes, but only by a certain kind of obedience. If we are obedient to an ideal, like someone in the military whose obedience is exterior, that is not true obedience and we pay the price. There can be a power struggle and we become unyielding. If it is for a good which is the true good, we can accept even things that cost a lot. If it is through love, for love and in love.

"Little by little, I learned what true obedience is. There were times when I said 'no' and when I said that I could not do what was asked of me. Once I refused to do what Sister Marie asked me to do and she asked me to do something else. I have never felt constrained when it comes to what is essential.

"I was more at war with myself, with my own darkness, than with what is exterior to me. If obedience is too much of constraint, it is perhaps because one doesn't have a vocation.

"If love dwells in you, that changes everything. The heart lives deeply.

"'The hardest war is the war against oneself,' as patriarch Athenagoras says."

At the end of fifty years of religious life, what more do you have to give? Do you think that you have given everything?

"My God, I am nothing! One gives and then takes back what has already been given. I didn't want to come and meet with you when my prioress came to get me! It is the miracle of obedience. I have an obsessive fear… it is the first time since I entered the monastery that I have managed to leave my hermitage to talk with someone. I do not believe in speaking. I do not believe that we can change people by our words."

It is not words, but actions. And you, you have fifty years of actions behind you.

"Yes, but we don't speak about that. I believe in the witness of communities that live something. Communities that love, that pray. There are people who start crying as soon as they enter our chapel.

"I believe in an invisible influence: a community that lives love. We must create communities that love: that is the sign. 'In this you will know Me': it is a great responsability for communities."

But the world is thirsty; is it our responsability to offer something to drink?

"In the desert one finds the well. The kingdom is a treasure that one must seek.

"God searches for us, but we also must search for Him. It is when we search for Him that we discover that it is He who searches for us.

"Man touches an abyss of distress when he realizes that he is not made only for material goods. There is a thirst that is lived in suffering. Who does not suffer today? There is deep suffering. And it is the opportunity for God to act."

Is it an opportunity or a trial?

"In real trials, when there is a dialogue, we end up finding God. That is the story of Job. Those who challenge God are closer to Him than we think. The worst thing is indifference. God manages when we dispute with Him."

2

There is no greater love…

In her letter to her aunt, Chantal Delsol, Sophie offered to explain how "God had entered in her life" and asked her to leave everything. She was kind enough to share her story with me. Our conversation was informal. Concerning her life "before entering the Monastery," I understood that she had been an adventurer… a missionary. Today, there is always an adventure! The big "adventure of the absolute – I'm not joking!" During our conversation, Sophie confirmed what I had sensed with my sister: a vocation is call that is lived in a particular religious order. We do not inevitably receive both at the same time and this sometimes makes the journey more difficult for some. Sophie explained that she received the gift, her vocation, and the parceled gift of Bethlehem together! "Bethlehem is a family where a mad radicality of the Gospel is lived in a flexibility and freedom which are also a kind of madness. It is an adventure of the absolute, of the most absolute love, an economy of impossible-possible. We recognize, with very deep joy, that we are miserable, very miserable, and that is how we live this magnificent gift. It is a matter of always trying to begin again to receive all from Mary, at every second, she who received everything and who continues to receive everything from God who is Love. As the Mother of humanity, a virgin Bride and an unconditional servant, Mary begets us to her life."

Sophie has been in the monastery for four years – four years full of life, joy, and humor. Sophie expresses herself with spontaneity and depth. In order to tell me about her "life before," she explained to me that she used to follow her intuitions:

"It was often like that in my life: I would have a very strong intuition and then I'd leave the next day." Brought up in Lyon in a Catholic family, she studied political science before leaving for her first mission in Mexico for one year. Despite the fact that she felt disoriented when she returned, she finished her studies with a diploma in communications before beginning work at Euro RSCG, a big communication agency. Carried along by Parisian life, "the subway, work, parties and a little sleep," she worked hard until the day when she realized that that life did not suit her. She decided to leave again, this time with the association "Children of Mékong" in Asia. Her boss offered to double her salary in order to keep her, but she was firm in her decision. The mission was in a little village in the mountains of Thailand, cut off from everything, and she was a teacher in a boarding school for ethnic minorities. At the end of one year, the association asked her to develop fund raising projects for the construction of schools. She traveled another year in Thailand, Cambodia, Laos, Vietnam and the Philippines. "During those two years, I was with volunteers, many of whom were Catholics. It was the first time that I was with young people who truly lived their faith and knew why they believed in God…They had something that I didn't have. I was envious and annoyed by the fact that I didn't have what they had."

She returned to France and to Euro RSCG… but not for very long. Sophie finally found the work of her dreams: a NGO that sent her overseas for missionary work. As for her work, all went well, but, in her personal life, nothing went well: "During the course of many months, I sank deeper and deeper into a life without God. It was not very healthy. I was deeply unhappy, and a dear friend from 'Children of Mékong' suggested that I go on a little retreat. At that time, I was completely rebellious, I was between two jobs…It wasn't exactly the right moment, but I turned toward God…I had to turn to someone!" Sophie left for her retreat in silence and gave God her first challenge: "Open my heart…this is the moment…afterwards it will be too late! And let it be clear, because I am completely closed." The answer was clear and precise: "I met an extraordinary priest who timidly offered to hear my confession… I had not been to confession for fifteen years. I had promised not to close any doors during that week. And it was there that everything was turned upside down... in the absolution!" Sophie snapped her fingers to give insistence to the memorable moment. "I came out... I wasn't the same... there were fireworks in my heart. I was immersed in love. That is how this mad story of love began with this God who is invisible to the senses and yet who reveals Himself in an extraordinary way when we want to open our hearts to Him. Everything changed in that moment." She returned to Paris, she attended daily Mass, and she immersed herself fully in her spiritual quest. She learned about all the aspects of the Church and discovered different prayer groups without any a priori. She did not consider even for one second a religious vocation. She was passionate about her work and traveled all the time. After two years, she had a new intuition: after a pilgrimage to Sinai, she decided to give one year "for the poor in France" and to deepen her theological knowledge. She went to Toulon, to the immigrant neighborhoods, with the association 'Le Rocher.' In her free time, she explored the region and its spiritual riches: it is there that she discovered the sisters of Bethlehem at the monastery of La Verne. "I went for a first visit and I had a shock: it was the shock of silence. For three days. I remember telling myself: they are the freest women in the world! But I didn't want to approach them or speak with them! I came back each month, but I always kept my distance from the sisters! And then, during another confession, my life was turned upside down once again. A priest I did not know said to me after having heard my confession: 'You should perhaps ask yourself if you have a vocation.'

"I was stunned...I wanted to say to the priest: 'Mind your own business!'

"And then he added something very important: 'Simply ask the Lord the question while remaining indifferent to the answer that He will give you!'"

Sophie was not at all indifferent to the answer...She had just turned thirty-one and she was very unhappy because she was not yet married. Convinced that religious life was not for her, she had completely closed herself even to the possibility of a vocation, but finally she took the risk of asking God the question one day when she was before the Blessed Sacrament: "Where do you want me, Lord, so that I may serve You? But again, give me a very quick and clear answer because I am still completely closed! I received a great grace: my heart was open and I didn't expect anything in particular. And God spoke. I returned to La Verne, and I met with a sister who said me in a conversation: 'You know, there is no greater love.' I was staggered, but I didn't understand right away. Later, in my little cell, it came to me like the fire of my first confession: it was clear and precise. It was obvious and I had an immense peace, an indescribable joy, an incredible relief...All was there, even the gift: the vocation and Bethlehem. The fire of love had seized me.

"There was always sadness in my heart when I was in the world, and yet I had a super job. There was always something unsatisfied in me, which I couldn't formulate. I couldn't totally live my Christian vocation and I couldn't see the Gospel truly at work, even in the 'Christian things.' At Bethlehem, I entered a space that is love, but not love as a concept or an idea. Love in action. A life for the Other and for others, in hiddenness. The gratuitousness of love.

"When I received that interior certitude in my little cell at La Verne, I no longer struggled. It was clear and it didn't come from me. Afterwards, it all went very fast."

Now that you are in the community, are you the freest woman in the world?

"I still have a hard time living this freedom, but it is I who am my own obstacle and I know that this is the place where I am most free. I traveled a lot and traveling is a kind of freedom. Today, there is an interior journey, which is a true journey and which opens all doors... In fact, the world is limited. That is why we are free here. We are in a milieu that allows us to go beyond our limitations in God because we are free to live everything in Him."

Do you also feel free to leave?

"I hope that that will never happen to me but, yes, I feel completely free to leave. I have seen some leave and I know that the sisters do not abandon them. We are in a relationship of love. Love means truth, simplicity. I never had relationships this deep in the world. And today, I have need of this dependency; curiously, it is this dependency that makes me free. What is deepest and truest emerges from a relationship of dependency."

What is this dependency?

"There is an absolute relationship of trust between the prioress and myself. I tell her everything including what shocks me and I feel completely free. Here, each one is welcomed as she is. We are not like sheep that all look alike. We are not zombies. We are in a space-time where each one can become what she is in her deepest heart. Dependency goes with transparency: that is what we live with our prioress."

Isn't this dependency in everything a bit infantile?

"We must enter into the intention of the one who asks us to do something on behalf of God. When my prioress asks me to do something, it is not for her, it is for God. My prioress doesn't intentionally try to go against who I am. She tries to help me to grow in love. It is to accept the will of God who only wants what is good for me. It is a dependency of love."

And that is what allows one to obey?

"Obedience is not a matter of having the right to do this or that. It is obedience to our deep heart. It is not a duty. It is a choice. No one supervises what I do in my cell. No one comes to see at what time I rise and what time I go to bed. True obedience is obedience to God, which passes through the mouth of my staretz.[1]"

Before coming to the monastery, you had a strong humanitarian streak in you; do you feel connected to the world when you are in your cell?

1. A spiritual guide. It is a word of Russian origin.

"Completely and much more than before, even though I am no longer in the world… It's strange. By our continual presence before the Lord, we are connected to the world in an incredible way. In a much deeper and perhaps truer way. If I let the world enter my cell, it is because I want to and it is gratuitous. And at the same time, I bless the Lord for those years when I traveled all over the world because I have faces, events and situations which I can offer to Him. They were given to me. I do not forget them.

"There is need of NGO, of people on the spot and of men and women who pray. There is a power in prayer, in the presence before God, a power in the struggle."

Do you feel like you are in a bubble?

"No, because at Bethlehem there is both a contemplative life and an extraordinary openness to the world, even if we do not leave the monastery. I believe that it is thanks to the Holy Spirit, who enters our depths, that we are always in a newness. There is no routine because there is the breath of the Holy Spirit."

Can we speak of femininity? Have you renounced your femininity?

"No, but what is femininity in the world? How can femininity be expressed in the world today when it is so tarnished? Here there is the space to be what we are. It is perhaps the place where it can be manifested in truth. I have not spoken much about Mary whom I truly 'met' during the retreat of the evangelical month. Mary tells us something about gentleness and about femininity, about openness, which is undying, funny, and full of life. That is what it is to be a woman."

Is it difficult to renounce motherhood?

"Not really. I am so convinced that there is a spiritual maternity that this does not pose any problems. All families are mine. I didn't have to make a big renunciation to not have a family or children. Perhaps one day I will have to do that. I don't know…

It's a mystery. There is nothing human in the call and yet, this call leads us to a plenitude of our humanity."

Do you ever think of the years that go by?

"Not much. Since I entered, I have the impression that time has become eternity."

Before leaving Sophie, I asked her for the text of the prologue to the Song of Songs written by André Chouraqui. She had referred to it in her letter to her aunt, Chantal Delsol, as the most beautiful answer to all the questions that arise when one enters a monastery. My sister also read it to me during my first visit to the Holy Land: it is the shock of an encounter and the craziness of a mad love...

> Could it ever be possible, one day, to see, face to face, the face of love and to experience such a deep trauma that one's being, realized in a new plenitude, be metamorphosed forever?
>
> Could it ever be possible that the shock of an encounter, like the encounter with the Burning Bush, could make man into a new being, make his former face disappear, suddenly effaced and replaced by the absolute of love, which has discovered him and which he has discovered, in the purity of an élan which raises him up and embraces him so powerfully that no other embrace could possibly make him forget its ineffable savor?
>
> Suddenly, the shadow is scattered and light inundates his being so strikingly that the dazzlement, it seems, will never end. This extreme plenitude seizes the new person, recreated and restored to his original perfection, and it seems that nothing ever again could alter his unity; the simultaneity is so complete that a fall becomes inconceivable.
>
> The voice which invites him to this union, is, above all, attentive to the "mutations" of his being, not to his progress, and it aspires to a metamorphosis so absolute of love that it appears at the threshold of redemption, of salvation. For that reason, it gives the order to remain absolutely faithful to the absolute of love, and, in a mad contemplation, to go to the end of madness[1].
>
> André Chouraqui

1. André Chouraqui, Prologue of the Song of Songs.

3

Give silence a chance

Is that what my sister had lived and what other young women were living today: "a deep trauma" which transforms a person forever?

It was the end of the last weekend of the retreat of the evangelical month. The voyageuses were leaving, one after the other. Some were going back to their families, others were going to the World Youth Day in Madrid, others to their work, and still others were going on vacation. Had they experienced this "shock of the encounter?" What had they decided? Had they already decided? Not necessarily.

Big suitcases and small backpacks: all the luggage was at the entrance of the monastery. I approached one of the young women: I had been touched, during the evening, by her gaze. Her tattooed hands had impressed me. She had a wonderful Canadian accent and funny expressions which brought a little levity to what still seemed to me to be quite difficult. She still had a little time before returning to Canada. She agreed to tell me her story.

T. is twenty-seven years old. She is the youngest in a family of six children. Her father is a sculptor, he has a Ph.D in theology, and he teaches moral theology and religion in a private school. Her mother home-schooled the children and later resumed her work as a midwife. Together, her parents had experienced an intense conversion, and the foundation of their family was their faith in God. They raised their children "in true love," which T. never doubted. She never felt deprived of love.

As a little girl, she grew up in the faith, and she noticed that her friends and their families did not live the same Christian devotion as her family: Mass on Sunday, prayer in the evening… and she began to ask questions: "God exists, but perhaps we can round off the corners! We can live our faith in another way." Progressively, she estranged herself from her family's values without ever challenging the existence of God. Quite rebellious by nature, she left school during her adolescence and entered the artistic world of Montreal. Life in an artistic milieu in this Canadian capital led her to a lot of partying. There were always more parties. A "dangerous spiral" began.

After studying to be a nurse, T. began to work at a hospital while living a double life: she spent her nights in bars and night clubs, and during the day she worked in an intensive care unit where she had an important and demanding responsibility with regards to the sick who suffered and sometimes died. The shock was strong, too strong: she drowned her questions and disillusionment in alcohol. She drank too much. "For me, life was absurd: I saw my patients die, I saw the suffering of children, of the elderly…How can one have hope in such a world? Can we speak of love in these situations? I had too great a thirst and nothing to satisfy it. I was at a point where life no longer had any value. I wanted to die. I didn't want to commit suicide. I had decided to drink myself to death. It was a way of settling the problem of the absurdity of life."

God had decided otherwise. Or perhaps Saint Therese!

Since her pious childhood, T. kept a statue of Saint Therese, which her father had given to her. It was still in her room. One day, in the wee hours of the morning, crawling on all fours to enter her home, blind drunk after a night of debauchery, she had a strange experience: "All of a sudden I saw myself as if I were outside of myself. I observed myself and I saw my tattoos. I had bruises everywhere from falling. I was standing in front of my dead body, and I saw that I had to make a choice: 'Either you stop drinking and you live, or you continue drinking and you die! Which do you choose?' I thought I had already answered this question, but this time it was like a last chance. I had one beer left in the fridge: I dragged myself to the fridge to get it, and I also caught hold of the little statue of Saint Therese, and then I collapsed on the floor in a sorry state. The beer in one hand and Saint Therese in the other…they were the same size! I looked at the beer, then I looked at Saint Therese and I said to her: 'Saint Therese, you will have to replace the beer. Can you do that?' That night I decided to give Saint Therese a chance. Just this one time. But I had also decided to start drinking myself to death again if it didn't work."

T. drank her last beer and smoked her last two cigarettes before calling her parents to announce to them that she wanted to return home. Two weeks later, after having resigned from the hospital and settled her affairs, she left Montreal, with Saint Therese under her arm, to go home to her parents, Normand and Madeleine. Her parents live in Chertsey, a village with one hundred and twenty-five lakes! After having lived in Montreal, they left for the countryside with one objective: to be close to a monastery in order to have daily Mass and attend the liturgical offices. It is there, in this little village, that they discovered a sanctuary dedicated to Mary Queen of hearts. The monastic sisters of Bethlehem had founded a monastery nearby.

The beginning of her weaning from alcohol was difficult for T. Added to the physical detoxification, there was also a psychological weaning. T. spent most of her time curled up with her dog close to the fireplace.

After a few months, almost without knowing it, she began to want to live again. Questions arose, and she found that she could easily speak with her father. She saw how her parents were living, going to Mass every morning at the monastery of the sisters of Bethlehem a few kilometers from their home. T. decided to accompany them once, then twice… then every day: "I was 'hungry'…I received communion, period. Don't ask me questions, Inès…At that time, I was not exactly giving theology courses!" The sisters and her parents, with much gentleness and discretion, answered her questions. Progressively, T. rediscovered the love that had been like a cradle for her childhood: the love of her parents, of course, and also that of God. She rediscovered true happiness, true joy… joy that lasts: "Having deeply tasted the joy that does not last, I know the difference, believe me! I found true joy in the Eucharist and in my communion with my parents. An enduring joy! The more I gave, the more I received. It was not like when I was drinking:

the more I gave, the less I had! One day, I found the answer to my thirst: the love of God."

T. spent three years with her parents and drew very close to the sisters of Bethlehem, whom she appreciated because they do not speak. They did not give her homilies. "In my experience, the monastic sisters were the best nurses I ever had. They work for the true Physician. And in my case, He was the only one who could heal my sickness. He is the only one who has conquered death. They allow the mystery to live, the intensity. They let the truth live, a truth which is too great and too beautiful to be named. We don't need to speak; there is nothing to say. Just give silence a chance. Give your life to live this mystery!"

Two months after our conversation, T. entered the monastery of Monte Camporeggiano in Italy, on the day of the feast of St. Bruno.

She had agreed to let me call her parents in Canada. I wanted to know how they had lived their daughter's difficult years and then her entrance into the monastery. On Skype, I was able to have a long conversation with them. Their responses were marked by the cadence of their Canadian accent!

"We must not judge our children. T. drank too much because she no longer saw meaning in life. For her, life was absurd and she took refuge in alcohol in order not to suffer from the absurdities of existence. She wanted to die quickly. We understood the thirst that she had for the absolute, but we didn't know how to prevent her from continuing on the path that she had chosen.

"T. lived what many people experience: everyone looks for happiness, joy, the absolute. Everyone hungers and thirsts for something. When we really know Christ, from Bethlehem to the Cross and the Resurrection, we know that it is He who unknots the mystery that is in us, He is the one who decodes the cryptogram of the human being..."

On the phone, Normand and Madeleine told me how they discovered the sisters of Bethlehem, their vocation, their liturgy. A deep friendship has developed between the community and T.'s parents. Little by little, they began to take responsibilily for the community guesthouse. Madeleine began making liturgical vestments and Normand prepared a commentary on the Gospel every day for the Sanctuary. Their six children, however, did not follow them in their journey of faith: "For them, we were reactionaries. They don't understand what we live, but they don't discourage us." When T. took refuge at her parents' house, she also didn't understand their life of continual prayer and, as Normand said, "we didn't push her." "She didn't want to be a nurse all her life, and we weren't looking for someone to take care of us in our old age. She bore her own mystery within her. Sometimes she accompanied us to the monastery. She had difficulty following us, but now we are the ones who have difficulty following her!

"T. gradually discovered that despite our isolation in the woods, despite the apparent emptiness, we had created relationships, friendships with the sisters and with others. She understood that the permanent quest for activity is only an escape from boredom, and that there is a deep passivity hidden behind apparent activity. Today people live in confusion and fusion: they are always spectators and never actors in their own lives. For us, it was important that our children achieve true freedom. We didn't want to constrain them or to compel them to live like us."

For these parents, the entrance of their daughter into the monastery was a great joy, a perfect joy, which they expressed as a "tsunami." They were witnesses of the fact that her humanity had been lost and then rediscovered. Above all, they feel that they are in constant communion with her in "her decision to follow Jesus and to participate in the construction of the civilization of love." Madeleine also explained to me that she had suffered from the fact that her children are indifferent to the life that she and her husband had chosen. Their life is centered on the Gospel. They are respectful of their children's choices. They had a life full of love and yet "nothing happened: that didn't change anything in their lives." Normand explained to me that suffering has a place in their life, but that this suffering is short-lived: "We must let the Spirit breathe: it is the Spirit who makes life lighter. In the final analysis, people get bogged down in a routine of constantly seeking the pleasures of this world in order to kill time because time is a source of boredom for them. They race towards nothingness. They are in an absolute state of passivity."

Before ending the telephone conversation, T.'s parents emphasized their satisfaction in knowing that their daughter is in a "Family of the Church," a family which is neither eccentric nor moralizing. Canada is a country where there is a proliferation of sects and where the religious habit is not always appreciated. Normand aptly concluded: "It is not appearances that count. The truth is that the sisters do not judge; they pray. They run towards Christ, in asceticism and in the gift of themselves."

4

The Father seeks worshipers

Every person's journey is very different: no two stories are alike. My sister's story did not in any way resemble the young Canadian's story nor Sophie's. And yet, each one of them was inhabited by the same Fire, by the same élan which nothing could stop. I no longer had any doubts about the "shock of the encounter" and the strength of the call. But one question pestered me: Were they really free?

Sister Isabelle agreed to answer my questions.

Are you really free? How can God's call be reconciled with personal freedom?

"It is definitely an act of personal freedom to enter a monastery. That is why it is also an act of deep solitude. The decision to give everything to God is, of course, in contradiction with a certain kind of human success. For a young woman who is twenty or thirty years old and who is truly free and is confronted by this choice, there are many possibilities to choose from. There are diverse influences, often contradictory, that come from the ambient environment or even from one's own family. What could be more healthy and normal? And a young woman in this situation can experience in herself both a powerful attraction and a huge contradiction. It isn't rare that, in the final stage of her journey before entering the monastery, obstacles arise, obstacles that strengthen or test her resolve, or even undermine the freedom with which she has made this choice. All of that is inevitable and even part of fair warfare, in view of a progressive discernment of God's call."

Is it therefore a question of the will, of a personal choice?

"Of course! It is like love between two people: as long as there is no true choice, the love between them isn't really 'knotted together.' But we must understand what this choice is. It's not a matter of making a list of pluses and minuses and then deducing where the advantage lies. That kind of approach will sooner or later lead to anxiety. And it becomes impossible to continue. The choice that I am talking about is a loving adhesion to someone.

"It is a love that little by little opens us to the other. Alone before Jesus, a person can make a choice. It is contact with Jesus, lived in faith, that determines whether or not a person will dare to take the plunge. He reveals Himself especially in the mystery of his Passion, his death of love and his Resurrection. It is nothing more than the folly of an encounter with Jesus in the fire of the Spirit. Seized by the Spirit, 'the head falls into the heart,' and it is as if one's interior eyes are filled with light and see the invisible, the Love that is invisible. From this is born the desire to surrender oneself to Him.

"But all that I have said with too many words reveals almost nothing about the reality as it is lived and experienced.

"Today, many of my brothers and sisters would tell you, if they were to break their silence, that for most of them the first decisive step was when they encountered Christ in his Passover of love. And this choice is continually renewed, day after day, throughout the life of a monk or a monastic sister. In the eyes of the world, it is an absurd choice, because there is no other justification for it than the gratuitous love of a God who cannot be seen, but who unceasingly touches our hearts."

Impossible without the Holy Spirit

Before leaving the monastery of Piquetière, I spent a lot of time with a woman whose presence intrigued me. She is not a religious. It is impossible to tell how old she is. She was there, often close to Sister Isabelle. I had not yet heard her voice, and I wanted to understand why she was here.

Piluca is Spanish…a language which I don't speak. And Piluca doesn't speak French: I needed an interpreter! How great was my joy when I saw a sister coming, my dear friend, who had interviewed Sister Marie with me in 1986! Since she is Spanish, she interpreted for me. Piluca is a passionate and fascinating woman. She is a woman who is marked by her past. She suffers physically, but she said nothing about that.

"For me, the Church was for the mentally retarded!" That is how Piluca began our discussion. She is an intellectual, passionate about science and philosophy. She explained to me that she lived the first thirty years of her life in a pagan world. After her father committed suicide, her life collapsed. Powerless to act in the face of this tragedy and filled with guilt, Piluca sank into in an existential emptiness. "I didn't kill my father, but a refusal to love is a way of killing a person." She began psychoanalysis, and one day she decided to go to a meeting of the Neo-catechumenical Way,[1] which she had heard about. "I decided to go to listen to them and my eyes were opened in a new way. I was able to listen to the Kerygma: Christ died, He descended into the hell of our life, He took upon Himself all of human suffering, He forgave our sins and He rose from dead. I understood that happiness was once again possible; because He had conquered death and every form of human slavery, He could also carry my suffering. I received Christ through suffering, through the Cross. I could do nothing for my father, but I was able to love once again. I experienced a new way of loving, having been wounded by the love, the treasure which is in the Church: the Kerygma of Our Lord Jesus Christ."

After discovering the "bomb of love" of the mystery of the Cross, Piluca began some self-searching: she considered entering monastic life, but finally committed herself as a catechist in the Neo-cathecumenical way. More precisely, she began to accompany young men and women who were searching for their path in life.

---

1. The Neocatechumenical Way is a school of evangelization. Kiko Argüello and Carmen Hernandez started the Way in 1964, with the approval of the Bishop of Madrid. Today, it is established in 1000 dioceses in over 120 countries, particularly in Italy and Spain.

She discovered the sisters of Bethlehem completely by chance when somebody gave her a brochure, though she doesn't remember the circumstances. "I read it and I had a shock: all was there. All that I was living was there… in the life of the Most Holy Trinity. I didn't feel the need to go there right away. What I had read was enough for me. I had understood and received the mystery of Bethlehem. I can't explain it. I knew that these monasteries were waiting for the return of Christ and that they were able to answer the Gospel question: "When the Son of Man comes, will He find faith on earth?" In 1986, Piluca went for the first time to a monastery of Bethlehem. Just to see. "Everything was confirmed. I could see that they were poor women receiving the mystery and living it out in great poverty. I never idealized Bethlehem. There is no ideal here. The mystery of love is incarnated in the life of these women who would not be able to live it without the Virgin."

Piluca doesn't have a special mission in Bethlehem. She spoke rather of a service that she offers, as in a family. Sometimes she welcomes young people who come to the monastery with questions about their vocation, but she doesn't try to make a discernment for them. Piluca has an immense respect for the human person. She listens deeply without judging others. She likes to define herself as a "gardener": "I meet a person and it is as if he or she is a climbing rose. I have a spool of thread and sometimes I attach a small branch here and if it doesn't work… o.k.… I let go of the thread. I don't have a project for the person who is before me; I simply try, in my poverty, to see what God wants. It is truly surprising and astonishing what God can do in a person's life. It is like when you look at a carpet on the reverse side, you see the threads and the knots, but if you turn it over it is a wonderful landscape. Every person's life is like that: God weaves us by means of the Cross, always the Cross. I learned in Bethlehem that a person is a mystery of God; we can't touch or manipulate the mystery, but we can contemplate it in the light of the Holy Spirit with the help of the Virgin Mary."

I don't know if Piluca met my sister when she entered the monastery, but she put her finger on one of the big questions that I had asked myself at the moment of her departure: why her? It is the mystery of the person, the mystery of the call, the mystery of the election. I must confess that, in my heart of hearts, I imagined that my sister and all those young women had something more than the rest of us. Something better? Or a greater depth? "God chose Jacob even though he was very sly and He rejected Esau. The Word of God is eternal: it chooses certain people gratuitously and not in function of their merits. The election of God is not in function of what we are but in function of a mission. If God chooses me, it is not so that I can lead a life of affected piety or live my little spirituality in my corner without caring for the rest of mankind. No. If I am chosen, it is for a mission. It is not an election of God's privileged ones. There is a gratuitous election for a mission, and when God chooses a person, He gives the grace." Piluca confirmed what Cardinal Barbarin had already explained to me. The sisters are called to accomplish a mission and not to be "unique in the world"…

A person's journey to the monastery can be long and difficult. To enter the monastery and to remain in it. I had seen, during the evening gathering of the retreat of the evangelical month, that all those young women were full of life when they were singing and dancing: I couldn't imagine them shut up in a cell. The word "cell" evokes a prison… and that is what they call their future residence!

"If we don't renounce our personal projects, it is very difficult," Piluca said to me, "and, without the strength of the Holy Spirit every day, it is impossible. They are not put in prison cells. In his homily, Bishop Cruz defined what the true prison is, it is the 'ego.' In silence, a person's balance is endangered if he or she is imprisoned in his or her ego and thoughts. All the time 'me, me, me' as in a centrifuge: it's impossible to live like that. It is necessary to discover, in silence, the mystery of the salvation of my past: to discover that my past has always been saved, that in the most difficult events of my life, God was there, Jesus was there in the process of constructing my life and the life of my family. I discover in my past, as in any vocation, that man is 'chosen before the foundation of the world to be holy and immaculate in His Presence in love.[1]'

1. Ephesians 1:4

"One cannot stay in Bethlehem, nor in any community, by one's own willpower or because of an ideal: it will crack. Of course, there are difficult moments and we cannot deny the reality, but we need to listen to the word of Christ: 'If you do not repent, you will all perish in the same way.[1]'

"Man has placed all his hope in himself: he wanted to make a paradise on earth without relying on God and everything collapsed. Without the Creator, there can't be creatures, for it is He who, at every minute, recreates each one of them and gives them hope. If man remains alone, whatever he may think, he can't find his purpose. The world is in bad shape because man ignores Heaven. The monastic sisters show us that Heaven is open, that the life of man does not depend on his belongings, his works, or his thoughts: 'If the Lord does not build the house, in vain do the builders labor.'[2] We have many false securities, which make us falls into very dangerous traps. As Psalm 39/40: 3 says: 'I set my feet upon a rock.' The rock is Christ. Christ is the true security of man who is called to live eternally.

"Our human capacities and our senses are useful for a time, but they are not eternal. Everyone needs answers to their existential questions. Where do I come from? Where am I going? If I have not discovered the answers, I will live in anxiety and try to solve my life and be my own savior of my past. Christ gave his life for us just as we are: there is nothing to fear. He prepared a place for us, we have Heaven forever, eternal life forever. Our society is so proud: we want to live without God, to control everything, to manage everything. China will be converted and Africa will be converted, because men are thirsty. In Europe, I don't know what will happen without God's mercy."

Piluca lives in Valencia. She is sixty-eight.

The desert continues to call

There is no otherworldliness in these first testimonies. Life behind the monastery grille is not a long and tranquil river.

1. Luke 13: 3
2. Psalm 127: 1

As I continued my "investigation," I read a book entitled *Sparks on the Snow*. Among the selected texts was this warning by a Carthusian monk:

> We often picture the desert as something idyllic, and yet, the adventure seems vertiginous. It requires most of all a tender and deep love, a solid endurance and the most extraordinary humility...
>
> The search for perfection cannot give rise to nor sustain in the long term such an undertaking... This vocation instead calls for the most total decentering of self and a single commandment shows the way to it: "You shall love God with all your heart, with all your soul, with all your strength[1]." If there is madness here, it is but that of a particularly absolute way of loving...
>
> No one can enter by exaltation or refusal of life...Solitude in a cell is something completely different from confinement: it is on the contrary the supreme experience of freedom...

Some of the sisters had spoken about this famous freedom and this mad love that dwells their hearts and their cells:

"It's true," Sister Isabelle said to me, "but we could also speak of the struggles, the aridity of the desert and, above all, of the uncovering of our indigence, of our mediocrity, of our impatient selfishness or of our impatience rooted in deep wounds. We could also speak about our secret thoughts, which sometimes have nothing to do with the thoughts of Christ and of the Virgin. True freedom, which is animated by love, consists in consenting to our poverty and to what is disappointing in us and in others, in the simplicity of a heart which has been softened. It is to be in union with God Himself, it is to give Him the freedom to transform this banal truth into the mysterious splendor which He alone knows. The Carthusian brother also says that 'the desert can very quickly become the place of illusions, of complaints or bitterness; the imagination catches fire and despair as well as revolt lie in wait. One must consent to stripping in order to meet a God who hides himself.'

1. Mark 12:29

"Whatever our poverty is, and it is very deep, we find ourselves in the same situation as some of God's great friends like Abraham, Moses, Elijah, John the Baptist and many others whom we find in the Bible or elsewhere. They were driven to the desert for a time, in order to be able to live in a continual relationship of intimacy with their Source, and to converse with Him as a friend converses with his friend. Jesus says in the Gospel, 'If you want to pray, go into your room, close the door and pray to your Father who is there in secret.[1]' Jesus unites the ultimate finality – the Father who is there in secret – to a very precise and concrete necessity: close the door and stay in your room. The life of the children of Saint Bruno is received in Jesus' word as an order which constitutes their life.

"Solitude can become the shrine of a Presence, of a love which is Someone. William of Saint-Thierry wrote in his 'Letter to the Brothers of Mont-Dieu' that 'the cell is Heaven.' It is not someone who is going to come in twenty years or after death… He is here. And if He is here, truly here, then the door of the hidden room opens to the infinite. It opens so that connivance can be established with what is most universal in humanity, and also most unknown. It is a complicity which will perhaps never be concretized on earth, but which is fully real with the millions of people who are wounded by an unbearable solitude because it is not chosen, but imposed by life: that of isolation, exclusion, humiliation and all the forms of poverty that deprive men and women of their dignity. It is an invisible desert of suffering which, in the silence of their cry, awaits the face of true Love.

"You guessed it, Inès, this solitude is Someone. It is the Only One who is recognized as unique. It is the choice of God alone in the absolute of a movement towards Him that has nothing to do with an ideal of perfection that is unattainable for our impoverished human nature. But it is He, because He is He, because He is Love and that suffices. Solitude pushes us irresistibly to encounter Christ in the most direct way possible, without any detour: to be before his Person, for He is here, present in secret, and, in faith, He reveals to us that the Father

1. Mt 6:6

is good, exceedingly good, and that He is entirely a Father and that He makes a gift of his paternity.

"The Virgin Mary is a star that shows us the path, a morning star but also star of the night, a woman of silence and solitude, the first disciple of her Son who, in faith, knew how to perceive the Father in secret and who grants us this knowledge little by little. She meditated in her heart all the words that her Son spoke. And she gives us, by her manner of listening to Jesus, of receiving His words, His actions, His life, a 'solitude of love' which is also a communion of love. She teaches us how to participate in the motherhood of the woman of the book of Revelation who gives birth in the desert."

But the desert can nonetheless be arid.

"Go and spend a few days in the desert of Egypt, Judea or elsewhere. Behind an apparent sterility, the desert is teeming with life.

"Solitude nourishes an intense life where one sees in the night, hears in silence, touches what cannot be touched. It is a continual awakening to a Presence that is truly present, that is offered to us and that sometimes even imposes itself without ever doing violence to our freedom."

Solitude. I had already questioned Sophie and Sister S. about it. I knew that solitude is one of the pillars of monastic life. As I continued my "investigation," I noticed that the solitude "diet" was not the same for all the sisters. They were numerous in the chapel, but I always encountered the same three sisters at the gatehouse of the monastery. I began to understand that perhaps solitude is lived differently by different sisters, and that there are different rhythms of life within the same monastery. Sister Isabelle confirmed my speculations:

"In Bethlehem, the life of solitude matures slowly. Some sisters, though they are not a majority, because our monastic Family is still young, have been living in the solitude of a cell for more than fifteen or twenty years. It takes a lot of time for a monastic sister to be stabilized in the solitude of her cell. In any case, the daily life of the entire community is marked by silence and solitude, whether the sisters remain in their hermitage all day long or not. It is true that some sisters, who are called 'monastic sisters of the cell,' leave their cells only twice per day in order to celebrate the liturgy (Matins and Vespers, and Mass always follows one of these offices), and only once per week or per month for their share in the services in the house. Others sisters, called 'monastic sisters of the house,' also live and pray in their cells, but only for part of the day, and the rest of the time they work in the house. There are certain sisters who welcome guests in the guest area of the monastery. Whenever possible, the so-called 'sisters of the house' offer their services (cooking, artwork, etc…) in the solitude of the kitchen or of workshops. Our Family is composed of these two different and complementary ways of living in solitude, and it is always possible to switch from one to the other. This back-and-forth rhythm can become a process growth in one's stabilization in the cell, or in the discernment of a less solitary call. This seems to us to be a great wisdom with regards to our human nature, which needs time and various experiences before it can be truly stabilized.

"A young woman of today who has a vocation to become a daughter of Saint Bruno needs to be closely accompanied in her progressive formation in the life of solitude. And this is even more delicate since there is a kind of interior tugging which only the fire of the Spirit and the presence of Jesus in the depth of her freedom can help her to discern little by little: the misery of the world doesn't leave her indifferent, and perhaps, before she entered the monastery, she even responded generously to this call. Where is the greatest Love? Is it in consecrating oneself totally to God and committing oneself to Him, letting oneself, little by little, be consumed and reduced to nothing for no other reason than that He is Love and that He can do everything, that is to say, that He can overcome our misery? Or is it in going to the poorest of the poor, to the most destitute, to those who are the most humiliated, and trying to love in truth by receiving, in each person and in his suffering, the face of Love which is also the face of God Himself? 'I was hungry and you gave me food; I was in prison and you visited me.[1]'

1. Mt 25:35,36

"This accompaniment that we try to live on both sides in a mutual listening to the Holy Spirit isn't without pitfalls and risks. There are always challenges. And those who accompany a sister, whether a prioress or an elder sister, unfortunately commit errors, blunders or faults. I feel myself personally implicated in these errors, which are painful on both sides, and they are for me an invitation to ask forgiveness. Thank God, Divine Mercy is poured forth into hearts that come together in truth, in mutual trust, in dependence to the Holy Spirit. And it is always possible for those who accompany a sister, and for the sisters who are accompanied, to discover the truth in humility of heart and then to continue on the path with greater clarity, trust and love, which God alone can give.

"I should add that a measure of prudence governs this accompaniment: as I said, a sister can receive the help not only of her prioress, but also of one of her elder sisters in the freedom of the children of God and in a communion of hearts. Of course, help from outside, whether spiritual or psychological, can also be part of the journey.

"In other respects, spiritual reading is also bread for the road, enrichment, a source of light and of the widening of one's horizons, indispensable to each one's interior journey in solitude. It is a privileged occasion for becoming acquainted with a saint who can become a friend, or with an event or with one of the many faces of the Church or of humanity in general.

"'Get up, Elijah, and eat, else the journey will be too long for you. He walked forty days and forty nights in the desert until the mountain of God, Horeb.[1]'"

Of all the sisters that I met, none was a "sister of solitude." And for a very good reason. I had been told beforehand: "If the sisters in solitude begin leaving their cells for interviews or to meet with people who ask for them, that will be the end of their life of solitude for God alone and also the end of our monastic family." I then asked if one of them, in writing, could explain something about the solitude in which she was immersed. By way of exception, my request was granted. I know neither the

1. 2 Kings 19: 8

name, the age, nor the face of the monastic sister who wrote these few lines, but, with great emotion, I received the testimony which she wrote in the secret of her cell:

"About fifteen years ago, I had already been in Bethlehem for more than twenty years when I received the invitation to enter into solitude. I never would have dared to ask for that by my own initiative. In fact, every Sunday evening, I was apprehensive about entering the desert day[1] during which I would be alone before God. I had the same apprehension before our annual retreats of ten days, and yet I was always renewed at the end, because of my prolonged contact with Jesus in Eucharistic adoration. But to live in solitude for a long time, or for my entire life, that seemed to me to be only for giants in prayer, and I knew the depth of my poverty and unworthiness.

"In fact, it was very simple: I began by making a little retreat, then I added one day after another and the boat found its cruising speed, and I was like…a fish in water!

"I can speak about many aspects of life in solitude. The first is that we are never less lonely than when we are alone, because the Father, who sees in secret, is everywhere present. Nothing separates us from this benevolent and loving Presence except for our thoughts and our imagination, which are the great protagonists in the spiritual combat.

"The second aspect, which is linked to the first, is obedience. The obedience of being where Jesus is waiting for me. When the alarm clock rings and it is still night, I get up in the joy of another gratuitous encounter with my Lord, simply for the sake of being with Him, or for praising Him for his greatness, his munificence and his goodness, entrusting to Him those who struggle in the darkness of the world, those who suffer in hospitals and for those for whom the night seems endless, those who lack love and who scream in their pain, those who torture or are tortured, those who kill, those who have no roof and are freezing or are battered by the rain. Evagrius, a monk of the 4th century who lived in the desert of Egypt, said that 'the one

1. The desert day, usually a Monday, is a day consecrated to prayer in solitude.

who is separated from all is united to all,' and this corresponds to what we experience: 'reduced' to existing only in the gaze of God, the heart of man becomes universal.

"The third aspect – which is the same as the first – is that the solitary monk is like the elders in the Book of Revelation, who throw their crowns before the Lamb's throne and fall down in worship: the monk knows that he has lost everything and that he loses himself to find himself. How? He doesn't know. That is the challenge of love. Why? He doesn't know why either, except that God is God and He is gratuitous Love and this gratuitousness gives birth to a reciprocity.

"'It would be tragic,' Thomas Merton[1] wrote, 'if a monk could give a clear, precise, easily understandable account of his monastic life, of his vocation as a man hidden in God, for this would mean that he believes, wrongly, that he understands the mystery of his vocation. The whole substance of monastic life is therefore buried in silence.'

"If the bell rings, nothing prevents me from leaving what I'm doing to go to my oratory: 'The Master is here and He is waiting for you.[2]' The celebration of a liturgical office in His presence is a *rendez-vous* of love where I prostrate myself like the elders in the Book of Revelation. The liturgical offices that mark the day are an ascent towards the Eucharist or a prolongation of the Eucharist, which is a nuptial feast in which the Lord gives Himself and consumes us.

"Solitude teaches us to bring into the light the most hidden recesses of our hearts which we wouldn't dare to acknowledge by ourselves. It is a work of purification and of interior reversal of a person who is by nature, more or less – more rather than less - self-centered, and who will become, little by little, Christ-centered by the work of the Holy Spirit. The monks of the East have a apt representation of a person's reversal: it is the icon of a monk who is upright and is seen from behind, his face and hands are lifted up towards heaven. Something similar to that occurs in the cell. Usually it happens 'quietly,' in simple activities such as prayer, the celebration of the liturgical offices,

1. An American Trappist monk who died in 1968.
2. John 11: 28

cleaning one's cell, washing one's dishes, gardening, manual labor and study. It is Saint Bruno's wisdom of life.

"Saint Bruno is a giant who used to intimidate me and yet, at the same time, I was fascinated by him because the little that he wrote resounded in my depths and answered a deep thirst that I had. It was by his letters and his profession of faith that I got to know him, and later I discovered his 'funeral titles,' which have nothing funereal about them, but are rather like little flashes of light that reveal his personality. How can you not love someone 'who was the son of Mary, whom no one ever found haughty but meek as a lamb, who never wounded anyone because he was always united to God, whose face was always full of joy, whose acts coincided with his words, who followed the naked Christ, who seized the Only One and was seized by Him,' etc.? I also very much enjoyed getting close to his sons by reading hagiographies or their writings. I always found in them a particular savor that we call 'spiritual virginity,' and that is so necessary, so sweet for the heart when we renounce human motherhood.

"I realized how fortunate I was to be able to delve deeply into the writings of the desert Fathers and of the Fathers of the Church who, in my life of solitude, quickly became very close friends: Evagrius, Hilary of Poitiers, Maximus the Confessor, etc., but also Louis Chardon, Hugh of Balma, Hugh of Saint-Victor, and also more modern authors like Yves Raguin, Anselm Stolz, and of course the writings of our most recent popes.

"But above all, I received great happiness and a lot of light in scratching away the surface of the Gospel so as to go deeper and deeper into the message of Jesus and of his disciples. That put me into deep contact with Jesus which helped me to overcome trials that came from elsewhere."

In the profundity of this testimony, I understood also that monastic life is not composed only of silent prayer and the liturgy. Solitude is nourished by prayer, work, the simple tasks of daily life, and also by reading and study.

Immersion in the Light

Sister M., who for many years has been responsible for studies, answered all my questions about the formation of monastic sisters.

How is the intellectual, spiritual and theological formation of monastic sisters organized?

"The primary goal of the formation of each monastic sister can be summed up as the acquisition of 'supernatural theology,' that is to say, a theology that directly contributes to the development of each monastic sister's supernatural and theological life of faith, hope and charity in her thoughts, words, desires and actions.

Every baptized person shares in the faith of the Church: it is both a necessity and an obligation to deepen and strengthen this faith by receiving the doctrinal and theological light of the Church's teaching. *A fortiori* for us, who are called to live a contemplative life in the silence of solitude, study is 'a necessary foundation for a life of prayer and true solitude.' Only revealed Truth leads to an authentic encounter with God. And it is clear that an objective structure avoids many of the pitfalls in a life of solitude."

What were the stages of the development of formation in your monasteries?

"In the deep poverty at the beginning of the foundation, our first sisters already had a library, small but significant: there were various copies of the Bible and the Gospel commentaries of Father Lagrange on the shelves. They had two copies of the *Summa Theologica* of Saint Thomas: the Latin edition and the edition of the *Revue des Jeunes*. There were also stacks of the Synopsis.[1]

1. Synopsis: a book which presents the first three Gospels in parallel columns.

"The orientation was given by assiduous reading of the Gospel and theological study of Saint Thomas. For more than sixty years, this orientation has been preserved and enriched by the patristic texts of the undivided Church. Several generations began their monastic life by consecrating one year to reading nothing but the Gospel, before beginning their theological formation. Now that it isn't always possible: one must first learn how to read the Word of God with objectivity and receptivity. And often one must also acquire a preliminary knowledge of the Church's doctrine. That is why the theological formation sometimes begins the first year.

"This formation unfolds in two successive and complementary cycles.

"The first is a 'doctrinal synthesis' of the Mysteries of faith exposed in an organic way that underlines their interconnection; this is coupled with a cursive reading of the Bible. The aim can be summed up as follows: the Mystery of God and his eternal plan of the divinization of the human person whom He created in his image and called to become a child of the Father, growing in resemblance to Christ through the grace of the Holy Spirit. This synthesis is rooted in biblical study and attention to the Magisterium. It calls upon the various theological branches. An initiation to biblical languages is sometimes added. There are, of course, things to learn, but we try to privilege what contributes in a monastic life to the unification of the person: the formation not only of the intelligence, but also of the will and of the conscience in view of one's spiritual struggle to achieve a life of union with God in continual prayer: an authentic theological work cannot begin or end except on one's knees. That is why we like to consider this work as an 'immersion in the contemplative light of the mysteries of the faith.' Each sister receives the Catechism of the Catholic Church and has frequent recourse to it as well as to the documents of Vatican II and the great encyclicals of our recent popes. At the points of transition of this *cursus*, each sister pursues a personal research project on a subject that has been studied, and she can eventually share it with others at a study meeting. In addition, monastic catechesis on the tradition of the desert monks of the East and of Saint Bruno is an integral part of formation. There are also short courses given by biblical scholars or theologians in some of the monasteries. Each sister is accompanied by an elder sister in this immersion in the light."

How is this teaching presented? Is it collective or individual?

"Both. Before each course (which lasts between one hour to one hour and a half), the sisters prepare themselves by *lectio divina* of certain texts. Then they listen to a broadcast of the course in the solitude of their cell. They have the text of quotations that are cited in the course and a list of vocabulary of the Greek, Hebrew or even French terms that are introduced in the course. Afterwards, the sisters receive a photocopy of the text of the course with questions which help them to assimilate the contents of the course. They also receive texts chosen from the theological and spiritual tradition of the Church. The photocopies of the courses also include illustrations from ancient iconographic traditions from the East and the West: frescoes, miniatures, mosaics and sculptures. Icons are reserved for liturgical celebrations.

"For the monastic sisters who have concluded this first synthesis, a structured study of realist philosophy is indispensable: anthropology, logic, and metaphysics. Saint Thomas's philosophy of being is privileged, because it is in accordance with revealed Truth and appropriate to theological research, as the magisterium emphasized before and after Vatican II.

"Monastic sisters then begin the second cycle of their formation which focuses on studying Saint Thomas's theology in depth, mostly in the *Summa Theologica*, but not exclusively. For more than sixty years, we have received instruction concerning his theology from the sons of Saint Dominic.

"The second cycle also includes study of the Bible, of the Fathers of the East and West and Church history.

"Though this second cycle is more demanding and often more scientific, it is transmitted in the same way as the initial formation. It retains the same contemplative goal and continues the monastic formation of the sisters.

"I should perhaps add a few words about our libraries: the books that we keep are chosen in function of what is essential. It has always seemed important to us, as Sister Marie said, that our libraries be kept from all that is useless chatter."

III

EASTERN LIGHT

Introduction

I had not forgotten what the Carthusian general prior said to the sisters: “You have received the influence of the first monks of the East.” What was this influence? I then wanted to understand where the light of the East came from.

I was struck by the beauty of Bethlehem’s liturgical celebrations. Though the eastern elements of these celebrations were sometimes disconcerting, I wanted to go straight to the source. I didn’t want to compare or oppose the eastern and western influences in Bethlehem’s charism and liturgy. I wanted, rather, to understand how these two “lungs” of Christendom can and should breathe together.

In Paris, I met with Father Michel Evdokimov, an Orthodox priest and a very good friend of the Bethlehem sisters. He had become acquainted with Sister Marie at the beginning of 1966 in Méry-sur-Oise. At that time, he was the choirmaster in the parish of the Daru Street crypt, a parish which had been founded by Father Pierre Struve. It was singing that led Father Evdokimov to Bethlehem. “Sister Marie,” he explained, “had asked us to help her. She had a deep intuition about how to adore God in truth. She sensed the Orthodox Christians’ fidelity to the original liturgy. We shared what could be shared. She also asked me to teach the sisters how to sing. She was very open, daring even, and at one point I would say that it was as if she were on a ridge where she might have fallen to one side or the other. And in all of that, she discovered her brethren’s riches, even to the point of asking herself many questions. In the end, she found her equilibrium: there was the contemplative liturgy, where she received the Orthodox influence, and there was hospitality, the love of people, openness to the world, which, I think, is characteristic of Bethlehem."

Do you think that Sister Marie was ever tempted to become Orthodox?

"The East remains the East, and the West remains the West; the risk is that we will lose our equilibrium, but we need one another. That's what ecumenism is: it isn't only a matter of offering what we are, but it's also a matter of needing what the other can give us.

"I should have begun with that – we met shortly after the Second Vatican Council. The Catholic Church had been shaken by many things. Any Church council is a shock, whether in the East or in the West, and a lot of time is necessary to digest and integrate all that a council, inspired by the Holy Spirit, has proclaimed to the people.

"At that time, Sister Marie felt the need to return to a tradition that had deeply moved her. She had read a commentary, which my father wrote, about the icon of the Holy Trinity, and it had moved her deeply, for at that time, the Church of the West didn't speak much about the Trinity. In the West, you consider God as a whole, whereas the Orthodox consider each of the Three Divine Persons in their unity."

I also asked Father de Laubier, who is an expert on the Russian Orthodox Church, if Sister Marie might have been tempted to convert. It is his opinion that she didn't suffer this temptation, for she always remained faithful to the successor of Saint Peter, never forgetting that "the Family of Bethlehem was born in Rome."

The monastic sisters were thus gradually introduced to the liturgy of the Christians of the East.

As early as 1966, Sister Marie received this advice from the prior of the charterhouse of Selignac: "Do not delay to contact the sisters of Greek monasteries. For in these monasteries, where the memory of the desert fathers is still strong, the absolute and maximal quality of the life of the first monks of the East, forgotten today, is still alive in truth." It happened that in

1968, Patriarch Athenagoras visited the Ecumenical Council of the Churches in Geneva. The Russian friends of the Méry monastery, among whom was Father Struve, invited the sisters to meet him. The patriarch gave them an exceptional welcome and advised them to write to the Holy Synod in Athens in order to obtain permission to spend some time in Orthodox monasteries. Having received a warm approval, Sister Marie went to a monastery located above Corinth dedicated to Saint Patapios. After her, other sisters left for the Holy Land, Greece and Cyprus, where they immersed themselves in the life of the monasteries that welcomed them.

Sister P. is one of the sisters who went to a Greek monastery: "From that time, something new began to take place. We discovered that Saint Bruno had recourse to the wisdom of the East: that of the lauras (the first monks living in solitude and fraternal communion). Without him, this way of life wouldn't have been introduced into the West. According to Arnaud d'Andilly,[1] Saint Bruno, in the 11th century, had brought the wisdom of the Greek monasteries – the lauras – to the terrible desert of Chartreuse. We discovered, thanks to Saint Bruno, that it was still possible to live according to the early wisdom of the East.

"Sister Marie opened her heart to a reality which was beginning to blossom and which came from the Council. At that time, there was a seed of unity, and she took hold of it. In her heart, she wanted to draw from the origins, to receive from the East that which would direct us to God and to heaven and add rigor to our monastic life. Before leaving, she had humbly asked the advice of Bishop Emilianos Timiadis, who was a member of the Ecumenical Council of the Churches. He was Orthodox, and he often visited the monastery of Les Montsvoirons.

"She was the first to leave; she spent a month alone in an Orthodox monastery. I accompanied her on her second trip in 1969.

1. In *Introduction to The Holy Ladder of Saint John Climacus*, Arnaud d'Andilly asserts that the tradition of the lauras would not have entered the West if Saint Bruno had not introduced it.

"It was a demanding and beautiful life. I saw students from Athens who entered the monastery. There weren't only old sisters. They used to rise very early; they were very fervent.

"In fact, we went to immerse ourselves in a life full of sap and fire. In order to sustain our nascent community, Sister Marie needed to experience a form of monastic life that has been preserved for centuries and centuries, for the Orthodox alone have kept this form of monastic life that has hardly changed since its beginning.

"Monastic life in the East is as necessary to the Church as the heart is necessary to the body. We received from them the liturgical office, the deep prostrations (also called *metanies*), and icons. Sister Marie was so keen on icons that she wished that we be formed in the authentic iconographic tradition. We are also deeply influenced by their tradition of obeying a *staretz* and of repentance. Our *staretz* is the one who guides us on our spiritual journey. Repentance means asking forgiveness for one's faults and being aware of one's own failings before considering those of others. All of that belongs to the eastern tradition, but the most important element that we received is the necessity of continually making the passage from the Passion to the Resurrection of Christ, which leads us to the light of glory."

1
The Rublev icon

There is a painted icon of the Trinity in the apse of the church in all of the monasteries of Bethlehem (except at Bet Gemal, in the Holy Land, for a representation of the Three Divine Persons might offend the Jews and Muslims who visit the monastery church or attend the liturgical celebrations). At the monastery of the Saint Désert at Piquetière, I asked an elder sister to tell me about the icon. "It is the source of everything: the Father, the Son and the Spirit. The three Persons of the Trinity are in constant motion, one towards the other. It is a circulation of love. The Holy Trinity dwells in each one of us: we just need to let the three divine Persons live in us."

Paul Evdokimov came to Méry-sur-Oise in 1967, and he offered a commentary of the icon, which has remained famous in Bethlehem. Sister Marie had this icon in her cell and Paul Evdokimov's words on that day revealed to her both her own vocation and that of the sisters: "As we listened to him, we discovered that it is as if each Person of the Trinity is hollowed out by solitude, and that each one bears a secret, in the silent celebration of an eternal joy that has neither beginning nor end. All of this is lived in such great love and harmony, that you need very deep silence in order to perceive it."

I asked Sister Isabelle about the meaning of the Trinitarian presence. "The real 'place' or heart of the monastery is the Most Holy Trinity. It is there where each one of us dwells. A monk's or a monastic sister's spiritual journey is not a matter of the gradual perfecting of his or her nature, but is rather a matter of a transforming and fascinating contemplation of his or her origin and goal or finality: God in Three Persons of light and love.

"If we look at the icon of the Trinity with the gaze of faith, with the eyes of our hearts enlightened, we enter the Fire, we enter Love. Father Cantalamessa (in his work on Saint Gregory of Nyssa) says: 'With regards to the Trinity, there is nothing better that we can do than to try to enter into the divine Being, that is to say, to enter into the Life of the Trinity which bears an incommunicable secret, the revelation of God as Love.' Father Lubac says: 'Let the world know that the revelation of God as Love drastically changes all that it could have grasped about the Divinity.'

"We are drawn, even burned, by the mystery of these Three Persons who are mysterious; They are inaccessible, and yet, at the same time, they are very close to us.

"It isn't easy for our human nature to remain before an icon, because it requires that we adhere to a reality that is beyond us, to Someone whom we can encounter only in faith. In a true icon, the faces are different from the faces in photographs – the features, the light and the proportions are different. One cannot contemplate an icon in the same way that one looks at a work of art. Contemplating an icon implies a participation, through faith, in the mystery that it reveals to us.

"Look at the icon: you can see a plenitude of relationship and communion among the Three Persons who lack nothing, and yet They seem to open a space to welcome you in their midst. As in any icon, the lines converge in the one who is gazing at it, there is an inverted perspective: the point of convergence of the lines is in the one who contemplates the icon. It is as if the Three Persons are there before us, in an intimacy with us, and yet completely other."

In the choir of the sisters' chapel, to the left and to the right of the icon of the Trinity, there are usually two big icons, one of Christ and the other of the Virgin Mary. During the liturgical offices, the sisters freely venerate the icons, whenever their hearts and their prayer move them to do so. Often, there is also an icon in the center of the chapel, either of the Resurrection, the Nativity or the Assumption, depending on the liturgical season. Visitors are often intrigued by the sisters' very spontaneous movements: "This liturgy seizes a person in his entirety: body, soul, heart, spirit and life. It enables us to express with great freedom our interior *élan*: we can venerate the icons or express our reverence by *metanies* – a *metany* consists in making the sign of the cross and then bending down to the floor. It is thus an immersion in the living Word which God unceasingly addresses to all people. It is also the answer which the Church gives to God in hymns or canticles inspired by the Church tradition or the lives of the saints."

Also on the subject of icons, I can't resist recounting two stories that one of the sisters told me. After their visit to the Greek monasteries, the sisters received instruction to deepen their knowledge of the East: theology courses by Father Boris Bobrinskoy, dean of the Saint Serge Institute in Paris and courses in iconography by Father Drobott. "He taught us something that is essential," she said. "There was a sister who seemed to be rather gifted. She took her paintbrushes and began. Father Drobott looked at her work, but he said nothing. Each time he passed by her, stopping only to help other sisters: once, twice, three times. Finally, the sister couldn't bear it any longer and she said: 'Please give me your advice. Say something to me!' Father Drobott replied: 'Go to confession!'"

There is also this other story, which illustrates that writing an icon is not like painting a picture. A monastic sister, who had previously studied art before entering Bethlehem, was at an iconography course with the same Father Drobott. She assiduously followed her inspiration, seeking the human satisfaction of completing her "little masterpiece." The priest-iconographer then said to her with his strong Russian accent: "Now, sister, painting is finished, begin icon!"

2

A short liturgy course

It isn't always easy to follow the liturgy during Matins, Vespers or other liturgical celebrations in Bethlehem. "The liturgy," Sister S. told me, "is first of all the celebration of a mystery. In a monastery, celebrating the liturgy means celebrating the mystery of Christ, it means immersing ourselves in the river of Life that flows from the Father and the Lamb and we are drawn, as we sing, into the circle of the elect. It means living in truth what we will be forever, and in the liturgy we already experience the new heavens and the new earth. Individually and in the body of Christ that we form, we taste in the Spirit the hope of glory. Is there anything more joyful than the moments of eternity when we sing to the Bridegroom who is full of grace and truth and who unceasingly pours forth his love upon us throughout the day? The liturgy that we celebrate in the church is continued in the *hodie* of daily life, burdened as it is with work and a multiplicity of things. We are called to impregnate our daily life with the life of the risen Christ, even though his luminous face is often hidden from us, covered by the veil of our sins; our daily life is often cut off from the spring that irrigates the celebration.

"In the monastery, the liturgical day begins in the evening: 'There was evening, there was morning.'[1] After giving glory to the consubstantial, indivisible and life-giving Trinity, the liturgical day begins with Psalm 103, which celebrates the bursting forth of creation. To receive the gift of God through creation and to receive oneself as a gift is first and foremost, even if the

1. Gen 1, 5.

experience of the fall operates a breach between us and God's gratuitous love. This breach gives rise to a new thirst and a cry of the heart to the One who is 'Joyful Light,' and then we plunge ourselves into the silence of the night. The night is important for a monk, for he is, above all, one who keeps watch. Keeping his heart free from the fantasies of the night, in faith he awaits the dawn of the Resurrection, the true Day, Christ, the One who is to come, the One who never ceases to come. The monk goes to bed early and rises early so that, even when he is sleeping, he can remain vigilant with a loving heart.

"During the course of the day in the monastery, there are 'big liturgical offices' and 'little liturgical offices.' Sister Marie used to say that it's like a medical treatment. There are big doses, and, from time to time, throughout the day, there are little booster shots. The little offices are like little reminders: in the midst of our activity, we stop to say hello to God. The bell rings, and we stop what we are doing. It is very important that we recognize that the Lord is our companion, step by step, on the path. He is the Light for our way and the Presence without which our life would be empty…Everything is centered on the Eucharist; the Body of Christ has set right the entire universe. Since we are all wounded by sin, we need the medicine given by the Physician who came to heal the sick, those who are lost, sinners. We need this medicine almost constantly. That is why our life is one long liturgy. Thanks to the Eucharist, His presence is renewed day after day. A liturgical day is a day where we are resonance chambers of the great Amen which Christ sings to the Father.

"It is God who sings in the liturgy. It comes from God, it returns to God and it passes through the little flutes that we are - our humanity, our life. Our whole life is a liturgy: walking down a corridor, meeting with people…"

Monks and monastic sisters bear a sign of their belonging to God: it is the rosary which is attached to their belts and its recitation gives a certain rhythm to the way they walk, pray and live each day. When they pray with their big rosary, their fingers pass rapidly from one bead to the next. I asked myself what prayer they were praying so quickly. This was Sister Isabelle's explanation: "There are two prayers that 'fit together' in our continual prayer: the rosary and the prayer of the name of Jesus.

"Right from the start of Bethlehem, we received the tradition of the rosary, which John Paul II marvelously enlarged. In the beginning, the rhythm of our monastic schedule was linked to the rosary. The event of each moment is the mystery of the rosary that we are praying, and not the fleeting incidents of our daily life. From the East, we received the treasure of the Jesus Prayer, which one prays unceasingly: 'Lord Jesus Christ, Son of the living God, have mercy on me a sinner!' It can also be prayed just by the repetition of the name of Jesus. Little by little, over the course of many years, the rosary and the Jesus Prayer were 'knit together' in our hearts, in a different way for each one of us.

"And so, in one's heart, there is an encounter between the Virgin Mary and Jesus, and the Virgin Mary teaches us to pronounce the name of her Son as she does and this leads us into the silence of the divine fatherhood."

Do you always pray with words or do you also pray in silence?

"Beginning with its most ancient traditions, monastic life bears witness to a disposition to silence which the Spirit inscribes in the monk's heart – a silence which is the very presence of God, the 'gentle Guest of the soul.' As everyone knows, the source of prayer is in the living Word, which is the bread that feeds, transforms and divinizes; there are stages of illumination, meditation and mental prayer. And the monk, a poor sinner who is always in the process of being saved, allows the sword of the Word to penetrate him during the long hours of solitary adoration in his cell and during his work. As it is written, the sword of the Word pierces to 'the division of soul and spirit, of joints and marrow, discerning the thoughts and intentions of the heart."[1] Little by little, he allows his own sentiments and thoughts to be visited by Jesus' thoughts and sentiments, by the Love of his heavenly Father, by the Spirit who comes like fire. Then the time comes to close the Book.

1. Hebrews 4, 12.

Without the slightest sound, God takes the initiative to teach the monk's heart a hidden and secret wisdom, as if unawares. This is pure prayer, the prayer of Fire that can be granted to him. The monk knows neither from whence he comes, nor where he goes. In his depths, love is ablaze."

In the East, there are no moments of silence in the liturgy, but in your liturgical offices, there are long periods of silence.

"That comes from the rite of the sons of Saint Bruno: a liturgy characterized by silence. The light of the East has given us a very vital way of entering into Christ's gestures and words. But we have also kept the treasure of silence, which has a significant place in the liturgy of the sons of saint Bruno."

Aside from the veneration of icons, which we have already spoken about, what other similarities are there between your liturgy and the liturgy of the East?

"All liturgical celebrations on earth are an entry into the divine liturgy of Jesus who celebrates an eternal liturgy in the presence of the Father. It is a sung theology by which the entire person is unified: heart, mind, soul, body and senses. To sing the liturgy is to profess our faith, to meditate in the secret of our hearts, to repent for our sins, to receive salvation, to share in the glory of the Kingdom and to unite ourselves to Christ the Priest in his offering of Himself to the Father in the Breath of the Holy Spirit. Of course, the Mass is the center and summit of our liturgical days, of our entire life. Every day we ardently await the celebration of the Mass 'more than watchman for the morning.'[1]

"By its movements, rhythm, duration and quality, the liturgy changes our perspective and we begin to perceive that everything cries that 'God is' and that everything in our life receives its meaning from the mysteries of Christ in the present moment and in eternity. It isn't only a matter of God coming to visit men, but also of men being at home with God.

1. Psalm 130(129), 6.

"We take part in the heavenly liturgy. This eschatological dimension, so dear to the liturgy of the East, does not make us forget the cry of man who longs for redemption. The immolated Lamb, at the heart of the Book of Revelation, receives all the blood that is shed by mankind; the Son of God is not indifferent to man's suffering. He appropriates it. And by the Blood of Christ, man's cry gains access to the sanctuary. This cry finds expression in the many and various *kyrie eleison* that are sung in the liturgy of the East. This supplication for mercy can be intensified and prolonged indefinitely."

That's right! Your liturgical celebrations are incredibly long! I was at the Easter vigil at the monastery in Paris. It lasted five hours!

"It is an absurdity to count the minutes during a liturgical celebration. In the East, they don't look at their watches. They leave behind them 'sick time,' and they enter into transfigured time which is close to eternity. It is the time without time of the Eighth Day."

You don't find it surprising that in Bethlehem there is a mixture of the monastic tradition of the West, which we are familiar with, and the liturgy of the East?

"They aren't in opposition. Saint Bruno died in Calabria. At the time, so many Greek monks had taken refuge in Calabria that the south of Italy was called 'Big Greece.' It is likely that he came into contact with some of those monks, even if he never spoke of it explicitly. For the nine hundredth anniversary of Saint Bruno's death, the Orthodox patriarch of Constantinople, Bartholomeos I, went to the charterhouse of Calabria. In his homily, he clearly stated that in Saint Bruno the East and the West were joined together: 'The fraternal relationships established during these past years between our monks who live in Calabria, or who come as pilgrims, and your monastic community come from the love which your founder, blessed Bruno of Cologne, had for the Greek Fathers whom he met and loved in this land where he lived in solitude, suffering from the painful separation that was occurring between our two churches.'

"It is wonderful for us that it was the Carthusian Fathers who encouraged us to get in contact with the East. In a way, it is the Saint Bruno of Calabria, the Saint Bruno of the East, whom they had us meet."

Saint Bruno did not decide to be ecumenical in order to create unity between Orthodox Christians and Catholics. Systematically, he sought unity between his heart and the hearts of all men. It was said of him that he was "the Goodness of God on earth." When he encountered someone, he was immediately "plugged" into the depth of God in that person, because he himself dwelt in his own depths. Inevitably, the fire of love was kindled. It was very simple. Saint Bruno's ecumenism was the ecumenism of mankind's deepest depths. If we faithfully live with Mary in our depths where the Holy Trinity dwells, we are rendered incapable of looking at a person without acknowledging that he or she is loved with a completely mad love by the Fire that the Trinity is, the Fire without beginning, without interruption, without end that the Father, Son and Holy Spirit are. We can no longer look at somebody without seeing that he or she is a temple of the Trinity. And so, instantly, there is a deep solidarity: we know one another and love one another in sharing the same misery, which is the consequence of original sin, and in the same predilection that God has for us. We are "one" in the paradox of an immense love and immense misery. We become a companion for all people, beginning by the "fraternal ecumenism" of daily life. God's infinite tenderness, which is all-powerful, and his devouring Fire unite us.

Sister Marie

3

A friend of the East

We were friends in our twenties, but we lost touch. He is a writer, and one of his recent books, *Inigo*, the story of Saint Ignatius of Loyola's conversion, moved me very deeply. When I was reading *Inigo*, I came across him outside our neighborhood elementary school, which our children attended. One day, when I went to Mass at the monastery of Bethlehem in Paris, at Victor Hugo square, I saw him seated in front of me: François Sureau. I was surprised and happy to see him again, and I wondered why he had come to the monastery.

"The first time I entered this church – I work nearby – it was like being in my own parish, Saint-Julien-le-Pauvre, a Catholic parish of the eastern rite (Melkite). I was astounded. Carpets everywhere…icons. Then I saw the sisters with a habit which I recognized; I have always had an affinity for Carthusian spirituality, which I discovered thanks to Father Ravier's books – he was the director of the Jesuit college where I studied. Augustin Guillerand, in particular, was very important to me. Two elements, which were particularly dear to me – the white habit with its two lateral bands, I forget the name, and the atmosphere of the East – made me want to know more about this community. It was five or ten years ago… I can't remember. That's how I became acquainted with the prioress of this monastery."

How did it come about that you were taught by Jesuits?

"There are several things. First of all, in the eastern rite, I found an answer to some of my problems, on an aesthetic level, at least, with the Catholic Church. For thirty years, I endured Masses that were blameworthy, aesthetically speaking; I didn't feel at all immersed in the sacred. Priests make comments, they add whatever they want, they improvise. By their strange way of dressing, they often seem to want to evoke life in Palestine. In the worst moments, with the women's shrill voices and the cold atmosphere of the churches inherited from the 19th century, it seemed as if I were in a kind of sect. The hymns change all the time. Many of them are absolutely ridiculous. I don't think that God is fond of inanity. That's why I found it difficult to attend Mass. I couldn't attend Mass without being distracted by the effort I had to make in order not to be astonished and to blame, and in order to bear with the ugliness. The beauty of God is in the same measure as his goodness. Then I became acquainted with the eastern rite. It was as if I came home. Everything spoke to me. Nothing seemed arbitrary. In the eastern rite, I found my spiritual homeland, that is to say, a world where the ritual is in place and where there is also great freedom; it is extremely incarnate in very concrete matters."

Does Bethlehem's partly eastern liturgy surprise some people?

"I don't know to what extent one can live, on a spiritual level, somewhere between the East and the West. I don't think it's possible, because it's all or nothing – in the East there is a totality and everything has its proper place. When I go to the monastery of Bethlehem, the use of microphones in the church bothers me. There shouldn't be anything other than the human voice in a church, one's own voice, nothing other than one's own nature before God. Nothing technical or artificial. That's the eastern tradition and that's why there's never an orchestra, an organ or other instruments in a Byzantine church. There's nothing but the human voice. We are obsessed by technology; the one moment when there shouldn't be anything technological… it's when we are in a church. I think there's a connection between the icons, the liturgy of the East and prayer of the heart. There's a definite order; everything is coherent. For me, it's difficult to pass from one register to another and mix the two traditions. In

Bethlehem, I can't help but feel the tension between the two opposites, even if both have their own beauty and depth. Can they be put together? I'm not so sure. But I don't want to push my reasoning too far on that point. The brothers and sisters of Bethlehem seem to draw great profit from the union of the two traditions. "

Do you find something of your "spiritual homeland" when you go to the monastery?

"Yes, but there's another thing, something less personal. When I discovered the monastery in Paris, I was, at the time, working with refugees. My wife had opened a school, located near the train station in Lyon, and then on rue de Bourgogne, where refugees learned French and about life in France. Most of them had just arrived in France, and they were almost completely lost and hadn't had time to adjust themselves to the new culture. The school had between one and two hundred students, of a variety of nationalities, but, at that time, the majority of them came from Afghanistan and Iran. I dealt with the juridical questions. Since I'm a lawyer, I represented them before the various institutions dealing with asylum. The law compels the administration to provide them with lodging, but the refugees often wait for a long time before receiving a place to live, if they receive anything at all. Many live on the street, which is hard, but most of all in the winter. At that time, a good third of the students at the Peter Claver School spent the night on the street, after having made their long and painful journey to France. My wife tried to find shelter for them, and I helped her in that task. I should admit that I did it with suspiciously too much passion: I was seeking to gratify my self-love in doing good works. In any case, I had the very naïve idea to turn to the 'institutional' Church, whose representatives used to lecture me ever since my youth, telling me that one should, before all else, care for the poor and for strangers, citing the Bible in support of their admonitions. I should have remembered that, as Jaspers says, one should always beware of those who try to instruct others about God. Since

I had not yet developed this mistrust, I was greatly astonished. Dignitaries preferred to write edict prescriptions and other directives and parish priests preferred to organize pilgrimages and other parish activities. Apostolic religious orders explained that the foreigners would interfere with the novices' studies. They feared that the foreigners might try to call home, or, God knows why, pull out the electric wires, or that they would seduce the young women in the parish. When they asked us if they were Christians and we said no, they were even less disposed to help. We met with closed doors everywhere. God's civil servants always made themselves unavailable. The mere prospect of dark-skinned refugees roaming about in the deserted corridors of empty convents gave rise to an insurmountable resistance. We were very far from the lofty declarations about 'the priority due to the service of the poor,' and the necessity of 'caring for the stranger.' And nowhere did we see them treat 'the other as the image of God.'

"There was a lot of snow, and there we were, with thirty or forty students without a roof over their heads. In that human desert, salvation came expectedly, and this will gladden those who admire what Grosjean calls 'Christological irony.' Salvation came through the sisters of Bethlehem. We had called them by chance. We knew that it's not their vocation. I still remember how they welcomed our first students. There were four. Two of them had been through terrible ordeals. They were a bit fearful. They weren't sure where they were going. The sisters welcomed them… I don't know how to express it… they welcomed them as if they were the Lord Himself, the God who appeared at Mamre, or Jesus at the well of Jacob, when He was tired. We almost cried. In fact, I think I did, though I hid it from the refugees. 'Behold, I am at the door and knock.'[1] They led them to a beautiful room on the first floor and they served them tea and cake. It was even amusing, because the tea, the carpets and the women with veils – it all seemed strangely familiar to our students. When I saw how they welcomed them, I understood that there is

1. Revelation 3, 20

no middle way with the Gospel and that it isn't a matter of speaking about the Gospel but of living it.

"One of the refugees had been in the war since he was twelve years old. He had seen and done a lot. He went to the back of the church during the liturgy, close to a statue of the Virgin Mary, and he remained there in silence. Another refugee told me much later, after he had learned French: 'That night, I thought I was in paradise. I should have stayed there.' Others came. With the sisters, they never found the door closed. Many of them, after having obtained legal status, found a job and got married. And whenever they asked us about the sisters, their voices changed, they spoke with a tone that is indescribable.

"Occasionally I would ask the prioress to pray for one of the refugees who had to appear before the court for asylum. She always asked me his name. That also reminded me of one of the rites in the East. When giving communion, the priest always pronounces the name of the person who is receiving communion: 'Inès, the Body and Blood of Christ are given to you for the remission of sins and for eternal life.'

"The sisters' help was entirely unexpected. But there were also others who offered unexpected help: friends, relatives, teachers at the school, some of them were far from practicing any religion. 'Many will come from east and west"[1]... And finally, since there were still about twenty refugees living on the street that winter, there was the Foreign Legion, at Fort Nogent. They opened their doors to them, and a warrant officer took care of them like a father. The legionnaires were fond of our students. Some of the soldiers had been in the war in Afghanistan. All of them had lived at one time or another in a war zone. They were very understanding, and they didn't make speeches."

To conclude my research about charisms, I asked François Sureau how he would define the word charism: 'Forgive me, but I should begin by saying that I'm not at ease with the word charism, nor with any of the other "isms," especially when they belong to a spiritual, or even clerical, vocabulary. In the final

1. Matthew 8, 11

analysis, it's just a question of people, or a group of people, and there's a certain 'something' about them, but I can't say more than that. I love the books by Guillerand who writes about the Carthusians, but I wouldn't know how to define the 'Carthusian charism,' and I suspect that the effort to define it would be utterly useless. I will simply try to express what strikes me the most in Bethlehem.

"I imagine that a life of faith, even more when it is a cloistered life, is, at least partially, a life of struggles. One can see it clearly in the writings of the first monks in Egypt. You go into seclusion, either by yourself or in a community. Then, there's no more dodging issues and the struggle begins: against oneself and against the Enemy. One of the Desert Fathers says, 'Go into your room, remain still for a few hours, and you will see what your passions will do to you.' That's also a Lenten experience that anyone can have. Yet, you see nothing of that struggle when you go to Bethlehem. The sisters are loving and present. Everything seems natural and easy for them. I don't know how they do it. You meet only with kindness and a smiling simplicity. It remains a mystery to me – a joyful and encouraging mystery."

At the heart of this mystery, the question of a vocation remains difficult:how can we reconcile a vocation with personal freedom?

"I suspect that for the one who receives the call, there is no question of freedom. The only freedom is the awareness of the need and the awareness of the need is to respond to the divine will. Apart from that, there is no being, there is no man or woman, there is no happiness, there is nothing. Nothing.

In theory, one is always free to say no to God… that is clear. Yet, practically speaking, can you imagine that such a tiny creature could actually say no to Someone so great? It has always seemed strange to me to consider that that could be possible.

Whenever there is an important undertaking, can one speak of freedom? Do we ask ourselves such questions? I don't think so. I believe instead in what is patently obvious, for it is there where the truth can be seen. It's true that sometimes there are bitter consequences. But the mixture of sweetness and bitterness is proper to the truth. There's a beautiful verse in the Book of Revelation about that: 'I took the little book from the hand of the angel and swallowed it; in my mouth it was as sweet as honey, but when I had eaten it, my stomach was made bitter.'[1] Anyone who has had the experience of a sincere and deep intuition knows that there is no room for freedom. There is only truth. When it is there, you know it at once and one is seldom mistaken. How can you say no?"

Is there also an eschatological dimension, which is proper to a religious vocation, but which also concerns all of us?

"I don't know if it's proper to religious life. Perhaps one can say that it is lived just as much among those who are in the world and whose life could even be an example for religious themselves? There was a monk in Egypt who sought perfection. The Spirit sent him to a craftsman in Alexandria and advised him to imitate him. The 'way of religious counsels' is foreign to the East, and, for my part, I think that it is best that way. There is also an absence of the hierarchy, which the Latin Church introduced to the world of believers . Of course, monasticism remains an ideal, but an ideal for everyone, for religious and lay persons alike.

When I see contemplatives, I have an almost visceral impression that they are already half-immersed physically in the age to come, in the Second Coming….'Watch for you know neither the day nor the hour.'[2] It is as if they are already partly beyond time, beyond human time. It is a sign. What is the age to come? Isaac the Syrian says that 'silence is the mystery of the age to come.' We will at last be happy in the age to come. The age in which we live now doesn't give us an idea or an image of the age to come, but it depends on it and draws from it. It is invisibly in contact with what will make us all personally and collectively happy.

1. Revelation 10, 10.
2. Matthew 25, 13.

4

Two lungs to live

Father Daniel Ange is also a great "lover" of the East. For him, it is a matter of spiritual vitality. One cannot live as Christian without two lungs:

"The thirst that Sister Marie had for the East, and the living spring from which the brothers and sisters 'drink' today is prophetic, capital and vital. You cannot be in good Christian health without breathing with both lungs. I myself have become very aware of the East.

"You can survive with only one lung, but you are in bad health. It is as if you are handicapped... A Christian who lives with only his western lung may be a good Christian, but he isn't in full health. It's a matter of equilibrium: we are in dire need of the dimension that comes from the East in order to counter-balance all the alterations brought about by centuries lived among Westerners. Thanks to John Paul II, among others, we are awakening to the riches of the great tradition of the East. It is like two streams that issue from the same spring, like a river that divides into two branches and whose water takes on various hues according to the regions where it flows. The water takes on the colors of the various cultures through which it passes... it's beautiful... and now it's a question of receiving all of our riches."

Father Daniel Ange enumerated all the riches that we have received from the East: the love of beauty, the love of the Virgin Mary, the Fathers of the Church, the sense of fidelity to the ancient ecclesiastical tradition, an acute sense of monastic life, the liturgy as Heaven on earth in all its splendor, a very incarnate liturgy that preserves the sense of the transcendent, etc....

"Love and beauty, the love of beauty has always impressed me in Bethlehem. Beauty for God, beauty for God's beautiful eyes and for ours also... everything should be beautiful. God has a right to beauty, because He **is** beauty. Beauty is one of the great themes of the theology of the East, which John Paul II admirably expressed in his wonderful letter *Orientale Lumen,* which is one of his greatest masterpieces. He insists on the divine splendor: the God of beauty and beauty made flesh... Jesus is beauty made flesh. Everything should be beautiful, not only in the liturgy, but in all of the smallest details. Beauty is manifested in little things, and that is part of Bethlehem's charism."

Is the eschatological dimension of the Bethlehem vocation drawn from the East?

"It is a prophetic life that anticipates Heaven, where everything will be praise, adoration, and a continual marveling at the beauty of the face of the Risen One. And it all begins in the shadow of faith. We are not yet in the full light, but we are in such a hurry to go to Heaven that we wish to start even now, to be with Jesus, to be completely for Him, for the sake of the beauty of his eyes... that's Heaven.

"We can hasten the coming of Christ in glory by our supplications and our ardent prayers. Evangelization also hastens his coming, for Jesus says that He will return. It will be the final and ultimate victory of truth over error, of light over darkness, of love over hatred: evil will be eradicated from the earth once and for all, and the entire universe will be transfigured. This transfiguration can begin in us if we allow ourselves to be transfigured by Jesus' glory, which is hidden in the Eucharist.

"That is the theology of the East. While the West speaks of being saved, the East speaks of being divinized and glorified.

"When we see so much evil, so many horrible things in the world, how can we not impatiently await Jesus' return in glory? Of course, He will come, and mankind will have to suffer a great passion in order to be purified, to be like gold that is taken out of the furnace. Jesus tells us: do not be afraid, lift up your heads, be happy. The worse things are in the world, the more we see that the end times are upon us. We are truly in the end times, because we have reached the point, at least in the West, where, after having completely rejected God, we no longer even know who man is."

Is it the East that has bequeathed upon us life in the desert?

"Of course. To live in the desert is to continue, in the Church, the Lord's life in the desert. His forty days in the desert must be perpetuated throughout all eras and in all the countries in the world. For lay people in the world, it is the life of Jesus at Nazareth that is prolonged. Missionaries continue Jesus' three years of apostolic life; monks and monastic sisters continue his time in the desert, those nights spent in intercession, in remaining in the Father's presence. This long time in the desert, in so many struggles… it's like watching over the city, on the ramparts of the city, like guardian angels who never cease to contemplate the face of God and who, at the same time, watch over human beings. That was also Therese's theological intuition, and it gave her the certitude that in Heaven she would continue to work for the missions. She said: if the guardian angels can do both at the same time, why can't I? That's the little Therese's boldness!

Angels ceaselessly pray and worship, and that's the way they protect and watch over us."

IV

THE MOST BEAUTIFUL OF THE CHILDREN OF MEN

How important it is that we associate beauty with love, and that we be able to discern what is merely "cold" beauty. For that, a conversion is necessary. The face of the most beautiful of the children of men and the face of the most beautiful of women tell us, in their splendor, what true beauty is. In the universe, in the stars, in light, there is something true that regenerates us, something that we feel is just and right; we must discern the difference between false beauty and true beauty. Let us be fascinated by our Source, for God's Beauty will never mislead us. His Beauty isn't deceptive, and it always leads us to love. It is never sterile. It leads us to his Being, to Being which is necessarily Beauty.

Sister Marie

The Church needs art in order to transmit the message that Christ entrusted to it. It must render not only perceptible, but, in the measure of what is possible, also fascinating, the world of the spirit, of the invisible, of God. The Church must therefore translate in significant formulae what is, in fact, unspeakable. For this purpose, art has a capacity, which is inherent to it, which allows it to grasp one or another aspect of the message and to translate in colors, shapes or sounds which reinforce the intuition of whoever listens or watches. It is able to do so without depriving the message itself of its transcendent value or its halo of mystery.[1]

1. Extract from the letter to artists by John Paul II, April 4th, 1999.

1

"Seekers of light"

Beauty... everyone I had interviewed spoke about it. In Bethlehem, there is a particular attention given to beauty; a beauty which is not always understood and which is inseparable from Love. Love and beauty. The love of beauty. The beauty of love. Claudel says: "What is beautiful reunites, what is beautiful comes from God." That is perhaps another one of the messages that the monks and the monastic sisters of Bethlehem offer when they try to make everything beautiful and when they invite us to contemplate beauty. Beauty that comes from God, beauty that brings us to God, beauty that is God. The sister who is in charge of the community's artwork offered this explanation: "Christ is beauty. He is 'the most beautiful of the children of men' who was born of Mary, 'the most beautiful of women.' Christ and the Virgin transmit this message of beauty. They are the archetypes of the beauty which Christ, in His person, entrusted to the Church which is his Spouse."

Upon entering one of the community's gift shops, one is struck by the atmosphere. The statues of the Virgin, in wood or in dolomite, some of them life size, attract one's attention. She is there, the Virgin; She looks at us and she invites us, in silence, to contemplate her. Near her are the angels and the saints. On the walls, there are several bas-reliefs of the Deposition from the Cross. There is also a big crèche, the kind that one often sees in parishes. In Paris, last year, at Champs-Elysées and at the foot of the Eiffel Tower, Bethlehem's statues of the Holy Family were there to invite the tourists and passers-by to pause for a moment of recollection, though a nearby Santa Clause competed for their attention! In the Bethlehem gift shops, there are also icons, medals, stoneware china, decorated pieces of earthenware, candles, incense and all sorts of essential oils and delicacies for the palate – the monks and monastic sisters keep their recipes a secret. There is a style that is proper to Bethlehem: "Like the art of the first centuries, our art expresses our faith," the sister in charge of artwork explained to me, "just as we say that the liturgy is in reference to the first centuries of the faith. We don't pretend to be artists. We try to continue the same work that the Holy Spirit inspired in more prolific periods, when faith was so deeply a part of daily life that all that came from the hands of men was the fruit of their life with God. There is no reason for the Holy Spirit to be less present today. We try to be receptive and attentive to the shapes, volumes and colors that the Holy Spirit inspired believers of the East and the West to choose in order to glorify God and honor the mystery of salvation.

"Sister Marie deliberately asked us to find our inspiration in the faith; we are not only disciples of ancient masters, but also of the Christian artists of today who wish to bear witness to their faith through their art. We seek to make of our artwork a source of prayer and of life, and we try to adopt an attitude of humble submission to the ever-new inspirations of the Spirit.

"There is a certain resemblance, in some eras, between the iconographic art of the East and the Roman art or the beginning of Gothic art in the West. Those artists were 'seekers of light'; their point of departure was a reality that cannot be seen or touched, and which is revealed by the Word of God. This reality is a mystery, the very mystery of God. A certain mendicity is necessary to perceive it. It is hidden in the work of God.

"This same characteristic marked eastern iconographical art, and that is why we love that art. At the risk of no longer being an iconographer, the iconographer begs absolutely everything of God: the inspiration, the will to undertake the work, the execution and the accomplishment of the work. The iconographer disappears to the point of not even leaving his signature.

"We find these same components among other artists who prefer God to their own glory: the anonymous builders of cathedrals and the sculptors of great works. They worked in teams, never leaving a signature or any other trace of their identity."

I didn't meet any of the artists in Bethlehem, but I would have loved to have met the sister who sculpted a breathtaking Deposition from the Cross: there is a man – Nicodemus or the apostle John – who receives Jesus' body in his open arms. "We wish to remain hidden," the sister said to me. "We aren't the creators of our artwork; in fact, our artwork is seldom the work of only one sister. The 'artist' disappears behind the monastic sister; by our renunciation of artistic ambitions and our humble collaboration, we allow the Holy Spirit to be the true artist. We manifest God by hiding ourselves like the Seraphim and the Cherubim, who accomplish their vocation by hiding themselves behind their six wings in the presence of God. Since we work in silence, prayer and adoration, the spiritual combat can become, if God gives us the grace, a kind of visible word."

So you aren't concerned about beauty?

"We aren't interested in aestheticism or in the effect that is produced. We try to manifest a theological reality in shapes and colors. Early Byzantine icons, Roman art, Gregorian music and singing in the eastern liturgy find their origin in the same theology. It isn't a matter of making 'beautiful' faces. The task is to unite one's physical gaze to one's faith. It is then that one 'sees' the invisible. In icons, the eyes devour the face. The eyes are never closed, except for very rare exceptions. And the onlooker gazes with all the intensity of his faith. That is why the glory of love irradiates his being: since he believes, he sees. 'In a little while the world will not see me anymore, but you will see me because I live and you shall live.'[1] It is in the strength of this promise of Christ that iconographers do their work of representing a life that is vision in the night, vision of the invisible. The onlooker's face is transformed. All the icons gaze at us from the invisible and they gaze at the invisible; that is why the eyes are so important."

1. John 14,19.

Are the faces in icons sometimes troubling?

"Those who are accustomed to 'photographic' representations of spiritual beauty are sometimes disconcerted by the manner in which monastic artists render beauty, for we don't follow the aesthetic criteria of prettiness and beauty when representing the beautiful face of an angel. When a monastic artist is before an icon, she doesn't look at it as much with her physical eyes as with the eyes of her heart. This gaze of the heart penetrates much deeper than the shapes and the visible expressions. She is in the heart of the mystery. When she sees furrows on an angel's face, she doesn't say: 'He has a lot of wrinkles!' But instead, she thinks to herself: 'What depth!' She is entirely in her gaze. In a human face in an icon, for example, there are places where the light is prominent and there are also traces of shadows where the iconographer has transcended all earthly seduction. The iconographer wanted to represent the fact that a person is a gaze, a tension towards, an intensity. Human charm is, as it were, eliminated.

We must listen to icons, and not only look at them.

We must let icons look at us, and not only look at them.

2

From beauty to glory

Monsignor Rey, the Bishop of Fréjus-Toulon, has known the community of Bethlehem for more than thirty years. His first encounters with the community were when he took refuge, even before becoming a priest, in the monastery of Poligny for moments of solitude. Today, his diocese is "rich" in contemplative communities, among which are counted two monasteries of the sisters of Bethlehem: Le Thoronet and La Verne, which I visited with my husband during a vacation. Located twelve kilometers away from Collobrières, in the massif of the Maures, the monastery of La Verne overlooks a landscape of rare beauty, which extends as far as the eye can see. There is a road that climbs its way through a big forest of arbutus, cork oaks and chestnut trees, and ends at the magnificent ancient Carthusian monastery, which dates from the twelfth century, and which restoration work continues to rejuvenate. There is no need to discourse about beauty in this monastic desert. Beauty is there in the midst of a mysterious splendor. Is it a dangerous beauty? A deceptive beauty? That was the first question that I presented to Monsignor Rey during one of his visits to the monastery in Paris where he inconspicuously celebrated Mass.

"In a cultural world that distrusts dogmatic and moral language," he explained, "it is touching to see manifestations of beauty. This manifestation is a first approach, a preparatory awakening. And then, at one moment or another, it should send the onlooker to seek deeper instruction and engage him in serving others. One must distinguish between, on one hand, beauty which is inherent to the mystery of God, and, on the other hand, a purely aesthetical experience which touches one's emotions, but which might be simplistic or even deceptive if it doesn't go straight to the rationality of the message of faith. Aesthetic experiences might even lead some people to an impasse."

Can beauty, therefore, evangelize?

"Benedict XVI spoke about 'the beauty of being a Christian.' That means that we must make our Christian life beautiful. Christ is 'the most beautiful of the children of men.' In the mystery of his Passion, in his disfigured face, his beauty is interiorized through suffering. The mystery of the Cross makes us go from an exterior beauty, which is disfigured by the Passion, to an interior beauty, to the splendor of the soul."

Is it important for a bishop and for priests to go to the desert?

"Of course. When one is immersed in action, one's existence is, as it were, reduced to action, and one is exhausted by too much action. Monastic life helps to humanize our time, to evangelize it, to bring it into harmony with the rhythms that are found in nature. Faith, which is inscribed in us, is lived in God's time, which is the time of creation and the time of the liturgy. Monastic life yokes together the words nature and praise. It is the art of living in union with the realism of the earth and the vision of the heavenly world.

"Time in our society is chopped, fragmented and determined by what is urgent and immediate; when one is immersed in monastic life, there is a deep interior restructuring that occurs as one enters into a new way of inhabiting time, which is both more natural and more supernatural, and which has the taste of eternity.

"Our mission is to go into the world, but it is also 'Come to me.' There are two movements: we meet Christ through his Word and, at the same time, there are places – sanctuaries – that speak of his presence, which bring us back to what is essential; a community such as Bethlehem is one of those places. Those who are seeking God come to this haven of peace, whether at Le Thoronet or at La Verne, and they have an experience that is intimate and profound."

One can therefore be a missionary in a monastery?

"The fact that young people – and in Bethlehem there are young people – choose to leave everything for Christ is an example that intrigues and fascinates others. Simply by their choice, they are missionaries. Contemplative life, and religious life in general, is a kind of image of what we hope for. It expresses what we will be: entirely for Christ and entirely for our brethren; it is a kind of prophecy of what we will live. This radical call and this eschatological hope are contemplated in the men and women who have left everything for Christ.

"The community's very name expresses hope: the Assumption of the Virgin Mary. We live in a world where time is crushed. We live in the hegemony of the present moment: a click on the Internet, and you are immediately on the other side of the world, you traverse space and time. Our memory is very short, and even atrophied: the future is purely technological. The political future is very uncertain: we have a short-term vision and we go from one election to another. There's no horizon. In this context, I believe that what is at stake for Christianity, the challenge, is to give hope. This hope comes to us through people who already live the mystery of 'not yet.'

"Mary is at the forefront of this hope. The function of the Gospel today is to say that the world can change, that we can change. If Christ is capable of changing bread into his Body, then He is capable of changing my life, which receives this bread so that it may be transfigured. There is a Eucharistic dimension in what is lived. And again, it is expressed by a community: it isn't only words that bring us hope, but also human beings who bring us hope and who bring us to hope."

3

What will it profit a man if he gains the whole world?

"It was through beauty that I encountered Bethlehem. It was at Lourdes, in Bethlehem's gift shop. Everything was so beautiful: the statues, the icons and even the photos of the monasteries and hermitages. I was drawn to Bethlehem by all of that, but in a somewhat romantic and artificial way…"

Maria's words were like an echo of what Monseigneur Rey had explained to me. She helped me to understand that beauty isn't enough to turn a young, idealistic woman, someone who is in love with beauty, into a sister. It took ten years for her to learn how to renounce her own projects and to answer Christ's call.

Originally from the Czech Republic, she was ten years old when the Berlin wall – and with it, communist ideology – collapsed. Her father was a manual laborer and her mother was uneducated and didn't have a career. Both of them were unbelievers. The living conditions were very difficult: "After the fall of the Wall, the biggest change, of course, was freedom." The freedom to travel, to work, to speak... and the freedom of religion. "We were 'thirsty.' The influence of the West was strong. There was a lot of enthusiasm for the Church. Sects and eastern religions also began to exert an influence."

Influenced by her friends, the young woman first discovered Buddhism and then Christianity: "When I lived in the countryside with my parents, I got up at six o'clock every morning. After putting on white clothes, I took my mat and went into the woods to do my breathing exercises and yoga. After finishing, I recited Christian prayers: the 'Hail Mary,' the

'Our Father,' 'Hail Holy Queen,' 'I believe' and a prayer to my guardian angel! After a while, I knew that I couldn't continue like that. It was incoherent. I had to make a choice. Since I was I drawn to the Eucharist, I decided to go to Mass every Sunday, even if I couldn't receive communion because I wasn't baptized. I abandoned Buddhism. One day, after Mass, I went to the sacristy to talk to the priest. He was a Jesuit. I asked him to baptize me. He wrote his phone number on a piece of paper so I could call him to arrange a time when we could meet together. On the back of the paper, there was a phrase which I still remember very clearly: 'What will it profit a man if he gains the whole world?'"

Baptized at sixteen, confirmed at eighteen, Maria's thirst was unquenchable; she traveled the world, pursued various studies and took one path after another. One can understand why, after all those years of restriction and restraint, she ran unbridled to the West.

She thought at first that she wanted to become a doctor, but she then she turned instead towards the social sciences after having passed an entrance exam in Fine Arts and learned several languages!

At nineteen, on Easter day, she experienced "an immense thirst for love": a love which she could name, but the struggle continued. She heard the call, but she couldn't respond to it. Maria was in love...why not consider marriage? She interrupted her studies, left the Czech Republic and committed herself for two years to work in France with Father Daniel Ange at *Jeunesse-Lumière*. During those years, she met the sisters of Bethlehem, first in their gift shop at Lourdes, and, later, during a retreat at the monastery of La Verne.

Maria went to Kazakhstan with Father Daniel Ange for a one-month evangelization mission, and then returned to Prague to study theology for five years. She regularly visited the monasteries of Bethlehem: Le Thoronet, La Verne and Montsvoirons for the discernment retreat, and then Currière for one month. But it was impossible for her to say "yes": "I knew that the great love of my life was passing me by, but I went back to my country to finish my theological studies and to write my thesis."

It was finally a university professor who put her back to the wall. She was twenty-seven years old when she confided in him about her desire to enter consecrated life and yet, at the same time, she asked him for a scholarship so she could continue her studies abroad! "That man saved my vocation and my life by advising me to do a thirty-day Ignatian retreat. I followed his advice, and it was during that retreat that I was finally certain of my call to consecrated life, to contemplative life. It couldn't be anywhere else than Bethlehem. A few months afterwards, I entered the monastery at Monte Camporeggiano in Italy.

"Today, I can say that my vocation is in some way a response to the invitation that John Paul II addressed to the young people gathered in Rome in the year 2000. I received his message in the depths of my heart: 'If you become what you should be, you will set the world ablaze.' In Bethlehem, we are often told that we must become Fire, that we must burn with love, that God himself is the Fire of Love, the devouring Fire that draws us to the desert and speaks to our hearts.

"Inès, I have told you my story because I truly want people to understand that the love of the Lord is stronger than everything else. He could have let go of me, but in his tenderness and his mercy, He didn't cease to draw me to Him so that one day I could say 'yes' to Him. When almost all was lost, He seized me. There comes a time when you just can't resist any more."

4

The builders of monasteries

"The companions"

In the autumn, I went back to the Saint Désert at Piquetière, a monastery which has been under construction since 1991, when the sisters began their work with few resources. Today, the monastery is nearly complete, and the community exercises important responsibilities for the whole "Family" (the general secretaryship, printing, architecture, artwork, etc.) The Family continues to grow and the work continues...I had already visited a number of monasteries, and I noticed that there is an architectural homogeneity, though the architecture of each monastery is also adapted to the site, country and climate. There is also always a characteristic style that doesn't leave room for doubt; one always knows when one is in a monastery of Bethlehem...

Who designs the plans? Who builds the monasteries? Who works on the construction sites?

It is here, at the Saint Désert, that I received answers to my questions, in a monastery above reproach. And I was left with extraordinary memories.

Within the monastery's walls, a few meters above the chapel, bordering the cloistered area, is "the companions' house." There I met Sister Jackie and her "guys": Maurice (nicknamed Mimi), Jean-Pierre, Henri (nicknamed Kiki), and Boule... the team isn't complete, but they are the entourage of the one whom they call our "little mother." We found ourselves in a dining room with Arabian coffee! I stared wide-eyed with delight: ever since I began visiting the monasteries, the sisters always offer me herbal tea. It's delicious, but I must admit that I miss coffee! There was even an ashtray and, since I'm a heavy smoker, I was very happy. The "guys" were a little bit intimidated at first, but their passion for their work and their love for the sisters made them quickly forget that there was a microphone.

Two of them have known Jackie since their youth. They were in Public Assistance homes for children, and she was their teacher. The two others came later to work on the sisters' construction site. They were supposed to stay for only one month, but they never left!

Sister Jackie was a young teacher when she first asked the sisters of Bethlehem to welcome her with "her" children for summer camp. She came back almost every year with the "little ones" who became adolescents and then adults and who, with her, took advantage of their visit to help in the construction work of the monasteries.

"I had to be a 'mother' before I could become a sister!" Sister Jackie explained to me. Thirteen years later, she finally decided to enter the monastery. She was thirty-four years old. She defines herself as "a free electron in the heart of Bethlehem," because she goes from one construction site to another, in France and abroad. The "guys" follow her, and they are proud to list all the countries where they have worked. Jean-Pierre has been to Canada, the United States, Poland, Portugal and Spain… His most beautiful memory is of Israel: "It's God's place. There's a different ambience. The light is beautiful." Mimi told me about his travels throughout the world: he visited the monastery of Bet Gemal in the Holy Land and the monastery near Lourdes, where they recently completed the construction of the church. They have had to tear down walls right after building them in order to move them just twenty centimeters away! They don't hide their admiration not only for Sister Jackie, who puts her hands in the cement doesn't hesitate to pick up a hammer or a trowel, but also for the other sisters who are courageous and work very hard.

I asked them to tell me the secret of how they construct the half-dome. In most of the chapels of Bethlehem, there is an icon of the Trinity in the half-dome. "It's like a beehive that is cut in two. I can't explain how we do it, but one day, Sister

Jackie almost fell right through it! She could have died...there wasn't any horsing around that day!"

They were visibly moved when they spoke about Sister Marie, whom they knew well, and about Sister Isabelle: "Both of them are just plain good." Jean-Pierre confided in me: "I was mistreated not only in my childhood, but also in my first job. By trusting me, Sister Isabelle gave me back my dignity. I found the light thanks to the sisters. They have big hearts. If I hadn't met Jackie, I wouldn't have met the sisters." Mimi told me about all the trouble that he got into in his life: "It's a good thing the sisters were there... if not, I would probably be a hobo."

Why hide all of that? I was impressed by those men who, battered by life, are the "artisans" of Bethlehem. They are eight in all. Three other men who are construction workers help them.

Materially speaking, "the companions" are responsible for "building" Bethlehem; when a house or a church is built, it's no small matter! "I'm nothing," Sister Jackie said to me. "Sister Marie received the charism and Sister Isabelle develops it in concrete situations, from all points of view, from the Rule of life to the construction sites. Then the charism passes through my hands and through those of 'my men.' They build Bethlehem by keeping the charism intact. Everything is connected: there's a hub with the spokes."

I understood that they are hardworking, tough men, but at the same time, they have an incredible respect for the sisters and a generosity and love which is equaled only by the generosity and love that they receive from the sisters.

They speak frankly, they are funny and they are also free. In the house where I met them, they eat their meals together. Sister Jackie cooks for them just as she did, for some of them, when they were children!

In that room, there is a big aquarium filled with very exotic little fish with magnificent colors... it was a gift that they gave Sister Jackie last year for Mother's Day... It was Alain, nicknamed Boule, who had the idea.

Alain is very reserved. He is the woodcutter of the "family": he cuts, saws and splits the logs to the dimensions of the wood burning stoves, and then brings them to the sisters' hermitages. Boule is quiet: he doesn't offer long discourses, but his beautiful gaze speaks volumes.

Henri's blue eyes are also very expressive. He is humorous, but also modest. He has been there less time than the others: ten years. "My encounter with the sisters is a beautiful story," he said. "I was working in a difficult world: in kitchens. I can't explain why I left the kitchens for stones. It's a call." Henri comes from Chartres… I couldn't help but mention the cathedral of Chartres, Our Lady of the Pillar, who was the Virgin of my childhood… He knows her, and being somewhat of an accomplice, he replied, "Here we live her and she makes us live. I can't say more than that. It's a secret."

It was nightfall – the time for those who didn't live in the monastery to leave. I remained with Sister Jackie and the pile of questions that I had for her!

Jackie's dream

After my conversation with "the companions," I realized that Sister Jackie is a sister who is a little bit out of the ordinary. As a result of the mission that she received to build monasteries, her frankness is often caustic. She often works day and night and she goes around the world to visit different construction sites. It must be difficult to live a true monastic life of silence and of solitude under such conditions. My questions didn't unsettle Sister Jackie in the least!

What is solitude?

"There's no deeper solitude than to do God's will. I live my solitude with God in my encounter with Him. That's my solitude. Of course, there have to be sisters who live in hermitages; I couldn't keep going without them. That's very important. My fidelity and their fidelity are like two halves of a whole. My poverty is deep with regards to that, but I try to be faithful to what is asked of me. My hands pray when I work.

"In fact, it's very simple. Jesus says: 'I am the way, the truth and the life.'[1] That's all that matters in the end… three words: love, truth and life. The rest is garbage. I've always said that I don't want to live in solitude."

I was delighted by her frankness. She continued: "According to my logic, Inès, love is all that counts. Whatever isn't love… It's love that leads us follow the rules. I wouldn't be able to bear it if someone were shouting all the time: 'Do this! Do that!' I'm not saying that we shouldn't force ourselves to do certain things, but it is God's love that makes it possible for us to obey human laws.

"Our Rule of life is wonderful. When it was written, I said to my prioress: I don't need anything else. Nothing other than the Gospel and the Rule of life. Life is full of paradoxes…

"Love is the only rule. Love and freedom: that's Bethlehem. Love is God. Love is first and God is the goal. If I love God, I also love my sisters and those who are entrusted to me. I can love everyone.

"Everything is grace. My work is to build monasteries, and I'm convinced that I have received the grace for that. Each sister has a particular grace. First of all, there is the grace of being loved by a God who loves millions of human beings, and there is the grace of being unique. It's crazy, but we have to believe that. There aren't any molds in Bethlehem. We are all here for the glory of God while respecting one another."

I asked Sister Jackie a few technical questions regarding the layout of the monasteries. "Whenever possible, a monastery of Bethlehem is composed of three distinct areas. First of all, there's the cloister in the upper house. That's a place of strict solitude. It's reserved for the community, and it's the heart of the monastery. The hermitages of solitude are there, far from any human gaze. Then, there's the coenobium, which is reserved for community life. It includes the church, the refectory, the chapter room and the library. All of that, of course, is within the enclosure. There's also the lower house which includes: on the one hand, a smaller cloister with hermitages for the sisters who

1. Jn 14:6

work in the house, and on the other hand, when it's possible, hermitages for the guests who desire to meet God in solitude. And finally, there's a guest area, a 'parvis of friendship,' which is accessible to all and where visitors and families are welcomed. It's set somewhat apart from the monastery, and sometimes there's also a sanctuary where they can come for adoration."

And the hermitages?

"I once visited Taybeth, in the Palestinian territories. It is said that Jesus may have passed by there… there is, what they call in the village, 'Jesus' house.' We studied it carefully and, in the car, with Sister Marie, we took a piece of paper and a pencil and we made a sketch of it. It serves today as a model for our hermitages.

"Now, when we arrive in a new place, we construct what is called a 'Casalibus.' It's a term borrowed from the Carthusians. We begin immediately by making provisory cloisters with little trailer homes (which remain sometimes for fifteen years) so that the sisters can live right from the start in solitude."

And the half-dome in the church?

It's a great story! I didn't have the slightest idea how to make one. One day, I went to look at some bread ovens and that night I had a dream. I had prayed to Saint Joseph and, in a dream, he explained everything to me: the next morning, I did exactly what I had seen in my dream!

There is often a search for perfection in the buildings and grounds of monasteries, particularly in Bethlehem. Some people might question this monastic "cult" of beauty. Is all of that really necessary?

"Beauty is inscribed in obedience. Like our charism, we received it from God. Beauty is connected to God's love, which is connected to the love of others. I already said that God is our goal, and God is beauty *par excellence*. The beauty of God, which we try to manifest in our monasteries, is for others.

"There are also technical requirements that are to be respected. There are certain norms in our monasteries for the half-dome that I spoke about, for the ceruse[1] in the church and stalls, and for the refectory and library. Other elements, like the icons, the canopy, the lamps, and everything else that we have received from the East, is adapted to each country.

"And again, there are many things that 'come from God' and are difficult to explain.

"I like Sister Marie's explanation: 'There are different ways to transmit a message: by speaking, by drawing, by writing … and then there is God's way.'

"For thousands of years, God has been revealing Himself to man. He has thought over the matter. His way is to create beauty that remains, that is visible; He remains, but in an invisible manner. He remains in the universe, in creation, but He disappears before the eyes of man; He remains only in the harmony of the colors and shapes that He has created. God disappears once He has clothed everything with His beauty and His signature. That's why it's so important for monks to live in very beautiful places: in order to have the right to do as God does. They try to preserve the environment as much as possible so that the message and spiritual heritage associated with those locations, which are inexplicable without God, without His saints and without the work of the Holy Spirit, whose presence in the Church dates long before the monks who came to inhabit those places.

"Beauty is a translation in created terms of what God is: Love and nothing else."

My conversation with Sister Jackie and "the companions" remains a pleasant memory. They helped me to understand that there can be a flexibility in monastic life that doesn't undermine its rigor.

1. It is the color white softened by a patina.

5
Two giants of love

When I left the Saint Désert, I couldn't resist making a detour to the monastery of Notre-Dame-de-l'Unité in Pugny, in order to meet with two builders of love of another genre. They are brothers. They are priests.

After having traveled around the world for more than forty years in serving the least of their brethren, they are now the happy chaplains of the sisters of Bethlehem. Father Raymond is at the Monastery of Pugny, near Aix-les-Bains, and Father Pierre is at the monastery of Montsvoirons, which faces Mont Blanc.

I knew that they would be together that day. It's not unusual that they are together, since they don't like being apart from one another for too long. They have been at the service of this monastic Family for six or seven years. These two youthful elderly men (one is eighty-five and the other is eighty years old) consider themselves the "happiest priests on earth."

I was impressed by my encounter with those two giants of love. Before meeting with them, I read the account of their incredible journey of love with lepers, children with polio and prostitutes. But there's nothing imposing about them: they are lowly like those whom they served, put back on their feet and loved unto the end. Every person whom they encounter, whoever he may be, is, for them, unique and to be loved with a preferential love. They welcomed me with big smiles that radiated goodness in the Inn of the Good Samaritan where Father Raymond (like Father Pierre at Montsvoirons) receives the numerous visitors who come to knock at the door of his heart. They are passionate about Jesus, and love to spend long hours in adoration in their oratory, but when a visitor comes, they come out to meet with him without batting an eyelid. Always ready to obey the call of Love, they leave their oratory, their eyes filled with the light of Him whom they have contemplated.

They could speak endlessly about the sisters: their youthfulness, their smiles, their radiance, the freedom with which they welcome all those who come to their monasteries. "They pray a lot, but, above all, they love one another! That's what characterizes them – love. There's an intuitive and respectful quality in all that they do. During the winter, they come to shovel the snow in front of my door, but I've never been able to see which sister does it. When they bring my meal, there's always a flower... those are just details but, behind those small things, there is something very deep which is directly related to their vocation.

"They live a life of intimacy with the Lord and with Mary. There's always a little flower that expresses something of what they are living. It's not for prettiness. It's because Bethlehem was founded by the Holy Virgin, and since she is the Prioress, there is always fraternal charity. The sisters are deeply marked by the Eucharist, in whose presence they live continually. When one sees a sister who has been in the monastery for ten or twenty years, and who spends a few hours every day in adoration, that isn't a spiel, it's for real!"

You who were on the "battlefield," what would you say to those who think that all of that is admirable, but in fact the world is collapsing around them and the sisters do nothing at all?

"I would insist that it's true that they aren't doing anything. Little Thérèse of Lisieux was proclaimed patroness of the Missions, and yet she did nothing, absolutely nothing at all; and she died when she was twenty-four years old. That's how the Church views contemplatives. They are indispensable to the Church."

Father Raymond then spoke about a young man named Robert, who died at sixteen, eaten away by leprosy. Then about another leper in Vietnam who was left on his mat for twenty years with no one to care for him… and so many others. "Do you see the connection with the sisters?" he asked me. "Those who suffer today are solitaries. Think of all the elderly who are left alone in nursing homes… The sisters' solitude is a presence, they offer an invisible presence to all those who are alone and suffer."

Father Pierre said to me: "Whenever there is a monastic profession, and I see a sister stretched out face down on the floor with her arms in the form of a cross, I say to myself: 'There are thousands of people surrounding her. Thanks to her, to the offering of her life, to her prayer, that all those people are going to be saved.'

"John Paul II said that the hidden life is 'a silent cross planted in the heart of humanity.' How can you explain that? There's nothing to be understood, we just have to believe it. We can't understand the mystery of Jesus. It's the mystery of love. It's the mystery of the Cross. Jesus came to plant his love in Mary's heart. Without Mary, it's impossible to understand. Mary let herself be led by Him…all the way to the Cross. The Cross is fecund: Jesus took upon Himself absolutely all the misery in the world, to such an extent that He died because of it. Jesus takes our side. He will never defend Himself. He takes everything, absolutely everything upon Himself. That's what Pierre and I have lived. The Cross.

"People often said to us: what do you do to keep from falling into despair? The lepers, the refugees, misery in all its forms, prostitution …? Saint Paul is a reference point for us: 'I complete in my flesh what is lacking in Christ's afflictions.'[1] We find Him in our deepest depths. We find ourselves in the mystery of the Cross and of suffering. It's true, we were immersed in human suffering, but we were never discouraged, because we kept in mind Saint Paul's way of seeing suffering and what Jesus said: 'as you did it to one of the least of these my brethren, you did it to me.'[2]

"The sisters are at the heart of Jesus' Passion, of his love. It's because they offer their lives that they participate in the Cross.

1. Col 1:24
2. Mt 25:40

"Remember Saint Paul's image: Jesus is the head and we are the members. Among the members, there are those who suffer terribly, and there are also others who perhaps don't suffer physically, but as chaplains here, we see that some of the sisters, sometimes, have terrible struggles. It's normal. In a vocation, there are always successive calls, which require purifications. Their suffering is a participation in the world's suffering. Without faith, it's impossible to understand, and yet, at the same time, there are some people who don't have faith, and yet they understand even better than some Christians, because Love is the key."

It was nightfall. I left the two priests whose love overflows from their words and illuminates their gaze – a love which has been intensified by the thousands of children, women and men that they have loved and welcomed in their own heart at the cost of their life.

In the name of all the least of Jesus' brethren, thank you!

Before I left, I slipped into the astonishing Byzantine chapel, Notre-Dame de l'Unity, which overhangs the lake of Bourget. This chapel, built at the beginning of the 20th century by Father Portal, a pioneer of ecumenism with Cardinal Mercier and Lord Halifax, was a meeting place for Anglicans and Catholics. Everything here speaks of Love and unity.

View on the monastery of Bet Gemal (Israel).

Each Sunday, the monastic sisters walk in « spaciement » (long way).

A monastic sister makes the great prostration during her monastic profession at the monastery of Montsvoirons (France).

A Eucharist celebration at the monastery of La Verne (France).

A monastic sister meditates on the Holy Scriptures in the "scriptorium" of her hermitage.

V

RENDEZ-VOUS IN THE PROMISED LAND

Introduction

I arrived in the Holy Land, in Bet Gemal, on the eve of the feast of the Exaltation of the Cross. I had already visited my sister there several times before, but the sense of otherness and wonder comes upon me each time I arrive there.

Half-way between Tel Aviv and Jerusalem, about 30 kilometers from Gaza, close to Bet Shemesh, the hill of Bet Gemal – whose name in Hebrew means "Gamaliel's house" and in Arabic "house of beauty" – is like the hills in the Song of Songs which are imbued with light and silence. As early as the 5th century, this hill became famous because of the discovery of the relics of the first Christian martyr of Jerusalem, Saint Steven. According to an ancient Judeo-Christian tradition, he was buried on the property of the famous rabbi Gamaliel, who was Saint Paul's teacher and a member of the Sanhedrin. Nicodemus and his son Abides were also buried there. It is this event that gives this place its signification, history and importance for Christians. Until 1967, this hill was farmed by an agricultural school founded by the Salesian Fathers, where they educate Arab children of the region. An unforeseen turn of events of a political nature led to the closing of the school. Part of the land is still courageously cultivated by the sons of Don Bosco. There are wheat fields, vines and olive groves. Bedouins come to pasture their flocks there. Sharing the same evangelical perspective, the Salesians and the communities of monks and monastic sisters on the hill welcome many visitors, whether Israeli or Palestinian, and also many pilgrims from all countries and backgrounds. In 1987, the Salesian Fathers generously offered the land for the foundation of the monastery of the monastic sisters. André Nathan Chouraqui, who once was the deputy-mayor of Jerusalem and a well-known translator of the

Bible and author of other works, encouraged the construction of this monastery in Israel. I had the good fortune to meet his wife, Annette, and one of his daughters, Elizabeth.

The sisters' monastery is comprised of three levels. Below is the cloister of the sisters' hermitages. There is a sandy path lined with pine trees that leads to a small cemetery where two monastic sisters are buried. It is a place of peace … a cypress is planted next to each of the tombs, as if directing to heaven the souls that they watch over… At the entrance of the cloister, there is a small Massabielle grotto in a rock… it is not uncommon to find a sister in prayer there…

Above is the guest house. Fuchsia bougainvilleas, oleanders and orange trees grow along the walls. Every morning, Yasuko, wearing a straw hat and carrying a small watering can, comes to water the plants while saying her rosary. Yasuko is Japanese and has been living there for several years… she is protected and loved by the sisters. In silence, she distributes to all those whom she encounters beautiful images of the Virgin Mary. The shop, visited by many people, especially the day of the Sabbath, lies under the terrace; the trunk of magnificent pine tree is in the middle and serves as parasol above. In the shop there are sculptures, icons, medals, pottery, books and candy. There is also a small kitchen for the guests: like most kitchens, it is a pleasant place, a place of confidences, laughter and also sometimes of tears… The sisters' families often meet haphazardly and exchange a few words, as they come to get the trays prepared by the sisters, always decorated with a little flower or a small orange branch, loaded with delicious meals no less savory than the immense love with which they are prepared.

To go the sisters' chapel, you have to pass by a small "synagogue," which was specially designed for our Jewish brethren, and then climb some stairs. There are two tribunes for visitors. In order to reach the highest one, you have to pass through a terrace that overlooks the whole monastery. There is a magnificent view on the surrounding hills, and, in the distance, the brothers' monastery is visible. It was there that I contemplated some of the most beautiful sunsets that I have ever seen.

The bell began to ring: I went to the first tribune for the solemn Mass of the Glorious Cross, feast of the Exaltation of the Cross. In the chapel, over the altar, hovers a golden dove that hangs from a whitewashed canopy with the star of Bethlehem. There are steps that lead to the raised altar. On either side of the steps, there are the icons of Christ and the Virgin Mary. For the feast, the cross was covered with multicolored flowers and there was a big earthenware jar of blessed water in the middle of the chapel. The sisters were in the stalls and the brothers, who were there for the occasion, were around the altar. In the tribune, I found Danielle and Robert, the parents of one of the monastic sisters. Danielle immediately recognized and pointed out her daughter, even though we only saw her back and she was hidden under her hood…a mother's heart is unerring. I tried to find my sister, but I wasn't sure that I had identified her. In the white-stoned chapel, sunlight and warm air from outside enter through the windows up above. Sometimes little turtledoves perch there and their chirping blends with the sisters' singing.

The monks and sisters began to sing a beautiful series of *Kyrie eleison* accompanied by "waves" of metanies: making the sign of the cross, they fell to their knees, touching the floor with their brow and then they get up again while making another sign of the cross. The priest presented the cross to "the four corners of the world"; he bent down, touching the cross to the floor as a sign of the descent into hell and then lifted it up again to Heaven. Afterwards, there was a long procession: the brothers, followed by the sisters, came forward to adore and kiss the cross.

"Cross of those who are far away, Cross of those who are near, we adore you."

The cross was then brought up to us in the tribune. There were also two young Philippine women, one of whom was pregnant: I was moved by the infinite meekness and tenderness with which they bowed down and kissed the cross…

At the end of Mass, some sisters brought large baskets filled with small loaves with aromas of the Middle East; the priest blessed them before distributing them to all who were present…for the monks and monastic sisters, it was a fast day, but a "festive" fast day, as they say.

After Mass, I meet with Sister Isabelle. She has been in the Holy Land for thirty years. She speaks Hebrew and Arabic. In 1985, Sister Marie sent her there, together with other sisters, for the foundation of this monastery.

Why are you here in the Middle East?

"We are in the Middle East purely and simply because of the *Orientale Lumen*, Jesus Himself, who was announced by the prophets. He is the Son of God and the Son of his people, who welcome us as we are, with our vocation, which, at first sight, seems strange to them. Because of our proximity, we receive the grace of the chosen people: an unexpected biblical savor discovered through the language and the landscapes. Our liturgy is shared with many Israelis in the tribune who come for a retreat of several days to listen to Adonaï[1] in silence. In the guest area of the monastery, there are many encounters, marked by a common love for the absolute of God, with many of the sons of Israel. There are also many encounters with Palestinian brethren, whether Christian or Muslim, in communion with their grief and sorrows, sufferings endured together, precariousness for each one of them and for all.

"Being in the Middle East is essential because, in a certain way, the Church was born there on the day of Pentecost, it is the land of the first Christians, of Judeo-Christians and of the first martyrs.

"The roots of early monastic life are also in this land: Jesus, the First Monk, lived there, and later vast multitudes of monks, madly in love with God, fled to the desert with the Gospel in their hearts.

"The Holy Land has been the source of the life of the Church and of Christian life for two thousand years and it will continue to be so until the end of time. The patriarch of Jerusalem is fond of reminding us that his Church is the Mother-Church. The Church remains, more than ever, thanks to the Mystery of the Cross, which is always present, an eschatological sign,

1. Adonaï, in Hebrew, means "Lord." It is one of God's names in the Bible.

an anticipation of the heavenly Jerusalem. Whatever happens here concerns all of mankind and its future, which is in the gaze of God.

"As for us, we were born in the Church of France, but it is in this soil that we set down our roots and where our charism has gradually unfolded, and so this land is essential for our Family. Because we live in the Holy Land, we have a share in something that is "ultimate" – according to the expression that Sister Marie used when referring to this monastery in Israel. It expresses the accomplishment of our *raison d'être*. Here, it is as if we are compelled, in the depths of our poverty, to strive to bring all things to completion in Christ. Everything leads us to this. It's nothing other than our vocation of 'assumption' in the land where Christ and the Virgin Mary were elevated into the Light of glory, a grace which was poured out upon our entire monastic Family, and which, in a certain way, is more concrete here because of an inescapable realism.

"In this blessed Land, which is torn apart by divisions, our life is anchored in the silence and solitude of the cell, as in all the monasteries of Bethlehem. Saint Bruno drew from the springs of early monasticism in the deserts that surround us. He teaches us that the person, the life and the teaching of Jesus guide all the decisions of those who live in solitude. Day and night, in this land of the first Pentecost, he teaches us to unite ourselves to Jesus and to his Father who give the Holy Spirit to the human family in numerous secret and invisible epiclesis.[1]

"And so, whether in their cells or in their silent work in the house, or in the guest area of the monastery, the sisters strive, by their watchfulness and their prayer, to become ever more fully 'sentinels of the invisible' and of a universal love.

"Allow me to share with you something that a sister who lives in solitude recently said to me:

'When we hear the bombers flying overhead, our heart is crucified with compassion and forgiveness: to the One who alone is Peace, we offer our hearts through the innocent blood of so many human lives that, in a few minutes, will be shattered by death and through those, on both sides, who know not what

1. An epiclesis is an ardent invocation of the Holy Spirit.

they do. It is in all of that that our spiritual struggles in the desert find their meaning. I learn to live day by day in a trusting abandonment that consents to the gentle will of the One who will one day return to his chosen Land. In any case, the Father who sees me in the secret of my cell invites me to allow myself to be reduced to Him alone and to remain interiorly silent in the gratuitous gesture of the woman in the Gospel who broke her flask to anoint the feet of the Lord for the sole reason that she had a very great love for Him and that alone was enough."

During our conversation, Daniel Facérias arrived. Daniel is a composer and musician, close to the community of Bethlehem. He recently recorded two CDs for Bethlehem: the liturgy of the Assumption and religious Jewish songs in Hebrew. Without hesitation, Sister Isabelle suggested that the three of us spend some time together.

1

Singing practice with Daniel Facérias

Daniel Facérias introduced himself as a "little mountain dweller" before telling me about his life. His Spanish mother dreamed that he would be a doctor, but from his early youth Daniel had a great passion for music. After studying musicology and writing a thesis on the troubadours of the 12th century, he started a double career: on the one hand, rock with Daniel Balavoine and Jean-Jacques Goldman, and on the other hand, sacred music. After a particularly violent rock concert, Daniel Facérias decided to devote himself to sacred music and to be the producer of musical theater: the first one was on the subject of Saint Bernard with Michael Lonsdale in a modernized medieval spirit, another one was on the subject of Saint John of the Cross, then another concerning the Virgin Mary at Lourdes. In all, there were about twenty shows, and records too, one of them on the subject of Saint Thérèse of Lisieux.

In 2005, when working on a project at the Marian center in Nazareth, Daniel Facérias became acquainted with the sisters of Bethlehem who, at Bet Gemal, welcomed those who were involved in the project.

"It's the liturgy that touched me in Bethlehem. Right from the beginning, I was captivated by the liturgy. I understood Bethlehem, from within, through the liturgy. We never had a theological discussion. I think that the liturgy resonates in me because I find in it a medieval aspect, in the true sense of the word. The Middle Ages achieved a spiritual maturity that seizes all of one's being on all levels, we find it in the music and in the painting. The liturgy in Bethlehem is somewhat like

Romanesque art where one finds a true unity between Heaven and earth.

"Bethlehem isn't just one more vocation in the Church, it's the Church of today and of the future. Bethlehem isn't the work of man: it's connected to the dogma of the Assumption, the Virgin's nature 'assumed,' or elevated, into glory, and her divinization. The Virgin does nothing haphazardly. There is also a vision of Redemption in all of that: to manifest and to bear witness to God's benevolent design; He wills that, by adoption, we be divinized like the Virgin Mary. That's what I feel and experience in the liturgy.

"In Bethlehem, one is both in reality and torn away from reality, or raised above reality, in the Virgin's Assumption.

"Monastic life, especially in Bethlehem, expresses in a particular way the splendor of beauty. It's not by chance that the great painters of the Italian quattrocentro were contemplatives or monks.

"Liturgical gestures reveal God's beauty. This beauty has nothing to do with aestheticism or prettiness, it's the splendor of Truth and Charity.

"For several years, I was pondering an idea, which is now being realized, of a ministry of beauty; the goal is to reconcile artists with the Church, not in an institutional way, but rather from the inside. Currently, there is, for artists, a crisis of the subject, a metaphysical crisis of the subject to such a point that express nothing but their narcissism or the prevailing cultural chaos of our time. It is imperative that artists be led to discover the dimension of the sacred and the fullness of their 'priesthood.'

"The cultural experience of young people is deficient, and art is the only means to express a certain depth to them. That is why this ministry is necessary both for artists and for the world.

"The Church also needs to rediscover a sense of sacredness and to learn anew how to be the silent partner in the history of art.

"This nascent project was entrusted to the prayer of the monastic sisters of Bethlehem. There is a retable of the "Coronation of the Virgin" by Fra Angelico that shows Christ placing a precious stone on the Virgin's crown. That's the ministry of beauty: this gesture by which Christ, in his humanity, adds the pearl of transfigured love...

2

On either side of the wall

I didn't have an interview with Monseigneur Fouad Twal, the Latin patriarch of Jerusalem.

Sister Isabelle had spoken about him during our last conversation. I wrote to him to ask him to share with me his thoughts about Bethlehem.

His Beatitude wrote about the contrast between the Holy Land, torn apart by war, and the beauty of those lives offered to God. This is his response: (next page).

PATRIARCHATUS LATINUS - JERUSALEM

بطريركية القدس للاتين

Prot. N (1) 1298 / 2011

Jérusalem, le 23 novembre 2011,

A l'attention des moines et moniales de Bethléem, de l'Assomption de la Vierge et de saint Bruno.

Très chers frères et petites sœurs de Bethléem,

En pensant à vous, à vos monastères, en réfléchissant à ce que votre communauté nous révèle, en contemplant la beauté de votre présence ici en Terre Sainte, un mot me vient à l'esprit, celui de « contrastes ».

Contraste de votre vie donnée et aimante dans un contexte de violence, de division, de séparation. On trouve chez vous un véritable oasis de paix, de prière et d'accueil :

- Vous participez par votre présence et votre prière à restaurer la véritable image de la Terre Sainte, vous attachant entièrement à la « sainteté » de cette terre alors que d'autres, dans une culture de violence, vont se concentrer uniquement sur le mot « terre ».
- Par la diversité et la richesse de vos communautés, vous êtes le miroir et l'image même de l'Universalité de l'Eglise, vous représentez la dimension mondiale de l'Eglise de Jérusalem car on retrouve chez vous des sœurs consacrées du monde entier, européennes, arabes et juives.
- Vous portez un magnifique message pour nos fidèles arabes palestiniens. Alors que beaucoup ont la tentation d'émigrer à cause de la situation économique et politique difficile, d'autres comme vous, qui ont le confort et la paix dans leur pays, viennent vivre ici à Jérusalem par amour de la Terre Sainte. Malgré les obstacles qu'il peut y avoir sur cette terre, cela vaut la peine de venir y vivre. Le Seigneur nous a prévenu d'avance de la croix qui nous attendait, «*Celui qui veut marcher à ma suite, qu'il renonce à lui-même, qu'il prenne sa croix chaque jour, et qu'il me suive*" (Luc 9, 22-25).
- Alors que le monde entier prêche la liberté et l'indépendance, vous avez un attachement filial et une confiance totale aux autorités religieuses.

Beaucoup font de grands efforts pour atteindre la paix par de nombreuses rencontres, discours mais vous, participez d'une manière extrêmement efficace à la cause de la paix, par votre prière et par vos sacrifices. Chers frères et soeurs, nous croyons à cette paix et je vous la confie à nouveau à vos prières.

En ce temps de l'Avent qui approche, je vous accorde de grand cœur ma bénédiction,

+ Fouad Twal

+ Fouad Twal, Patriarche

PATRIARCHATVS LATINVS JERVSALEM

Jaffa Gate, P.O.Box 14152 - Jerusalem 91141 • Tel. + 972 2 628 23 23, 627 22 80 • Fax. + 972 2 627 16 52
E-mail: chancellery@latinpat.org • website: www.lpj.org

PATRIARCHATUS LATINUS – JERUSALEM

November 23, 2011
Jerusalem

To the attention of the monks and monastic sisters of Bethlehem, of the Assumption of the Virgin and of Saint Bruno.

Dearest brothers and little sisters of Bethlehem,

As I think of you, of your monasteries, as I think about what your community reveals to us, as I contemplate the beauty of your presence here in the Holy Land, there is one word comes to mind: "contrasts."

It is the contrast between the loving offering of your lives in the context of violence, division and separation. Your monasteries are a real oasis of peace, prayer and hospitality:

-By your presence and prayer you contribute to the restoration of the true image of the Holy Land. You occupy yourselves with the "holiness" of this land whereas others, in a culture of violence, concentrate only on the word "land."

-Through the diversity and richness of your communities, you are the mirror and the very image of the Universality of the Church, you represent the global dimension of the Church of Jerusalem, for one finds among you consecrated sisters from all over the world, Europeans, Arabs and Jews.

-You bear a magnificent message for the faithful among the Palestinian Arabs. While many of them are tempted to emigrate because of the difficult economic and political situation, others, like you, who enjoy peace and comfort in their own country, come to live here in Jerusalem out of love for the Holy Land. In spite of the obstacles that are found in this land, it is worth the trouble to come and live here. The Lord warned us that the cross is waiting for us: *"if any man would come after me, let him deny himself, take up his cross daily and follow me"* (Lk 9, 23).

-While the entire world preaches freedom and independence, you have a filial attachment and total trust toward religious authorities.

A lot of people take great pains in order to achieve peace through various encounters and discourses, but your contribution to the cause of peace, through your prayer and sacrifices, is extremely efficient. Dear brothers and sisters, we believe in this peace and once again I entrust this intention to your prayers.

In this time when the Advent season is drawing near, I heartily grant you my blessing.

Fouad Twal, Patriarch.

"Contrasts": that is indeed the word that characterizes the monastery of Bet Gemal and what is lived there. The contrast between the stillness of the monastery and the violence of a country that is torn apart by an endless war. The contrast between a life of prayer in solitude and the influx of people of every nation, race, people and language that one finds in the gift shop or in the tribune of the chapel. The contrast between the silent prayer of the monastic sisters behind the enclosure and the terrible noise of the bombardments. The contrasts of the encounters that I planned to have in the Holy City...

Two sisters accompanied me in the car as we headed for Jerusalem for a series of interviews. The monastery is located about thirty kilometers from the Holy City, and I took advantage of the trip to chat with the sisters! But it was time for Terce or Sext...I'm not too clear about their liturgical schedule...one of the little offices that all the sisters normally pray at the same time, but in solitude.

In the car, they adapted and continued their monastic life as we rolled along. After a "Hail Mary" which they prayed in order to ask for the Virgin Mary's protection, the sisters then prayed their office together. I listened to them while contemplating the landscape. We first crossed the town of Bet Shemesh, which in Hebrew means "the house of the sun," the town closest to the monastery, where there is a Jewish community of ultra-orthodox religious.

We then drew near to Bethlehem, which is enclosed by a wall. It was the first time that I saw Bethlehem and it was a shock. Bethlehem, the birthplace and also the name of this monastic Family. Bethlehem which, today, two thousand year after the birth of Christ, is no longer a crèche, but rather a tomb for the population that is enclosed there.

When we reached the gates of the Holy City, the sisters sang a greeting to Jerusalem, psalm 121:

> I was glad when they said to me,
> "Let us go to the house of the Lord!"

Our feet have been standing
within your gates, O Jerusalem!
Jerusalem, built as a city
Which is bound firmly together,
to which the tribes go up,
the tribes of the Lord,
as was decreed for Israel,
to give thanks to the name of the Lord.
There thrones for judgment were set,
the thrones of the house of David.
Pray for the peace of Jerusalem!
"May they prosper who love you!
Peace be within your walls,
and security within your towers!"
For my brethren and companions' sake
I will say, "Peace be within you!"
For the sake of the house of the Lord our God,
I will seek your good.

As we drew near to the Jaffa gate, I continued to repeat one of the verses: "Pray for the peace of Jerusalem!"

I left the sisters at the entrance of the souk. I had an appointment with Abu Taher.

The secret of Jerusalem

Abu Taher sells fabrics. In all the monasteries that I visited, I was struck by the beauty of the priests' vestments and of the altar linen… In Paris, in particular, the church has a Middle Eastern style.

Abu Taher's shop is a real treasure-trove: cushions with brilliant colors, and everywhere there are rolls of fabric: velvet, silk and Egyptian cotton. A small staircase jammed with yet more rolls of fabric leads to the second floor where there is a variety of pashminas, stoles, expensive and elegant dresses, mantels, brocades, silk vests… clothes-conscious as I am, my head was spinning!

Abu Taher welcomed me in a way that I'll never forget. After having served me delicious mint tea and loaded me with gifts, he told me his story and that of his family. "I have six brothers and four sisters. I had an older brother who died in the United States in 1969 in a car accident. Like my grandfather, my father also sold fabrics. He used to go from house to house with the rolls of fabric on his shoulder. Life wasn't like it is now: life was more simple. He lived in Jerusalem. After a few years, he invested a little money in a shop in the old town. It was a market for Arabs who wanted galabiehs. Afterwards, he purchased this shop, which I now own. And then another one nearby, which one of my brother's owns. Then a third one. Together with his brothers, he extended the trade to Jordan, in Ramallah and in Hebron. Having started out with rolls of fabric on his shoulders, he ended up by owning almost thirty shops.

"My mother's family lived in Egypt. Her parents had left Jerusalem to settle down there in 1910. I went to visit my grandmother in Egypt because I was considering studying there. I didn't know anyone. I met a wonderful woman, my Egyptian cousin; I fell deeply in love with her and married her. I was twenty-two. My father needed my help in his shops: so I left my studies in Egypt and returned here in Jerusalem with my wife. We worked together for about ten years before my father died in 1985: he was only fifty-five, but he had worked hard. I was thirty-five. My brothers were still young and my father had given me instructions before he died: "Take care of your brothers until they get married, don't allow any divisions among you and make your decisions with your mother." I was faithful to his instructions. Only recently we divided up the shops with my brothers. Now I am working with my oldest son who is thirty-four." Abu Taher has two other sons, one daughter and three grandchildren. He told me how difficult it was for he and his wife to have children: "I'm a Muslim. I could have married another wife, but she is the one I love. There's no room in my heart for anyone else!"

He told me the story of his encounter with the sisters of Bethlehem in 1983. "My father was still alive and, one morning, the two of us were in the shop. Two sisters entered and at once I understood there was something special about them.

They were different. They had an 'open heart' and they weren't fussy. They chose a fabric which I then offered to them as a gift because I sensed that they brought with them the "baraka". The *baraka* for us is a blessing. It's not a matter of fortune or fate. There's no such thing as fortune. It's God who leads us. God leads those who are pure of heart...

"That was twenty-eight years ago...twenty-eight years of love. The sisters continued coming back. It's not only business between us. There's friendship and love. As for money, it's easy to get it in all kinds of ways. But it's much more difficult to become someone's friend, and it's easy to lose a friend. It's not just a matter of business with the sisters. Our relationship is more than just fabric. Today, they are part of my family. That's life: business isn't the only thing that counts. There's love that comes from the heart."

Where is love in your country that has been at war for so long? How can people like you and the sisters, whose cultures and religions are different, have so much love for one another?

"It's very easy. We are all human beings, whether Christians, Muslims or Jews, whether one goes to a church, to a mosque or to a synagogue. We should forget the difficulties in the past. Everyone tries to set Christians against Muslims and vice-versa. Here it's different. We are in Jerusalem and here it's different than other Arab countries.

"The relationship between Jews and Arabs is destroyed by the political situation but, in life, we get along very well. I have two shops. Here, I meet mostly Christians, Jews and tourists. In the other, most of my customers are Arabs. In this shop, I sometimes have customers from as many as seventeen different nationalities in a single day: I see Christians and Muslims, and people from India, China, Africa, Canada, Greece, Germany, Algeria and Asia... Before the euro, I had twenty different currencies. I remember my father always said: if you do nothing but remain seated on the chair in this shop, you will see the whole world...

"If you take me out of my shop, it's like taking a fish out of the sea. I have three houses: in Jordan, Jericho and in Jerusalem.

But whenever I travel, I always look forward to the day when I will return to Jerusalem."

What is different here? What is so special about Jerusalem?

"There's a secret in Jerusalem: it is a magnet for Christians, Jews and Muslims. One comes to Jerusalem to pray. That's why everybody wants Jerusalem. It's a beautiful city. We should take care of it. If we were intelligent, all of us, Christians, Jews and Muslims, we would carry Jerusalem on our shoulders. Not wage war for it. There's no such thing as an Arab Jerusalem or a Jewish Jerusalem or a Christian Jerusalem. Jerusalem belongs to God: it's our responsibility to protect it, love it and take care of it. Together, we should carry it on our shoulders like my grandfather carrying his rolls of fabric..."

Do you think that the sisters have a special mission in the Holy Land?

"Of course. In the Holy Land, which is crammed with churches and history, they can and should bring people together so that they may love one another. So that good may come from evil..."

Have you ever gone to the monastery?

"I 'live' in the monastery! The sisters are angels of God, they bring peace."

I must admit that I was a bit shaken by my conversation with Abu Taher. His faith, his openness, his understanding of the situation in Jerusalem and then, of course, his relationship with the sisters, a friendship shared "in God," in a God who always bears the same name... Love.

Peace is the sign of the cross

Before leaving the Holy City, I stopped at "Versavée," a restaurant at the Jaffa gate. It is owned by a man, Elias, whom I wished to meet for two reasons: because he is an Arab and a Christian, an identity difficult to live here, and because, a few months ago, he married Violaine, a young woman who had spent a year at Bet Gemal before discovering her vocation to marriage. We had a serene interview during which he said nothing about his sufferings endured in a town where it is not easy to be a Christian. In a certain way, this interview was like an echo of the one that I had just had with Abu Taher.

"I'm a Christian Palestinian and I have an Israeli passport. I was born in the old city of Jerusalem in a family of seven children. My mother is Greek Orthodox and my father is a Roman Catholic: we were raised in the Catholic Church. I was educated in a Lutheran school that no longer exists."

A Catholic father, an Orthodox mother and a Lutheran school...that put me in direct contact with the Church of Jerusalem, heiress of the Church of Pentecost, which, at the beginning, was Judeo-Christian, Mother of all the Churches and guardian to this day of the most ancient eastern rites and open to the newness of the Spirit: Roman Catholics, Greek Orthodox Copts and Catholic Copts, Ethiopians, Orthodox Syrians and Catholic Syrians, Chaldeans, Maronites, Melkites... Anglicans, Lutherans. The Church of Semites and the Church of Arabs, the Church of the nations, the Church of Golgotha and of Easter morning, the Church of Elias and of his relatives.

"God led me to Bet Gemal when I was a child, since I went there several times as a Boy Scout. I rediscovered it three and a half years ago, thanks to Violaine, my wife who is French, and who has a brother who is a monk there. Yet we are more in contact with the sisters than with the brothers; my wife wanted to become a sister... but God had another plan since she became my wife!

"From the start, my relationship with Violaine has been built on true love rooted in Christ, a love that kept bringing us back in one way or another to the monastery where we found support through prayer, advice and love. We always receive a warm welcome at Bet Gemal, especially from Sister Isabelle. I will never forget my first encounter with her and how she helped me to grow in love. A love that was a long and profound path that led us to the altar."

Is it difficult for a Christian to live in Jerusalem?

"I had the privilege of growing up within the walls of the old city where my parents raised us to live in harmony with Jews and Muslims. It's not easy to speak about that situation, for there are good people and bad people in both religions, just as there are among Christians.

"In 1987, the first Intifada began and many Christians migrated to Europe, America and Australia. Still today, very skilled and well-educated Christian Arabs continue to leave: it has been very detrimental to us and we live under a kind of tutelage. Before 1948, we comprised 28% of the population, now just barely 1.5%. We need the help of European Christians who love us: it isn't so much a matter of cash, but rather of the necessity to have better lodgings, better education and career prospects so that our situation might become more stable, and especially our work.

"For example, my wife makes mosaics, and I want her to have a workshop and a shop. But in the Christian neighborhood, 95% of the shops are rented to or belong to Muslims, and the houses are sold to Jews who are coming to live here little by little. We need help in order to survive here. So that we Christians might remain in the Holy Land, we need help to bring our plans to fruition. The pope himself urges the Christians of the Middle East not emigrate: I'd like to drink some cognac with him and talk to him about this subject!

"A few years ago, this neighborhood of the Jaffa Gate was filled with drug addicts. Several Christians managed to buy houses or, like myself, to open a restaurant, under very modest conditions, with a single room then adding another one and still another one. Now there are almost no more drug addicts in the area.

"There aren't many Christian Arabs, but they aren't weak. Many of them are very skilled. They need help to be 'visible,' to bear witness, to be radiant Christians in this holy place."

Elias, what does peace mean for you?

"It's difficult to define peace: it's in the heart. Peace is the sign of cross that has two directions: vertically, it is the relationship between God and men and between men and God; horizontally, it is the loving relationship among men. And we Christians, we truly strive for peace.

"I would really like to meet someone with whom I could deeply examine the situation of Christians in the old city and discover new perspectives."

The doves of peace

When I returned to the monastery, there were still more surprises in store for me! While I was seated peacefully on Bet Gemal's terrace, I saw the thundering arrival of another great friend of the sisters. Abu Issam is a Palestinian sheik. With a keffiyeh on his head and clothed with a white galabieh, I was struck by his nobility, his craggy face, his white beard and his piercing gaze. He was accompanied by his son and daughter-in-law, both of them carrying boxes filled with cookies (still warm) filled with a sesame paste... there was more than enough for the whole monastery!

Abu Issam had come from Jericho where he lives. He was on his way to attend his nephew's wedding and he stopped to greet his dear friends...the sisters! It was obvious that he felt entirely at home, and he went directly to a small room for guests for our interview. The interview, in fact, was completely spur-of-the-moment since Abu Issam had called just a few minutes before arriving!

In the guest room there was a big statue of the Virgin Mary; he sat down next to her, lit a cigarette and invited us to help ourselves to the wonderful cookies.

After warm preliminaries and an invitation to come and enter "the heart of his family for a big feast," Abu Issam told me his story. The interview was in Arabic; a sister translated for me. "My name is Abu Issam. I have eight children: five sons, three daughters and a lot of grandchildren. I don't know how to read. For a long time, I made tin trays and pots. It's an important job because we Arabs eat together from one single platter and everybody eats with their fingers. When I grew old, my children wanted that I stop working. My tribe acknowledged that I have a gift of wisdom and that I could be the tribe's wise man. I solve problems of all kinds. The problems of daily life. Not religious problems. There is a fatwa for that. I teach them to forgive one another and to dispense justice.

"I should also tell you about my wife... the Malika... the queen! I was nineteen when we got married and she was fourteen! Today, it is forbidden to marry so young. I love her as much as on the first day. She is clothed like a queen, she cooks like a queen and she has the heart of a queen. But now, her heart is very tired. We went to Mecca together two times: that's why they call me the *Hadj*, the Pilgrim."

How did you come to know the sisters?

"Since they are our neighbors, we went to visit them one day, and ever since the bond has grown stronger: we know how to love and respect one another like brothers. I hope that this loving relationship that exists between us will last forever. We are one heart and, in our heart of hearts, we are one religion. We have the same desire: that true peace may come."

But you are Muslim and they are Christians?

"Their Lord Jesus is also mine and the Virgin Mary is the mother of us all. There are differences in our religions but we wish to live together in peace."

Is peace possible after so many years of war?

"Today there are rebellions everywhere in Egypt, in Syria, in Yemen, in Lybia. In our Arab countries there's no democracy and the people are fed up. Such things could never happen in France because there's a democracy. Here, people don't have the right to speak up. For me, the sisters are white doves of peace. When I see them, each one is like a little 'Virgin Mary.' The Virgin Mary has chosen the sisters to be like her on earth!"

Who is the Virgin Mary for you?

Before answering, Abu Issam turned towards the statue of the Virgin and blew her a kiss... "Maryam...she is first of all a mother, but not like other mothers... she is a virgin. Everybody knows that Jesus was born in Bethlehem under a date palm..."

Then his son began to speak: "As my father, the Hadj, just said, your Virgin Mary is the same as our Virgin Mary. There's only one Maryam and one God in Heaven who is for all of us. We are one family and Mary is the mother of us all: it is written in our Koran..."

And then his wife added: "We learn tenderness from the Virgin and how to take care of our children. We receive all that we can from Maryam. I would also like to welcome you in this land of Palestine. We love welcoming guests in our country. It's wonderful that there is friendship, love and strength between us. We shouldn't emphasize the differences between our religions, but rather what we share in common: we have the same God and we want to love one another. I'm very grateful to journalists who take the time to ask us Arabs about our situation."

Abu Issam stood up: it was time to leave. We took a few pictures in front of the statue of the Virgin. Before leaving, I told him that I will continue to pray for peace here. "If there's peace between us, there's no problem," he replied. "It's the dignitaries that cause problems. Peace comes from love. God did not create us to make war but to love one another." Inch Allah!

I was impressed by the simplicity and warmth of the relationships that the sisters have with their Muslim brethren. No proselytism: each one remains who he or she is, and there is a deep mutual respect. Sister Isabelle accompanied Abu Issam back to his car. I saw only their backs, and he put his hand on her shoulder... like a brother.

The one who loves God has nothing to fear

When I was at Piquetière, Sister Jackie had spoken to me about Abu Jado, the foreman of the construction work at Bet Gemal. The companions had also spoken about him. Once again my curiosity was roused. I went to meet with Abu Jado in a little house that had been equipped by the sisters for the workers at the monastery. By providing them with work, the sisters enable them to earn a living for their families.

Abu Jado has been working for the sisters for twenty-three years. For several years, he lived at the monastery and was able to return to Bethlehem to be with his family only once a month. For the past three years, he has been able to return home every evening. But not without difficulty: he has a permit to work outside of Bethlehem between 7:00 a.m. and 10:00 p.m., provided that access to the town isn't suddenly closed without reason!

For Abu Jado, life has never been easy. His father died before he was born, and he lived alone with his mother who never re-married. She struggled to earn a living for them by cultivating vegetables on a small plot of land. When he was fourteen, Abu Jado left school in order to work. He made concrete for construction sites. When he turned twenty, he went to Jordan in order to earn enough money so that one day he could get married: he lived the "life of a slave" for one year, and was then able to return to his country and marry Fatmeh. He was very happy to tell me that he has four children: a son who is a lawyer in Bethlehem, a daughter who is an artist, another son who is studying in Abou Dis in the Palestinian territories and Nour, the youngest, who is still at school.

During their first years of marriage, Abu Jado worked with his father-in law, who, like himself, works in the construction business, and he discovered Christian monasteries and convents. He enumerated for me an impressive number of construction sites where he has worked: the university of Bethlehem, Our Lady of Jerusalem, the basilica of the Nativity in Bethlehem, the Franciscans' Casa Nova guest house and also their school Terra Santa in Bethlehem, for the sisters of the Rosary, the sisters of Saint Joseph, for the nuncio of Jerusalem, in Abu Gosh, for the Salesians. And then one day, when the building contractor in Bethlehem took him to Bet Gemal to build a guest house and to lay the tiled floor in the main building. "I immediately felt at home," he explained. "I love this place. One day, I found myself unemployed and life became even more difficult. I had no more money to pay for the school that my children attended. The sisters were very attentive and kind. I think they saw that they could trust me and that my work was good, and they invited me to continue doing construction work at Bet Gemal.

"I'm going to speak the truth...it's a secret. The sisters don't live like other people. They love God, they fear God and they protect all that comes from God. The secret is that there is someone who binds me to the sisters: it's the Virgin, the *Hadra*... it is She who watches over this monastery. And she is also my Mother."

I asked Abu Jado to tell me a little bit more about the Virgin Mary, to explain to me what she represents for him. He saw that I was a bit perplexed. "I'm a Muslim," he replied, "but I love the Virgin Mary. She is a Mother for me too. It is she who gives me direction in my life, who shows me the path to follow. If I've been here for twenty-three years, it's because She asked me to do so. She has sown love among us and she asks me to protect this love. It's a gift that I have received from God thanks to Her.

"I've worked a lot here... my hands know almost all the stones of these new buildings. If I'm alive, it's because I receive life, water and breath from this monastery."

I thought of the Little Prince who looked for a well in the desert because he was thirsty. "What makes the desert even more beautiful is that a well is hidden somewhere...water can also be good for the heart."

Abu Jado has found the well, and I asked him if he thinks it's important to lead others to it.

"Mrs Inès, we are God's guests on earth. All people, whether great or small, should seek God. They should lift up their gaze to Him. They should fear God. Everyone should pray with his heart, his soul, his mind and draw closer to God. If we do so, God opens all things before us. Everything is open before us: knowledge of the Virgin Mary and love for her, for Jesus, for Mohammed, for Moses. If someone fears God, God answers him."

Abu Jado, do you ever pray with the sisters?

"Every year, there is a blessed feast here: the Sunday of Forgiveness. It is just before Lent. The sisters are like everybody else, sometimes they get annoyed...but that doesn't last for more than three minutes, and afterwards they ask forgiveness and it's over with.

"I'll tell you a funny story. I worked a lot with Sister Jackie, and sometimes she gets annoyed. One day, she said to me: "Awad, you have the head of a Muslim, but the heart of a Christian!"

"I always attend the liturgy of the feast of Forgiveness. If God is angry with me, that day we ask forgiveness. It's a grace and a blessing: everything is forgiven. If I die on the day of Forgiveness, I know that I'll go straight to Heaven."

For years, I've had little compartments in my mind, one for Christians, one for Muslims and one for Jews; but these conversations led me to start calling into question my mental categories. My Cartesian mind was all in a muddle. And since Abu Jado had opened the topic of forgiveness, I followed his lead."

Abu Jado, you live on the other side of the wall with your family. Do you forgive those who built it?

"I'll tell you something: we are all God's children. It is God who has created us. We were all in gestation for nine months in our mother's womb. Jews love life, Christians and Muslims also love life...everyone would like to have a beautiful life. This land belongs to God: why can't we live here together? I have a lot of Jewish friends with whom I work. I pray to God that we may all share the same freedom and that Christians, Jews and Muslims may pray in their holy places so that peace may come.

"I will speak from my heart, if you permit me: when I am before God and before the Virgin, I forgive others for everything... I forgive everything and I also ask forgiveness.

"Mrs Inès, to tell you the truth, I don't like blood. I don't like war. If only we could consider true peace. Why can't all of us, Christians, Muslims and Jews, and our religious leaders, fall to our knees with our heads bowed to the ground and pray to God, beseech Him to open our hearts so that we might live like human beings?

"I will say it one more time before God: I forgive them for everything."

There was a long silence filled with emotion. Then Abu Jado continued: "There is an Arabic proverb that says: 'Whoever sows eats what he has sown.'

"It's the sisters who have sown that in my heart... what I just told you. For us lay people, it's difficult. The sisters and brothers live for God alone, for Jesus and for Mary. They don't run after material goods, they have become very wise. You and I, we aren't like them, but we can receive from them their capacity to forgive.

"If someone lives with good and respectable people, he himself becomes respectable and good. He receives from them a lot of love and respect and he desires to follow the same path. God has sown these monastic sisters that they can teach us how to draw closer to Him.

"Today it's very difficult, very hard. Whoever we may be, the solution is the same: that we should pray more and draw closer to God. Today everyone runs after money, honors and power. Because of that, many people forget God. We should continue to pray and to draw close to God, so that our Lord may grant us a way of life that is pure and just. Palestine is a sacred place and we should watch over it, that is why God wants to put an end to this difficult life. From Heaven, God blesses all the communities of all religions.

"If there were no more monks, who would ring the bell? If there were no more sheikhs, who would say *Allah akbar?* If there were no more rabbis, who would transmit the Word?

"Remember this, Mrs. Inès: anyone who loves God and fears God has nothing to fear."

We can live together

It was nightfall. The night comes early in Israel. Some of the little sisters went to the guest house for a medical consultation. Rahib is a physiotherapist. He is an Arabic Christian, and he was born in a village in Galilee called Ibillin. It is the village of Mariam of Jesus Crucified, an Arab Carmelite whom Pope John Paul II beatified in 1983.

Rahib is married. He has four children. Two girls and two boys: Issa, Mariam, Lamar and Charbel.

I waited until the consultations were over to spend some time with him. I was surprised by how much time he spent with each sister, considering how many appointments he had. "I'm very happy to work here," he said. "When I come, I have more energy, even if I work a lot. The sisters give everything from the heart, from within. You can see that all is true and clear, whether in their words or their gaze."

I still had in mind my conversations with Abu Taher, Abu Jado and Elias. Each of them had spoken about the possibility of peace in this land. "Peace on earth to men of good will," as Saint Luke says.

Rahib, do you think that Christians, Jews and Muslims will one day live in peace in this country?

"Why not? It's politics that creates problems. If you were to take a survey in this country, you would see that more than 50%, or even 60%, of the people believe that we can live together.

"The first thing that we need to do to promote peace is to improve education. How can I live with Jews if I don't know their education and their customs? I speak of these things with my patients, and we know that we have to change interiorly.

"We should continue to believe. I explain that to my children. When there was a war in Gaza, we saw on TV a child who opened the fridge and there was no food left in it. Then I said to my children: 'Did you see that child? You cry when you want to buy something in a store, but there are people who have nothing. You should thank God that you have everything that you need.'"

"My children come to my clinic which is twenty meters away from our home. They see me talking to Jews, Druzes, Muslims. They see that we are friends and that I invite them to my house for a drink. That's how things change. Children understand by watching, and then it's imprinted in them.

"It's very difficult to be a Christian here: people don't understand our importance. In the West, people think that all Arabs are Muslim. You have to come here to understand that one can be both an Arab and a Christian."

Are the relationships between Israeli Arabs and Palestinan Arabs difficult?

"I sometimes work in Palestine, and I also know the University of Jenine: that helps me to understand what life on the other side of the wall is like. It's sometimes difficult for Palestinian Arabs, both Muslims and Christians, to understand our situation as Israeli Arabs; as for them, they think that an Arab who lives in Israel is living a compromise. The question of our future isn't simple. I think about my children: in twenty years, will they be able to live here?

"If I had the chance to emigrate, I think I'd be tempted to do so. A lot of Christians have already emigrated: 60% of the Christians who were in Bethlehem now live in Canada or the United States. I understand. Yet, it's very important that we stay here; it's our country, it's Jesus' country...

"It's important to believe. Lord, bless us and grant us what is best. Amen.

"I'd like to tell you a little story... a true story...to illustrate that peace is possible. Once, when I came here to treat the sisters, I found a note at my door that said: 'Rabib, we are sorry, we don't have any more water.' Yet, there was a container at my door with a little water for me. I asked them why they had no water. They didn't know why there was no more water, and it had been like that for two days. I asked myself, how are they able to manage without water? I spoke about the situation to a friend, a Druze and member of the government. He promised that he would help, and he did. He came here to Bet Gemal with five members of the government and four Druze friends. They were all very surprised to discover that there are sisters here who only pray, pray, pray. They were very moved by their encounter with the sisters and they promised to help them.

"One of the Druzes said to Sister Isabelle: 'Give me a model of Christ or of the Virgin, and I will make a stone statue for you.' He was a sculptor. You see how a common cause can bring Christians, Jews, Druzes and Muslims together.

"It's only one example, but it's a path toward peace."

3

Our Lady of Palestine

The sanctuary of Our Lady, Queen of Palestine and of the Holy Land, is located a few kilometers away from the monastery of Bet Gemal: some sisters even walk there sometimes. It takes a good two to three hours.

Situated halfway between Tel Aviv and Jerusalem, it was built in 1927 in order to ask the Virgin Mary for her protection. For a long time, it was a place for children, then it became a house for spiritual retreats. It is an "emblematic" place, a place of hope, since it was, from the beginning, a convent including a sanctuary, Our Lady of Palestine, right in the middle of Israel! Bordering the desert, it is a place very dear to Christians in the land of Jesus who like to gather there on the last Sunday of October. On that day, pilgrims flock from all over Israel and the Territories for the feast of the Virgin at Deir Rafat.

In August 2009, the Patriarch of Jerusalem, Monseigneur Fouad Twal, asked the monastic Family of Bethlehem to send some sisters who could pray and adore there, in accordance, as much as possible, with their vocation of solitude.

When I arrived at the sanctuary, I realized how bold and open-minded the monastic sisters had been in accepting the Patriarch's request to devote themselves with all their heart to this site, while remaining faithful to their life of silence and prayer.

Bertrand accompanied me to the sanctuary. He and his wife, Catherine, live in the guest house in Bet Gemal. He had had a very busy professional life, and two years before retiring, they "were bowled over in a way they couldn't ever have imagined." Just as they were about to begin a peaceful retirement – they had dreamed of producing their own wine – various circumstances led them to the radical decision of leaving everything behind in France in order to be of service to the sisters. Bertrand and Catherine have two children who now live in Jerusalem.

"I help the sisters according to their needs," Catherine explained to me. "I do the shopping, I take sisters to the doctor, I take care of the library and the honey, and Bertrand is the Mr. Fix It of the monastery! We are very independent and very free, and we are happy to welcome the families and other people who come to the monastery." It's true that they are happy to welcome others here – several times I went to talk with this remarkable couple.

Welcoming lay people in a monastery who help the sisters and preserve their contemplative life is an experiment. It's especially suitable when there's a big project that requires a lot of time – as is the case for Deir Rafat.

Before going there, Bertrand explained a few things to me: "In the monastery-sanctuary of Deir Rafat, there is the life of solitude and prayer and there is also the welcoming of people for an hour, a day or a short retreat. In addition to all of that, we lay people have conceived a project that has both spiritual and humanitarian goals: our idea is to welcome young people who are destitute, particularly young Christians from the Territories, for a period of four, five, six months or more. During that time, we would teach them job skills in a spiritual environment while living close to a community.

"In one wing of the building, a small community of about ten sisters lives within the enclosure. The other wing is for guests and visitors.

"There were already guest accommodations when the sisters arrived, but they weren't complete. There was no kitchen, no dining room. Our first task was to turn the guest area into a guest house in the spirit of Bethlehem. With the help of volunteers, the renovation work took two years. It's now a place where families can be welcomed; there are also Arab pilgrims who are welcomed, and pilgrims from Europe and elsewhere.

"This guest house will also soon provide lodging for our volunteers. We still have to equip our first two workshops: one for baking the other for carpentry. It might also be possible to cultivate olive trees.

"The project is adapted to this country, but it's not completely new. In the monastery of Mougères, in France, there's a workshop for twenty-five salaried people. It provides work for the people in the neighborhood and it helps the sisters.

"Do you think that in a country like Israel, the sisters can retreat into their ivory tower saying: 'We have big walls around us, we are here to pray. It's true, there are people who are starving, humiliated and tortured twenty kilometers away from here, but there's nothing we can do for them?!' Of course not, and more can be done for them than just welcoming them for the duration of a liturgical office.

"At the heart of their 'desert' life, the sisters remain connected to the country in which they live. Concretely, the sisters don't do the construction work, but they keep vigil and pray and remain present. The work is supervised by lay persons, always with the agreement of the monastic sisters."

We began by visiting the buildings before meeting with Serge and Brigitte, lay-friends of Bethlehem who made a one-year commitment to this project.

The playground of the former school is lined with seven gigantic ficus trees. There's still a basketball hoop, and the volunteers enjoy taking a little break there!

It was interesting to walk in the immense hallways of the guest house which is gradually taking shape, as Bertrand explained to me. In the refectory, there's a large fresco of the Last Supper. The parlors, decorated with icons and Middle Eastern furniture, are ready to welcome guests. On the first and second floors, the bedrooms are very simple and sober in the typical Bethlehem style.

What a surprise when I stepped out onto roof terrace! There's an exceptional 360-degree view. One can see the Bedouin camps that border the desert, and in the distance, the sea. And then, when one turns, the landscape changes: there are the verdant hills of Judea, the cotton fields and the pomegranate and olive trees. And, on the roof, there's an immense statue of our Lady of Palestine, bigger than life-size, who watches over the eastern territories. At that moment, when I was admiring the view, I saw several war helicopters equipped with a gun in front arrive with a deafening noise. We then returned to the church whose ceiling is decorated with the words of the angel's greeting to Mary, "Ave Maria," in 280 languages.

Love without boundaries

Serge and Brigitte were still in their work clothes when I met with them; one had been working the vegetable garden and the other in the flower garden. We sat down in one of the guest rooms and sipped lemonade. Both of them are from Switzerland; they have four children who are adults now, and one is a sister of Bethlehem. They are lay-contemplatives in this monastic Family.

The lay-friends of Bethlehem are men, women, families or single persons who, while remaining in the world, commit themselves, according to their personal vocations, to live in spiritual communion with the monasteries and to share in some of the material tasks.

Brigitte explained to me that she had been Protestant, though she rarely practiced her religion. After her marriage to Serge, they began to seek God in order to deepen their own relationship. "It was, above all, when I met the monastic sisters that I met Him and that my thirst to know Him deepened," she said. "About twenty years ago, some friends took us to the monastery of Les Montsvoirons. The first time I saw monastic sisters, I was struck by how radiant they were... that aroused my curiosity! We began to take part in the meetings of the small team of lay people at Les Montsvoirons at that time. Then, things gradually developed.

"I was bowled over by the discovery of the living Christ in the Eucharist. God was no longer a distant personage in Heaven, but Love that is close to us, so close that He wants to make His dwelling in us. It's incredible! I then received catechetical instruction in my diocese in order to become Catholic.

"Together with Jesus, I also received Mary. In the beginning, She was very unobtrusive. She never imposes herself. Little by little, I learned, and I am still learning to turn to Her. At first it was mostly when the times were difficult or when I had an important question. Then, She became more present, and I know now that She's close to me also in daily life, that she guides me when I entrust myself to Her." For Serge, it's a bit different. His long-time spiritual director invited him to conversion through his actions. "With the sisters of Bethlehem," he explained, "I discovered how precious silence and solitude with Jesus can be. Through *lectio divina* and long hours of adoration, I gradually learned to live in Jesus' gaze and to allow Mary to direct my life.

"Both stages, *lectio*/adoration, and conversion through my actions, go hand in hand."

Is that why both of you decided to leave everything in order to commit yourselves for one year to the renovation of Deir Rafat?

"It's not quite as simple as that," Serge replied, "but it's true that we had to make some choices. Once the children left home, it became easier. We organized our life accordingly, but we had already cut out a lot of things. We wanted to nourish ourselves much more with what comes from God."

And Brigitte added: "One of our reasons for coming here was to make a concrete commitment, as Serge said."

You are married and you have also been called to live a life of poverty, abandonment and gift of self. Would you say that you have a double vocation?

Serge replied: "I don't know if one can speak of a double vocation. The fact that we have added a more contemplative dimension to our life has given another dimension to the sacrament of marriage."

And Brigitte: "It's a grace to be able, as a couple, to share our life with God. We are blessed to have both received a call to live this charism. The sacrament of marriage is received and assumed at the very heart of the Holy Trinity. Our conjugal love is drawn from Trinitarian love, and we are immersed in this love individually and as couple."

Serge and Brigitte are spending their year at Deir Rafat with people whom they have not chosen, of different cultures and who are not necessarily lay-friends of Bethlehem. At lunch, we ate with a single woman who is Portuguese, a French woman, a young English woman who is an evangelical Christian in search of her vocation, three Christian Arabs from Palestine and Rabba, a Muslim. "It's true that we never would have chosen to live all together, and perhaps it would seem to some people impossible to do so. But it's because it seems impossible that God chose to bring us together here. It's a gift to welcome the other just as he or she is. We learn to not let ourselves to be deceived by appearances and to always seek a person's deep heart. Everyone has a deep thirst for God. It's the passage from the 'exterior' to the 'interior' that is sometimes difficult.

"It's not so much the project that is important, but rather the spirit in which we wish to realize it. We strive to be in relationship. Loving relationships that go beyond our cultural and religious barriers and our prejudices. What's important is to welcome the other, different as he or she is, and to want to work for a common goal. It sometimes means that we have to change our ideas, our projects or our way of thinking. It's a very rich experience for our personal growth and we enjoy it very much."

Rabba's wisdom

After lunch and before leaving Deir Rafat, I went to the kitchen... just to see if there was anything going on there! I found Rabba who was making a little "bouquet" of mint leaves. It was very fragrant and we began a conversation. Rabba comes from Beer-Shev'a, the great Bedouin empire. In 1960, she arrived at Deir Rafat with her very large family. She was ten years old. Her "Baba" is a shepherd and a farmer. Her mother takes care of the children. "I have seven brothers and seven sisters and a twin brother," Rabba told me. "We are the fifth. Eleven of them got married. I don't know how many grandchildren there are... perhaps seventy-five... in our family we don't count!

"Usually, Bedouin women don't work. But I worked a lot and I didn't get married. I paid for my younger brothers' and sisters' studies. My older sisters don't know how to read or write. When I was a child, I went to school here. There were Italian sisters of Saint Dorothy who ran Deir Rafat and they had a school there. For us Muslims, sisters don't exist, but my parents eagerly agreed to enroll me in the Christian sisters' school. In my family, there are no differences between Christians and Muslims. Also, my father worked on the property of the Jerusalem's Patriarchate.

"It was a priest who took care of me when I arrived here as a child. In the beginning, I only spoke the Bedouin's language and the sisters didn't have the patience to listen to me. I went to the priest and spent the whole day with him every day. He very was Arab and he taught me "good" Arabic: every day, he wrote vocabulary lists for me. It was interminable! But he was a very good man, and he taught me patience.

"A few years later, he became sick. At the time, I was the sisters' cook and I asked permission to visit him at the hospital. They didn't permit me to go, but I went anyway. He was in a French hospital which was very dirty. They did almost nothing for him and he went from bad to worse. I called the Patriarchate to ask them to take him to an Israeli hospital, and he was transferred. He stayed there for one month and then he died. I saw him only one more time, but he couldn't speak, just a few words. He said to me: "Rabba, take care of Deir Rafat." He loved this place. The next day he died. May God have mercy on him...

"The night after his death, I couldn't sleep. I had a dream. He came to visit me and he asked me for some tea. I'm convinced that he was in the monastery that night. When one dies, the body is lifeless, but the soul continues to live. Jews, Arabs and Christians in the East believe that the soul ascends little by little. It's not instantaneous.

"The next day, his grave was dug, and I said to the man who was responsible for the upkeep of the Sanctuary to dig a bigger grave. It hadn't been dug properly and it wasn't straight. It wasn't right to give him such a small grave.

"Afterwards, I escaped from Deir Rafat, and then I returned. It took time to get accustomed to his absence, but I had promised...

"The Sisters of Saint Dorothy remained a little longer, and then one day they announced to me that they were going to leave. Sister Isabelle came to Deir Rafat, and the sisters asked her to promise to keep me at Deir Rafat."

I asked Rabba how she lived the "changing of the sisters"!

"El mahabé...love! I immediately sensed that the sisters love the poor – a lot, really a lot. They never made distinctions between Muslims and Christians."

At that moment, I wanted to film Rabba... her smile. Poor Rabba, a little like Abu Jado, for her all is so simple: "I pray and they pray. It is love that unites us. When my father speaks about the sisters, he says that he greatly respects them. We live together: between us, there are no problems. I make mistakes, and the sisters do too. One should never keep inside whatever might spoil a relationship. When I'm angry or when I see something that isn't right, I tell them immediately. They also tell me when something isn't right.

"I really love the sisters: they are my life. It's the same for all my family: my brothers, my sisters, the grandchildren... Everybody loves the sisters!

"There's someone who unites us: the *Hadra*."

It's always the Virgin!

"In the Koran, there is a sura concerning Maryam. During Ramadan, we are required to pray this sura every day. For us, she is a very great person because she said 'yes.' She didn't ask the angel any questions. She didn't say 'What?' or 'How?'

"She is the Mother of the Messiah: it's written in the Koran. Everybody knows that.

"I know that some Christians don't believe that. At Zababdé, a little village nearby, there was a Protestant teacher who doesn't pray to the Holy Virgin. I asked him why. He said that he doesn't pray to the Virgin Mary, only to Jesus. So I said him: "Forgive me, but if the Virgin Mary hadn't existed, the Child Jesus wouldn't have existed either... If there's no mother, there's no child!" He didn't reply. Still to this day, I don't understand!

"As for me, I love Her one hundred per cent. I'll tell you a story. Not long ago, all the Bedouins who live in this region had to go to court because the Jews wanted evacuate the Bedouin camps. My brothers went to visit the Jewish authority in this region to ask him why we had to leave. They wanted him to defend us, but he didn't want to talk to them. In the end, nothing happened, and they left us alone. I had the Miraculous Medal, and I hid it in the encampment... I think that the Holy Virgin protects our land."

Rabba is very talkative. Time was flying by, but I couldn't stop her. I asked her if she respects the sisters' silence! She burst out laughing: "In the beginning, I talked all the time. The sisters responsible for hospitality said me 'Shhh! Shhh!' I grew accustomed to the sisters' silence. They pray and work a lot... always in silence. I have a lot of respect for them, because it's a life of sacrifice...it's the most beautiful life that anyone could choose! If had been Christian, I would have been a sister. No question!"

It was then my turn to burst out laughing. Everything is so simple in Rabba's heart. She is nothing but joy and spontaneity. Her common sense and her understanding of the Holy Virgin made me reflect on my twenty years of catechism in our good Christian schools...

As I prepared to leave Deir Rafat, Rabba came to meet me at the car and invited me for tea at her parents' house.

Accompanied by one of the guest sisters, we went to the encampment where her family lives. The encampment is situated on the monastery's land, bordering the desert. After crossing an olive grove, we arrived at her home and were greeted by her father. He wore a white North African scarf wrapped around his head and his face was serious. I was impressed by his great dignity. I saw in him a son of Abraham in the Promised Land. He explained to his daughter that he couldn't come to talk to us immediately because he was waiting for visitors who are not of "the family." In such cases, tradition requires that women be sheltered from the men's gaze. So we joined Rabba's mother who is also a Malika[1] and who was waiting for us in the shade of a big tree. She was beautifully clothed, covered with

1. In Arabic, a queen.

a dark veil, which didn't hide her beautiful face. Rabba served us mint tea and watermelon, and she gave me some advice: "People don't know the path. You have to show it to them. Tell them that they have to speak with God, otherwise He won't know their voices. It's very important."

I watched her mother who was invoking the ninety-nine names of Allah as her fingers passed over the dark beads of her rosary. Next to her, the monastic sister was praying the Jesus Prayer on her white cotton rosary...a beautiful communion of hearts...

4

God is God

I was struck by one of the things that Rabba had said to me. It was this simple sentence: "I pray, they pray: it's love that unites us".

Muslim, Jew or Christian…what's important is prayer. That was her message.

Rabba, like Abu Taher, Abu Jado, and Abu Issam are Muslims, friends of the sisters, while remaining faithful to their religion. None of them ever raised the question of conversion…a question which I would never imagine asking. I saw that it was a non-subject, and I never saw the sisters attempt to proselytize anyone.

What I experienced, however, in their testimonies was the power and strength of a universal message which didn't come from the monks or the monastic sisters of Bethlehem, but from God. It's a message that we have all heard: "Love one another as I have loved you."[1] I thought of a text by Christian Chabanis, which had deeply struck me:

> Love is not the genius of man, but the genius of God: that of man is the infinite need to love and to be loved, despite all the oppositions that existence presents to this need. The obsession with an absolute love, an eternal love, a lasting love, is simply another form of our obsession with God – in it's most universal, constant and irreducible form.

---

1. John 13:34.

Rabba helped me to understand that, at Deir Rafat, this need is satisfied. It is satisfied by the monastic sisters' love, but above all by the great, unconditional and eternal love offered and shared in this monastery, in particular, by men and women of all races, cultures and religions.

What Rabba had suggested to me, others had confirmed through their testimonies. "It was here that I was cured," one of the volunteers had said to me. "It was first through the sisters' love, but also through a kind of intuition that their love is connected to God's love. There was at first a little light in me, and I sensed that it was the reflection of another bigger light. I don't know if the bigger light is God, but what I live here is connected to God. Of that I am sure."

I met Merav in the monastery's tribune. I had often seen her come and go. One day we found ourselves together on the large terrace, and we had a long discussion.

Merav comes from a liberal orthodox Jewish family. Her childhood was shattered by a mentally ill father. Her mother, an artist in "a state of survival," eventually left her husband and went to live in an Orthodox Christian monastery with her daughters. A long path of wandering and reconstruction began for Merav. "I no longer had an identity, no longer a stable reference point," Merav told me. "In my childhood, there wasn't a boundary between good and evil." But there was the spiritual testament of her great-grandfather, who was a guide for the entire family: "Be good and follow the path of God. Draw near to Wisdom."

Merav began to find her path. "Like my mother, I sought peace. I knew the monasteries; I had begun visiting them when I was seven. It was like an open space for me, not at all strange or unfamiliar. I didn't fear churches or Christianity, as is the case for some Israelis.

"The first time I came here to Bet Gemal I was studying anthropology. After that first visit, I always felt the need to return. After three years, I asked to meet with a sister. I wanted to stay at the monastery to write my thesis. They welcomed me, but I didn't write my thesis or finish my studies! But I continued to write and to pray. From meditation,

I progressed to prayer. I sought a relationship with God. I remained for hours in prayer in the tribune. One day, while looking at the icon of Jesus, I was seized by a question: 'What are you doing here, Merav, in a church and not in a synagogue?!' The answer came to me spontaneously and naturally. All the paths that I had trodden in my life led me here. There was a reason that I was here; it wasn't a coincidence. I felt that wisdom was at work, that there was a meaning to my presence here.

"Then another answer came to me. I had been wounded in my childhood and I needed a kind of unification – to become one. To be Jewish and to be with Christians unified me in a certain sense. I understood that one shouldn't remain alone with one's suffering and accuse the other. We should share and be together.

"Now I can go to a synagogue, but at that time I needed serenity, silence and peace in order to face myself and to face God. In the synagogue, there are a lot of people and a lot of words.

"Here, in this monastery, there is a great respect for all people, religions and cultures. We can pray together. There aren't many places where that's possible. I listen to my inner voice. If something inside of me says: "There!" then I go directly there; nothing can stop me…I go directly towards God! And for me, here, this is the house of God…that's what I call it.

"What's important is to have roots…Jews, Christians, or Muslims, and…God. I needed to believe in God. Bet Gemal was like a beacon on my path, a house of light. I believe that this monastery could be a place for contemplation for all those who seriously seek the truth without rejecting their roots. It's so good for me…why should it only be for me?"

"Today Merav continues to write. She is finishing a book: *Become who you are*…a phrase taken from St. Augustine.

Merav is married to Kobi. They have three children: Rotem, Roï and Taliah.

Merav had spoken of a "beacon" and yet I continued to think of a well! They are both images of the same reality. The light of the beacon, the water of the well reveal the same secret, the same mystery: God. And I clearly saw that those who are "thirsty" are there for Him, for this love…

When Merav left, I saw a couple coming towards me. They had been there on the terrace with us for a while, and they probably heard some snatches of our conversation. They introduced themselves: Idith and Shay. Idith is a therapist and Shay is an engineer. Idith resumed the conversation naturally, as though she had read my thoughts!

"Man is thirsty: he looks for a well! If we dig deeply in ourselves, we can find our well and we share it. When I come here…this place is unique, very special," she said that as if confiding in me. "I carry my water and the sisters carry theirs… then the well becomes bigger. They never try to convert others. They could say to us: 'OK, since you are here, we are going to put you in our well and you will belong to us!' But that's not at all what they say. Instead, they say: 'OK, you have drunk our water, and you liked the taste, now go and dig in your own well, in your own religion, because God is everywhere. That's what I like here: I speak to them of my religion, and they speak to me of theirs. It's an exchange…God is God.'"

As I was collecting my thoughts, I ask Idith some questions about her family and her work. I was at the bottom of the well, so to speak! Everything seemed so simple, so obvious. Why all the debates? Everyone can go to God and drink. Or maybe that's simplifying things? I don't know; I don't know anymore….

"I'm a Jew and I grew up in an observant family," she explained. "For many years I tried to encounter God, but I couldn't. I went to the synagogue, I tried to be observant, to practice the law, but it didn't work. In my work as a therapist, we practice "breathing therapy," and one day we came here with my professor – a friend of a friend who knows the sisters brought us here. We even spent a night or two at the monastery, and we discovered that there is a higher level here of what we had been practicing on a lower level."

I grew more and more perplexed, and I think my perplexity was visible. Idith continued even though I didn't ask any more questions! "It was as though something in me opened more and more to God. What is special here is the feminine side of God and of religion. Today, religions, Judaism and, I think, also Christianity (though I don't know much about Christianity) have become very masculine. This feminine aspect adds something more open and less strict.

"I told you that I had had trouble encountering God, perhaps because in my childhood there was only the God who said to me 'if you do that, it's good; if you don't do that, it's not good.'" (I was back again to the scolding father of my childhood!!) "It was black or white, good or bad. Today, I can say that for me God is Love. And I believe that one can deeply feel this Love when one comes to Bet Gemal.

"With time, thanks also to my work with breathing and thanks to what I have discovered here, I was able to open myself to a more feminine and softer dimension of religion."

At that point in our conversation, I spoke of the Virgin Mary, of her presence here in the monastery, and, above all, of her gentleness, which is specific to her. There was a deep silence. Idith was overcome by emotion, and her husband gazed tenderly at her. "The fact that I'm moved by your question should tell you something," she said. "For me, Mary is the Mother. I had a very difficult relationship with my mother. With the breathing and God's help, something has changed in me on the maternal level. I don't know how to explain it.

"I don't need to tell you, everyone experiences that everything that the sisters do is animated by love, a love that has something maternal about it. That is very powerful for me, and part of my healing: to discover the maternal side of Mary and of the sisters, and also to discover it in myself."

Before leaving, Idith confided in me: what she lives here at the monastery helps her in her therapeutic work. "I'm often confronted with the question of suicide – either people who are affected by the suicide of someone close to them, or people who themselves threaten to commit suicide. What can one do to help them discover a good reason to live?

"The answer is in something greater than ourselves. We all have challenges in our lives, whether it's a matter of illness, of terrible things in our families. What can we do and how can we believe that life is worth living? For me, the only answer resides in the relationship that we can have with something which is above us, that surpasses us, that is greater than that which we have and see. One can, then, find a reason to live.

"I can't speak directly of my patients. I begin with their reality, the reality with which they live and I remain there with them where they are. There is a moment when something changes, something opens thanks to the breathing exercises, and then they discover a relationship with something above them. And then I can speak to them."

"I would like to conclude with this example: I had a patient whose mother had committed suicide. It was a terrible story. One day, while we were working together, she said to me: 'It's bizarre; there's a phrase that keeps coming to mind.' It was a verse from Psalm 22: 'Even though I walk through the valley of the shadow of death, I fear no evil.'"

5

In memory of André Chouraqui

It was a Friday, and Orna, who teaches the sisters Hebrew, was waiting for me in Jerusalem for my first Shabbat. I took advantage of my trip to visit Annette Chouraqui before arriving at Orna's house. Very deep ties unite the Chouraqui family to Bethlehem. It was Sister Marie who took the initiative when, during her first trip to the Holy Land in 1968, she went to visit André Chouraqui and it was then that a strong friendship began. After that first encounter, he did a lot to help the monastic sisters of Bethlehem to remain in the Holy Land, and it's thanks to him and his family that they were able to stay. It was thanks to his support that the monastery of Bet Gemal was constructed and recognized by the State of Israel.

Annette is André Chouraqui's second wife. There is something universal about André, who was animated by a deep ecumenism, and who devoted his life to the reconciliation of Jews, Christians and Muslims. He also translated the Bible from Hebrew and the Koran from Arabic into French. André died at the dawn of his ninetieth year in 2007. Born in Algeria, it was in France that he received his education before returning to Israel, to which he had always remained a loyal child. He is buried in Jerusalem, the city which he loved more than anything in the world. He once said: "When I'm at home, at every minute I see all of humanity passing before me, all peoples coming from all countries. It's fascinating because of all the dramas that one sees. I would like to be buried on the Mount of Olives; it's just opposite my house."

When I found Annette Chouraqui in her living room, I was fascinated by the view from her home. She lives on the top of a hill facing the old city, which is surrounded by ramparts. The Church of the Dormition is prominent in the landscape, and in the distance is the Mount of Olives.

Annette is a very reserved and attentive. I had in mind the conversations that I had had with my Jewish and Muslim friends, especially what they said about the possibility of peace...

Annette, do you think that in this blessed land we will see the peaceful ecumenism to which your husband dedicated his life?

"In the long term, André was convinced that it would be realized. He truly believed that. His vision of the unity between Jews, Christians and Muslims was spiritual and even mystical.

"He didn't concern himself with tomorrow... he saw farther ahead. He believed that there would be peace with the Palestinians, and he advocated a confederation between Israel and the Palestinians, and Jordan and other surrounding countries. He thought about the possibility of a union of the Middle East based somewhat on the European model."

And do you think that that is possible?

"Yes, in the long term."

In the long term? But so many years have already passed by.

"Yes... it has been two thousand years! Have a little patience..."

We then spoke about the *Prologue to the Song of Songs*, the text that Chantal Delsol's niece had chosen as the most beautiful response to the questions of our hearts. It's a true hymn to love, and, in my opinion, it's one of the finest texts that André Chouraqui wrote. Annette kindly allowed me to publish it. "Love was truly André's charism: he always brought everything back to love," Annette said to me, before returning to the subject of the bonds between her family and the monastic Family of Bethlehem. "What unites us to the sisters is fraternity, love of the land and love of one's neighbor. Our friendship with the sisters is precious, and it is based on listening and attentiveness. Even our children and grandchildren share in our friendship. Bet Gemal is our second home: that is where we celebrated André's eightieth birthday and many other family events. André stayed there for long periods of time in order to write."

At that point in our conversation, Elizabeth Chouraqui-Chemla arrived, Annette and André's daughter. She is very dynamic and warm. I didn't even have the chance to ask her a question before Elizabeth declared: "Ines, we are just ONE big family with the sisters, not two! Sister Isabelle and all the sisters are part of MY family. I saw the beginnings of the roots of this love grow deeper and deeper between us. I remember everything that preceded their arrival at Bet Gemal. My father helped them to find a place.

"And today the monastery of Bet Gemal is a place without borders, an oasis of love where one receives a shower of love that comes from heaven.

"It's also a place of convalescence and of healing. In Hebrew, the word for healing is *havraa*: in this word is the root of the verb "to create." Bet Gemal is a place of re-creation and rebirth. That is why we feel like we are between Heaven and earth there. Of course, we are on earth when we are there because the food is very good and we don't eat only with our mouths but also with our eyes, and there are all the different fragrances too. And yet, at the same time, we enter another state of mind. And that's a miracle... you can't find that anywhere else. My four children, aged between twenty-seven and thirteen, love to go to Bet Gemal. They feel that there is something extraordinary there... beyond the ordinary.

"The secret of Bet Gemal is their openness, their giving, their prayer, their presence to others. The sisters give entirely of themselves; they are entirely given. There's deep purity and silence that foster communion.

"I'll tell you, Ines, some people think that the sisters are crazy, but it is we who are crazy. We are so rooted in all that is earthly and material...

"There's something in the monastery that allows for freedom, detachment and a certain *élan* of the spirit. My father wrote a book about the "duty of the heart," that is to say, first there is the *élan* and detachment, then light and love. Love is an *élan* of the soul, which, by detachment, is united to pure light.

"Another thing that's astonishing at Bet Gemal is that there's no flesh, no human flesh, nothing physical, no barriers. There are no judgments, no barriers between Jews, Christians and Muslims, the rich or the poor, blacks or whites...what they live is beyond all of that."

Before leaving Elizabeth, I asked about her father and what she thinks is the most important thing to remember about him. "My father didn't have an 'earthly' presence. He was more like a spiritual father than an everyday father. He was in his own world. But he was deep as a well, and he was radiant like the rays of sunlight; he had a strong presence. I have great treasures in me thanks to him, but what he gave me wasn't verbally expressed or expressed otherwise in our relationship.

"We are five children and each of us is the depositary of something that we received from our father. He is still very present: his optimism, his hope, the fact that he never classified people according to 'their clans.' He didn't have prejudices.

"As for me, I work in the field of psychotherapy, of psychology, and I can 'tap into him.' I always feel his strong presence. My father often spoke of the 'new self,' a person who can be at peace with himself, with the world and with others. That's what I strive for in my professional life. From that perspective, there's something like a ray of sunlight from my father that lives in me.

"I also had the great misfortune to lose my husband, Moshe, last year. He was fifty-three years old. In my deep suffering, I had a certain strength which I had received from my parents. My father said to me one day: "I have set before you life and death…choose life." [1] Those are the two paths in the Book of Deuteronomy. That phrase is engraved in me."

1. Deuteronomy 30:19.

6

A First Shabbat

Orna had been living with her very elderly mother who had recently "gone to His world." It was Shabbat, and, in one of the newer neighborhoods in Jerusalem, she was waiting for one of her daughters, Madi, who has been a stewardess for one year on El Al and Shir'el, one of her sons, who is doing his military service, and his friend, Shadok.

There was a lot of commotion in the house for the preparation of Shabbat. While Madi was making herself beautiful, her brother and his friend left for the synagogue to pray. Orna was busy in the kitchen while talking to me. That night, the sun set at 6:08 PM, and that was the beginning of Shabbat. The end of Shabbat would be the following day at 7:20 PM. Every week, the *Jerusalem Post* publishes the hours of Sabbath. At sunset, Orna lit the candles while pronouncing the blessings. Two candles were "to guard and remember" and two were in honor of her mother.

Orna has been teaching the Hebrew language and Hebrew literature for forty-three years. The sisters had inquired about a Hebrew teacher at the Jerusalem tourist bureau, and it was there that they were put into contact with Orna. At first, Orna wasn't too enthusiastic, but she was persuaded to try a small "ulpan," or a Hebrew class, for three months. "That was in 1990. I taught the sisters Hebrew for several months," she explained, "and then at different intervals during the course of twenty years, when new sisters came to Bet Gemal."

When she began to teach them, there were fifteen sisters, and Orna remembers the discomfort and fear that she experienced when arriving at the monastery. "When I entered the room where I taught my first class, the first thing I saw was a cross, and I asked myself what I was doing there. But when I looked at the sisters, I thought I was seeing angels. Then they began to sing, and it was as if I were in paradise! I immediately had a feeling of plenitude and serenity. Hebrew is a very logical and simple language. French is much more complicated. My teaching method is difficult: I teach Hebrew in Hebrew and I don't provide a lot of explanations in French. In the beginning, discussion isn't possible. There are two hours of classes with only a little break.

"How can I explain it? I sensed that the sisters were very motivated, and I was fascinated by their smiles. You can't speak of a sister of Bethlehem without speaking of her smile. It's very contagious. They smile all the time. But the most important thing is that it's a smile that comes from within. I took that smile with me each time I left the monastery to return home.

"In general, after I've taught the basics, I use newspapers to help my students learn to speak. But that doesn't work to well in a monastery. So I decided to ask them to talk about their names. (When a sister receives the monastic habit, she receives a new name.) Later, we talked about Jewish and Christian feast days. It was a kind of catechism for me, which I found interesting, since I knew nothing at all about Christianity. Before, it had been a taboo subject for me. The sisters taught me everything, and I dared to say to others that I had Christian friends."

Before your encounter with the sisters, what did you think about Christians?

"I'll tell you very bluntly: for me, Christians were pagans and idolaters. The idea of Christ and of the woman who gave birth and yet considered herself a virgin, for me, it was ridiculous! And then I met the sisters. I said to myself that such beautiful souls couldn't possibly believe such nonsense. And then I realized that it was I who was ignorant, and that I had to change my ideas. I was able to take that step because we share the same fervor in our faith."

What does that mean?

"I'm very religious, and I had to be very Jewish in order to accept their Christianity. We have the same fervor – I, in my Judaism, and they in their Christianity. I'll give you an example: the *Avinu she ba shama-im*[1]. The sisters recite it at the beginning of our classes, when it's time for the break, and at the end of the classes. The first time, I listened very attentively to that prayer, to every one of the words. Obviously, there are words in that prayer that are in our Jewish prayers, but it's not a Jewish prayer. I closed my eyes and I listened. I watched them with my head lowered in meditation. It's like a song that floods over them, and I let myself be flooded by their prayers. But I kept quiet, and I prayed in my heart...

Orna, in Judaism, there's no consecrated life?

"Not only that, but it's even forbidden! The first *mitzvah*, that is to say, the first commandment that we receive, even before the Shabbat, even before "you shall not kill," and "you shall not steal,"[2] before everything else, there is the commandment to "multiply and fill the earth."[3] One must procreate. Consecrated life goes against this first commandment. And yet, since you asked me the question, I've never seen such feminine women. It's as if they have lived ten pregnancies!"

As we continued our conversation, I realized that Orna had the same questions as I did. Many of her questions are the same questions that led me to conduct my "investigation." "The truth is that I asked a lot of questions about them," she admitted to me. "What is this madness? Is it a choice, an election? A young woman has nothing better to do with her life than to lock herself in a monastery? Why isn't there the sound of an infant's cry in this house? Those were my first questions, and I quickly forgot them when I saw the sisters. When one enters

1. The "Our Father" in Hebrew.
2. Deuteronomy 5:17,19
3. Genesis 1:28

the monastery, it's clear that these questions are stupid. These women are so radiant, serene and, one would say, complete. They taught me to listen to their inner happiness. They are full of light, and that's not just words. Today, I realize how lucky I am to know these women, to have met them, to live with them and to breathe the same air with them. No one would be able to imagine all of that from the outside. You have to meet them.

"As for religion, they gave me the possibility to consider another religion. They opened the Christian perspective to me. In our heart of hearts, we're not so different. But again, if I weren't so entirely Jewish and they so entirely Christian, it wouldn't have worked between us. That's the fervor that unites us."

The time came to move to the table and to celebrate Shabbat by singing the traditional song "*Shalom aleichem malachei ha shalom*"[1]. Shir'el, the man of the family, said the prayers of blessing, taking the cup filled with kosher wine – the *kiddush* cup – which was passed around to all the guests. The table offered us all the flavors of the East. We also asked one another questions about our respective families, about France and Paris.

The hospitality and generosity of Orna and her children deeply touched me. I was not in a foreign country. I had received the hospitality of an "older sister."

1. "Peace be with you, angels of peace".

7

Who are these people dressed in white robes?

What the spring sang

I was always at my "post" in the chapel's tribune for all of the liturgical offices, but I must admit that I was often distracted in my prayer by my observation of the "white hoods." The sisters rarely look up to the tribune, but my sister assured me that she always knows when I am there because she recognizes my perfume!

A pleasant memory returned: it was eight months after my sister's departure for the monastery, and we went to the Holy Land to visit her. Our youngest child, Juliette, was three years old. We went to the tribune at the time of vespers, and we saw only the backs of the sisters who were all wearing their hoods. It was impossible for us to pick out the sister whom we had come to visit!

As only children know how to do, Juliette waited for a moment of deep silence to voice her disappointment: "But where are you? I can't see you?" My sister kindly stepped just a little bit out of her stall and turned around, for a split second, to look up to the tribune. That was enough to provoke Juliette to exclaim her admiration: "You are beautiful in your white dress!" And then an elderly sister looked up at the tribune for a little peek-a-boo with Juliette. The monastic sister and the child were of one heart.

My sister later confided in me about the elderly sister who had been one of the "foundation stones" of the monastic family. She was well loved by the young sisters who often asked her about "the humble beginnings" of the Family of Bethlehem. This is her testimony:

"THE VIRGIN IS ALIVE! That's what we lived at Chamvres, the village where the first community of the sisters of Bethlehem was born. The Virgin was there, and we didn't even have to make an act of faith to encounter her. She was there! Really there! It's difficult to explain. But don't misunderstand me. At Chamvres, there was nothing affective, in the negative sense of the word, in our relationship with her. No female emotions. It wasn't a relationship of emotions, but of naked faith. Naked faith is solid and stable, but emotions are changeable. It was a presence that we could always count on, and that had nothing to do with our interior state, our difficulties or our euphoria. It was very simple because, no matter whatever happened, we knew that she was there. The big event of each day was her presence. But, of course, we also had to make acts of faith. But our acts of faith were spontaneous, whatever situation we were living personally or in the community, and that helped us in our prayer and made life very simple. Simple! Very simple! The Virgin was always there: whether we felt her presence or not, that was secondary. And the greater our indigence, the more we were filled!

"Lately, I've been reflecting on all of that. It's incredible! We were living a completely banal life. Exteriorly, our life was totally simple and completely void of events. There was only one event: the presence of the Trinity and the presence of the Virgin. That gave a certain color to all the events that we lived, whether they were pleasant or unpleasant.

"At Chamvres, there was a tiny spring of water. Like children, we crouched down to listen to it:

> If any one thirst,
> let him come and drink
> let him who desires take the water of life without price.[1]

"There was nothing else to do. There was nothing more interesting than that. We had nothing, because we had everything.

1. Jn 7:37; Rv 22:17

It was a tiny little spring, and we had to bend down to listen to it. And we enshrined it, so to speak, with a lot of silence.

"Our silence was spontaneous. The silence just kept expanding like an enormous tablecloth and covered everything. It descended into our hearts. God was very present, amicably present.

"We were all very different, but we agreed on what was essential: the goal of our little *ecclesia.*[1]"

Wasted by illness during the last weeks of her death, that well-loved sister flew to Heaven like a dove after having sung the Song of Songs to her Beloved day and night. I understand why the young sisters were always so happy to listen to her.

The unexpected child

I met with one of the sisters who had recently had her first profession. She had a good rosy complexion as a testimony of her youth in Provence, and a big smile. There was depth to her gaze and a twinkle in her eye. She was, as it were, blessed with good luck in life.

Z. grew up in a non-practicing Catholic family. It was her friends that introduced her to the Church and to "Jesus' presence in the Eucharist." When she was seventeen, she asked to be baptized, and a few months later she went to Rome for the World Youth Day in 2000. Her older sister accompanied her, and later, she too, asked to be baptized. When she was eighteen, she entered the monastery of Thoronet. "I was deeply drawn – irresistibly drawn to the monastery – because it was 'Heaven.' And yet, at the same time, it seemed impossible for me. How could I leave everything to enter the monastery? I then put my desire on hold, but I continued to have little retreats in the monasteries.

"Several months later, I went to the monastery of La Verne, and, when I was before the Blessed Sacrament, it was as if Jesus wrote on a billboard for me: 'Do you want to enter Bethlehem?'

1. Latin for church.

It was very powerful. I understood that God is like a beggar with us, and I no longer had any fear. He awaits our 'yes.' And He waits for the right moment.

"I waited another four years in order to finish my studies. I studied for the entrance exam in literature, and I studied in a university, but I knew that all of that wouldn't lead me anywhere but here!"

When she was twenty-one, Z. announced to her family that she was going to enter the monastery in Israel. Her parents' lives were turned upside-down by her announcement, and her brother and sister were torn apart. She spoke to me about the beginning of her monastic life, which was relatively easy and free of troubles. "What struck me the most," she explained, "was the sisters' freedom in the Holy Spirit. I had come from the world, and they were much freer than I was. I lived in a world of stereotypes. And what I discovered here in the monastery completely changed my little categories, my preconceived ideas and my prejudices. Little by little, I began to understand certain gestures that are part of the liturgy or of the sisters' lives. I was sometimes surprised by certain things that I saw, but I knew that all that they did was in the Holy Spirit. And then there's obedience, which is essential. Obedience doesn't prevent the 'old self' from lashing out. Our sin emerges."

What is the 'old self'?

"The 'old self' is the part of us that bears the marks of sin and that sins. It's the part of us that can't receive the Holy Spirit and that makes a lot of noise! All of us, except the Virgin, have an 'old self.'"

I would imagine that a feminine concern about one's appearance is part of the 'old self,' and therefore something that one renounces upon entering the monastery.

"The Lord demands everything. It's more or less difficult depending on the person. For me, it was very hard. But don't think that monastic life entirely erases our femininity. The Virgin imparts something very respectful and feminine.

Through her, we discover another kind of femininity, another way to live our femininity.

"I've been in the monastery for seven years, and there are still times when that returns and it's terrible.

"It's one of the great struggles in the world today because all of our reference points with regards to femininity are attacked. The Virgin is the Woman. She is a mother, a virgin and a bride. We enter the monastery with a very distorted image of what constitutes a woman, and sometimes that reflects what we have lived.

"The Virgin reveals to us, through our wounds and through what we have lived, the mystery of what constitutes a woman, a mystery which is connected to the mystery of what constitutes a man. It's a mystery of relationship with all people, and it's connected to the mystery of the Church. When we enter the monastery, we have no other model of what a woman is than the Virgin. Christ is the only true man. Christ and the Virgin are our only beacons. I don't know how to explain it, but it's a struggle that extends even to our flesh."

What do you do in the monastery when the struggles become too difficult?

"We are accompanied by a prioress and by sisters who are more experienced than we are. But sometimes we are completely alone. Solitude is the place of struggles: it's the place of Christ's agony, which He asks us to live everyday. In the cell, we experience all the colors of the rainbow. There's a moment when God 'breaks down': He answers us and shows us His face. He never leaves us flat on the ground. The daily Mass is the privileged place where He lifts us up by His Love."

Do you know that some people don't understand your life, and that they think that it's completely egocentric?

"We are very egotistical because of our sins. But come and spend one month in a cell, and you'll see. You'd have to give it a try in order to find out if we have a nice and comfortable life in our cells!"

After our conversation, I had the joy of meeting with this sister's parents who were visiting Bet Gemal when I was there. I laughed a lot with Danielle and Robert, and, above all, they taught me generosity and how to tone down the drama of our common experience. Nothing had prepared them for their daughter's vocation, and I learned a lot from their manner of having accepted it with love, simplicity and good sense. I would have liked to film them. Paper and ink can't convey the warmth and mirth of their southern French accent.

Danielle had been very busy in the guest kitchen when I arrived for our interview.

"I'll tell, you, Inès, our family wasn't at all socially programmed for what we are living now! I certainly never thought that I'd be in a monastery kitchen making vegetable soup with pesto for forty monastic sisters! Some people think that you have to have been born in Versailles to know the good Lord or to be a good sister, but I'll tell you, I don't think Jesus even knows where Versailles is! Jesus is everywhere! I'll explain everything to you, but you have to help me cut the vegetables!"

There had been a mountain of zucchini, squash, carrots, tomatoes, onions, garlic and basil. We chatted while chopping the vegetables.

Danielle and Robert are retired. Danielle had taught English and Italian, and Robert had taught gymnastics. In their little village in Provence, Danielle is deputy mayor in charge of culture and associations.

Their eldest daughter is a comedian, their son is a jazz musician and their youngest child is a monastic sister. "All of that," she said, "with the same parents and the same education!"

With great tenderness, Danielle explained that their youngest child "has become the angel" of the family. In her maternal heart, she knew early on that she didn't belong to this world.

"Without love," she continued, "a vocation can't be understood. We have to respect our children. I accepted that one be a comedian, a journalist and appear on television, and the other be a musician. Why not accept a monastic sister? We have to accept everything.

"Welcoming somebody else's vocation makes us reflect on our own identity: who am I? What can I do in order to accept the vocation? There are families that are very poor and that suffer, parents who cut themselves off from their child and refuse to accept him or her. They need to ask themselves what kind of love they have for their child. Perhaps they don't love themselves. Or perhaps they love their plans for their child more than the child himself or herself. It's true that we make plans for our children, we imagine all kinds of things, and when the time comes to let go of all of that, we are lost and we don't understand anything. What it comes down to is that we have to love our children more than ourselves. Nothing other than love can help us. If we refuse to let go of our pride and if we think about what others will say, it's a lost cause!

"A vocation concerns the whole family. The child's vocation becomes our vocation. A religious sister is a treasure for the entire family and their friends. But not everyone is ready to accept this treasure, and so it's our responsibility to make a little nest for the treasure. For some people, it takes time to make a little nest, but it works out in the end. Nothing but love makes it possible, otherwise there's no exit. We have to be lenient with ourselves, love ourselves and know how to forgive ourselves in order to love our child."

Do you think that giving one's child to the Church and to Christ is the biggest gift that parents can give?

"I never had the feeling that I gave my daughter because I never felt that she belonged to me like an object. I love her too much to be able to say that she belongs to me. It is she who gave the gift of herself. I didn't give her away. I remained with her in her decision. I never thought that my children belong to me, and yet I gave my life for them without hesitating for a second. I'm responsible for them, but I don't possess them. They belong to God, not to us. And when we are able to understand that, we have already turned the corner.

"I had imagined all kinds of things for Z., but never that she would be a monastic sister. The greatest mistake parents can make is to attach their ambitions and desires to their child. Our children don't belong to us. We must do all that we can to help them, to enrich their lives and their personality, of course, but afterwards? Suddenly, we realize that we were mistaken, that we hadn't foreseen the choices that they would make... Those are life's lessons."

But wasn't there also a separation that was terrible and definitive?

"Of course we are separated from her physically. But, believe me, I feel closer to her than if she had been glued to a computer or a television all day long. It's not at all true that the sisters are cut off from their families. We know that there are times when we can't see her, but it's not an effort for us because we have accepted that it's like that. I don't like suffering. I prefer happiness. Our visits here to the monastery enrich us enormously. We have made friends with Palestinian Christians and Muslims and also with Jewish families. We have met people that we never would have met if we had remained in our village."

How did you experience the day when she received the monastic habit?

"I had a lot of emotions. I even lost my eyesight for thirty seconds or one minute. I saw a big white curtain and I said to myself: 'O.K., I've lost my sight!' I saw absolutely nothing. Afterwards, I saw clearly. And when she came up to the tribune to give us a kiss, at that moment, I felt as though I had completed my mission. It was as if I had unburdened myself of very heavy baggage, because I had arrived where I had to go. I had completed my mission. I had completed my role as a mother. It was a deep joy. It's not easy to be parents. We give everything, and yet sometimes that's not enough."

Danielle, what do you say about the sisters to those who are outside the monastery? How do you explain their life?

"First of all, I explain that monastic sisters aren't repressed neurotics. They are women of light who could have done fifty thousand other things in their lives, but they were called by Jesus. People are intrigued by the fact that they are called by Jesus.

"Then I tell them: it might very well be for you that she went to the monastery! If there weren't sisters in monasteries, you would probably be living much more difficult situations. They don't enter the monastery for themselves.

"I emphasize that it's not at all a self-centered life. They aren't there for themselves and to be sheltered from material concerns. They work a lot. Sometimes it helps to explain that their vocation is a service for others: by their prayer, they carry the world. I believe that it's true. The world would probably be worse without their prayer. They save us from many dangers. They aren't imprisoned. We are much more imprisoned than they are! We live according to the dictates of our consumer society: we have to remain young, we have to be beautiful, thin, rich. All of that is false. We know perfectly well that when illness strikes or when we are in mourning, even if we have all of that, we have nothing at all. They are much freer in their hearts than we are. We lose our lives in trying to gain all that the world tells us is necessary. But the big difference between the sisters and us is that they don't judge our lives."

Before concluding our interview, Danielle offered me one last memory in the form of a poem. One day, it had started to rain. The sisters had prayed a lot for rain, and it was a blessing in this sun-scorched land. Danielle had run to the terrace to taste the first raindrops. She heard the sisters crying for joy and spotted her daughter in the midst of a group of sisters. It was a Sunday, the day when they take their weekly walk together.

I saw her dancing…a joyful saraband
thanking Jesus for the falling rain,
which was inundating her laughing youth with happiness
and she lifted her arms to the heaven that she had implored…

I saw her running joyfully,
her sisters full of wonder followed after her,
playing cheerfully in the woods like flowers of the field,
their laughter joined to the murmuring wind.

I saw that she who had been praying was enveloped by silence,
where walls of praise rose up to heaven,

I was in the tribune, and she lifted up her eyes,
her smile lighted up her face…sublime evanescence
I received with all my heart that precious treasure.
She slipped away, a slender silhouette,
there where only the Lord was with her…
The night bore delicate aromas.
She traversed the cloister,
there was a resplendent statue in the midst of greenery,
and I saw her kiss the hand.

You who don't believe in eternal life,
when you see these white doves,
with their fluttering wings,
let them touch your hearts which are
asleep to the promises of heaven.

Danielle explained to me: "Robert's way of communicating with the sisters and of being in communion with them is to work for them. As soon as he arrives at Bet Gemal, he begins to work."

And so I went to the woodworking workshop to look for Robert. He was happy to take a break. We sat down on the terrace with our tea and cigarettes. Robert spoke as if confiding in me. At times he paused to seek the most appropriate word. His words were full of tenderness and respect for his daughter. At times, he didn't quite know how to express himself, and he took the time to reflect. Sometimes he simply let silence speak for him.

"I'm not going to tell you the story of my daughter's life, " he said. "She probably already told you everything. What I can say is that there are as many destinies as there are people. We already had two children. I was forty, and she was an unexpected child. All children are unique, but she had something different than the others. We saw that little by little she became more serious. We can't remain a toddler all our life. She was becoming a young woman. She sensed a kind of confusion or turmoil, a call, a mysterious event that was in the process of developing. Afterwards, we understood. There's always a thread that connects everything, but we don't see it immediately. Later, we understand. When we are in the present moment, we can't decipher the signs. It was like that with Jesus: the apostles deciphered everything, but afterwards. In the present moment, they didn't understand. Only Jesus knew what was happening. Those close to Him didn't understand anything. It was a shock when she announced her decision. I had retired after forty years of activity and routine. My first reaction was: 'Oh great, our relationship is already over!' Time had flown by, and I hadn't been sufficiently present to her. I was dejected and I started brooding. We Westerners, we always seek to understand and to make clear and coherent whatever goes beyond our understanding. In my worst moments of delirium, I imagined all kinds of things: perhaps she was unhappy, perhaps she had been disappointed in love… And then, in the end, I understood that there is a mechanism or a process that we didn't understand and that even she didn't understand. After that, I was more calm, and the turmoil was turned into admiration and rapture."

Are you at peace now?

"There were two very powerful moments. First, when she received the habit. That was a moment of offering. She renounced her own ego, she forgot herself and made of her life a permanent offering. We entered into another dimension. We who are close to her, we were filled with admiration and pride, and at the same time, we were deeply struck because it was 'supra-natural.' Not supernatural. It transcended what is natural. That offering transcended what is human. It's a call. I've had conversations with elderly people who had also received a call, but couldn't respond to it. They were unhappy all their lives. Then, two years ago, she had her first profession. She received the wimple.[1] That was very powerful. I cried. It's ridiculous, but I said to myself: it's the last time that I will see her hair. You have to know what it is to be a father. It was very powerful."

Robert, what did that change in your life?

"For seven years I've been becoming an expert on monastic sisters! I became a historian: the history of the order and their art. Before, religion interested me, but I approached religion

1. A cloth headdress that surrounds the face.

the way one approaches astronomy, films or architecture. For me, it was simply an element of our humanity. Like fishing, there are churches, monks, monastic sisters and the pope. But with our daughter, we discovered all of that on another level. Since I was personally concerned, I began to search and to dig a bit, and that's when I began to enter into the mystery of humanity and I realized that I couldn't put religion on the same level as the natural sciences such as physics or chemistry…nor on the same level as films or songs. No, religion isn't part of our consumer mentality. It's different. Then one enters into the mystery of the divine, of Creation and of our humanity. The more one advances, the more things become simple, and, yet, at the same time, also complex. The thread is always there. And the more one advances, the more it becomes complex in what is infinitely small and infinitely big, in the infinite varieties of manners of seeing things, whether in the East or in the West, all the rites and other religious traditions. We were living all of that from the outside, but now I read things and I seek to understand. For seven years, I've been meditating on all of that and seeking the connecting thread."

Do you know the parents of other sisters?

"Yes. Some parents are in a state of rebellion and denial with regards to their child. I know a lot of parents who are in that state, and that makes my stomach turn. When one has loved one's child and continues to love her, I can't understand how someone can dig his heels in, to resist stubbornly and to reject his child. Sadly, there are even some who are here."

What do you say to those parents?

"First of all, I tell them what I have lived. I try to make them feel the weight of the mystery, the weight of what is essential and of the thread, which I spoke about. I tell them that we are all called to the same mystery and that love is above everything else. And then there's forgiveness. We have to love over and beyond our capacity. It's not a question of relinquishing our feeling of love that we had for our child; it's a question of going above and beyond in love, of loving even more, in a different way. I tell them what Jesus asks of us: to stop moaning and complaining. To go beyond ourselves and to be stronger. To go beyond our egotism.

"I advise all fathers who are living what we are living with our daughter to change their position. Those who have reacted egotistically, I advise them to ask their daughter to forgive them. They are poisoning their hearts and their souls. Pride and egotism are poisons."

What do you say about the sisters when you speak with people who don't know Bethlehem?

"It isn't good to antagonize them. First of all, I speak about the concrete elements of their life: what they do every day, their beauty, their kindness, their gentleness and their patience. I try to speak about the incredible aspect, which transcends what is human, in their commitment and in the mystery of prayer.

"Inès, I seize hold of every possible occasion to bring them to God. To open their eyes, their ears and their hearts, and to help them abandon their banality. In fact, I try to tell them that a life without God is a life without a compass, but it's difficult to explain that. I try to help them to think in another way, to think about things other than soccer, the weather or traffic jams. Sometimes it works, and it touches their hearts. The ambient culture tries to inculcate certain things, but we have to look farther, reach higher and keep the thread of truth. And this thread, almost everywhere in the West, is beginning to unravel. We need to rediscover the light, the original thread which is slackening, but it can lead us to the well of truth, happiness and salvation. Salvation passes by Mary: She also suffered as a mother who gives birth. All mothers are attuned to that. There are mothers who have experienced terrible things. A lot of people live what Mary lived when she lost her Son. Our only resort is Mary; she intercedes for us."

It's rare that a man speaks of Mary the way you do.

"She's essential. For me, She is the feminine aspect of the divine message. She represents motherhood and, at the same time, femininity, but a virginal, immaculate and intensified femininity. Mary tells us what is essential: that humanity, desired by God, desired by a divine power – let us call that divine power God – come forth from a woman. He wanted humanity to be represented by a woman, by Eve. And that puts in place, once and for all, the foundation of humanity. Neither two men nor two women can procreate. It's the woman who is the source of love, forgiveness, motherhood, affection and breast-feeding. It's the woman, not the man.

"In our contemporary world of confusion and relativism, Mary represents the truth, the original reference point for humanity. That is to say, childbirth. A test-tube child isn't conceived in love. When the genes are in their early stages and the chromosomes are in disarray, Mary is Mary. Of course science must do everything to understand and to help people. But Mary teaches us respect for life and how to accept life. It's more difficult to turn to Jesus because of the sacrificial aspect. We turn to Mary because She is the Mother of Jesus, of God. In the West, we try to deny the fundamental elements of women and mothers. Here, in the Middle East and in Asia, they could care less about our raving! O.K., that's enough…I have work to do!"

Remove the garment of your sorrow and affliction, O Jerusalem

"When the Lord is enamored of one of his little creatures, He never abandons him. And He never abandons his plan of love for each one of us. Never be troubled when something takes time, for time always works in favor of the truth."

One of the sisters told me the very long story of an unimaginable 'voyage' that lasted many years, a voyage with multiple trips between the U.S. and Israel, Israel and Sweden, and in Italy. It's at the end of such a voyage that we can say that we've come full circle. It's the voyage of a back-packer of the faith who was desperately seeking her religious identity and her vocation. It was a voyage which, in a certain way, ended in the tribune at Bet Gemal during Adoration. Born of a Catholic mother with Hungarian roots and of a non-practicing Jewish father, she is now a monastic sister of Bethlehem after having been a charismatic Messianic Jew!

Born in Pittsburg, Pennsylvania in the U.S., Judith was baptized and raised as a Catholic with her father's approval. She remembers having loved Jesus as a child, and having a fascination for religious, whom she considered to have something special with God. But after a minor event, Catholicism soon became a religion of fear. When she was eleven, during a Girl Scout outing on a Friday, she ate a ham sandwich. Sin! One can easily imagine the ambient Puritanism of the time. The priest who heard her confession said to her concerning her "terrible" sin: "Perhaps God will forgive you." That phrase haunted her, and she never forgot it. Overwhelmed by guilt, she thought that she was condemned to hell!

Several years later, Judith left to study psychology in Alabama and then in Texas. It was the late 60's: the war in Vietnam, hippies, Woodstock, marijuana and drugs. Her life was in total disarray. She was a brilliant student, but the rest of her life was a disaster. She had numerous addictions and deep interpersonal problems. In the small town where Judith was studying and working, she adopted a very anti-Christian attitude, which antagonized those around her.

"I was almost anti-Christian," she explained, "perhaps because of the wound that I received when I was eleven. Even the sight of a cross irritated me. The lie that I continued to believe – that I had been created in order to go to hell – gave rise to deep anger in me with regards to God. Why did He create me in order to suffer in hell for eternity? Since I worked with a lot of Christians, I took pleasure in pointing out their hypocrisy and their weakness. And I also felt rejected by them.

"A young woman came to work with us. We spent a lot of time together and we spoke a lot. For the first time, I felt truly loved. She was an evangelical Christian, and she didn't reduce me to my sin. She always brought Jesus into our conversations, but I was totally blocked. How could I go towards Jesus when He had rejected me? To bypass the impasse, I turned to the New Age movement and I had spiritual experiences in the occult. But nothing worked; nothing set me free. Tension mounted. Finally, I collapsed, and I gave Jesus an ultimatum: 'Jesus, if You really exist, tell me now.' When I got up, I had only one idea in my head: the Bible! I read the Bible all night long. It was like a torrent of purification. The next morning, I wasn't the same."

Judith joined an evangelical community where she began to find stability. She deepened her knowledge of Scripture. It was by reading the genealogies in the Bible that she rediscovered her Jewish identity. She experienced this rediscovery as a call to seek her paternal roots in Israel. One year later, she left her job, sold everything and left for Israel. In Jerusalem, she met two brothers, Reuven and Benjamin, members of a Messianic Jewish community,[1] and she learned that it was possible to be Jewish and to believe in Jesus.

At the end of one year, Judith returned to the U.S. to be with her family and to continue her work in Texas. Involved in a charismatic community (there weren't any Messianic Jews in her small town), she met Ulf and Birgitta Ekman, Swedish charismatic Protestants, who are the founders of a biblical school and a church called 'Word of Life,' which is comprised of 250,000 members in Sweden, the U.S. and Israel.

It was then that Judith decided, in the hidden depths of her heart, to consecrate her life to the Lord and to remain celibate. The years passed, and again she felt called to return to Israel. This time, the call was definitive. In order to immigrate, she needed to obtain a letter from a rabbi to verify that her father was Jewish.

---

1. Messianic Judaism is deeply influenced by Protestantism. Messianic Jews, in fact, have exactly the same faith as Protestants. For a Messianic Jew, his faith is the very faith that has endured throughout the centuries: it's the faith announced by the prophets in the Ancient Testament. They also await the Parousia. They have retained many elements of traditional Judaism, but they are not in any way bound to the Jewish rabbinical tradition.

"I told my parents about my desire to immigrate to Israel, and I asked my father to help me to obtain the letter. That's all that I needed. The Lord touched my father's heart, and he obtained it for me. In his heart of hearts, he was very proud of me for adopting my Jewish identity, even if he couldn't understand that one could be Jewish and believe in Jesus. My mother didn't understand in my life, neither as a Protestant, nor as a Messianic Jew, but she was respectful. When I received my papers, I became a Jewish citizen. That was in 1998, the Jubilee year in the state of Israel. Fifty years!"

She had barely settled in as a new immigrant, when she met a young Ukrainian Christian who spoke to her about the Swedish biblical school 'Word of Life' founded by the Ekmans, whom she had met in the U.S..

"The Lord surprised me again. One year after having immigrated, He put in my heart the desire to go to the biblical school in Sweden! I was forty, and with my background in psychology, I had a hard time finding work. I also felt that the Lord was calling me to something else. I applied to the biblical school in Sweden and I was accepted!"

Judith packed her suitcases again, this time to go to Sweden, in Uppsala, where she met with Ulf and Birgitta. After one year of formation, the Ekmans proposed that she return to Israel to participate in the foundation of an office and biblical school of 'Word of Life' in Jerusalem. She agreed, and after two years, again she questioned herself about the direction of her life.

"In Israel, I had obtained an equivalent diploma for my studies in psychology which allowed me to work, but I wanted instead to return to Sweden for a second year at the biblical school. There was a second intifada, and the situation in Israel was very difficult. For three months, I worked as a volunteer policewoman for the Jerusalem security services before leaving again for a blessed and marvelous year in Sweden. When I returned to Israel, I found a job in a souvenir shop in a Jewish neighborhood. Of course I knew that that wasn't part of my call, but I lived according to my faith. I evangelized a lot."

Ulf and Birgitta were in Jerusalem to launch the biblical school, and they invited Judith to do secretarial work for them. She accepted. At that time, her interest in the little Messianic Jewish community was renewed, and she became more and more involved. Benjamin and Reuven were also connected to a charismatic Catholic community, the community of Saint Egidio in Italy, founded by Andrea Riccardi. They encouraged Judith to go there for a short retreat.

"It's a very lively and joyful community, and it was the first time that I returned to the Catholic Church. They had decided to go to Saint Peter's for the Christmas vigil. It was John Paul II's last Christmas, and we found a place in the basilica. I was deeply struck when the pope arrived in his wheelchair, because he was radiant with love. It was incredible. He was very sick, and I saw how he gave all his strength in celebrating the Mass. Something happened in me. The idea that I had had of the Catholic Church changed completely. After the Christmas vigil, we had the second part of the retreat. Father Ricardo spoke about life in the Church before Vatican II: how some people suffered because of the legalism at the time, which prevented them from encountering Jesus, and they also lived with a lot of guilt. It was as if he were recounting the story of my childhood and my wound. A path opened for me to return to the Catholic Church, which I no longer tried to avoid.

"During the liturgical celebrations, there was always a big crucifix. It had been a long time since I had approached a cross. In looking at Jesus on the cross, I realized what He had done for me, and I understood that the cross could be a source of joy and thanksgiving. I was very happy to rediscover the crucifix in my life and to be able to look at it."

Messianic Jews, who wish to keep their Jewish identity, never display the cross. They speak about the cross and they preach the cross, but they never display it. For them, the cross is the sign of the persecution of their people: Jews are accused of having killed Jesus, and for them, the cross is the symbol of that accusation.

After her return to Italy, Judith met up again with Ulf and Birgitta. One day, they invited her to visit Bet Gemal's gift shop to look at the sisters' artwork since they had heard people speak about it.

"It was Shabbat. The idea didn't interest me much, but I was happy to spend time with them. When we entered the gift shop at Bet Gemal, there was a sister there, and I had never seen a sister who was as happy as she was. In Jerusalem, all the religious are in black. I was deeply moved, and immediately I thought: 'That's what I want!' The sister spoke about Jesus with such faith...I held back my tears as I looked at all the beautiful things in the shop. I was stunned, as if something had taken hold of me. I continued to fight back my tears. We walked up to the terrace that leads to the chapel. There was Adoration. I think there must have been a sister, but I saw nothing but the altar and the monstrance. It's hard to explain, but it was as if there were a fire, as if I had been knocked out, as if someone had taken possession of me and had drawn me to Him. I knew that it was Jesus. A door was opened in the depths of my memory, and all the memories of my childhood fascination with religious and my desire to become a religious came back to me. At that moment, I knew that the Lord was asking me to live here. He invited me to enter. I no longer had any doubts.

"Ulf and Birgitta saw everything. They didn't offer any commentaries. The only thing they said to me was that I shouldn't speak about it to anyone, and that I should keep everything in my heart and pray about what I had experienced. The following Sunday we returned for Vespers and Mass. I met with two sisters, and I told them what had happened in the chapel and the call that I felt very deeply in me. 'The door is open,' they said to me.

"For nine months, I went every weekend. I went to the evangelical month at Les Voirons. I met with Sister Isabelle, and I understood her special love for Jews. She understands the soul of a Jew. She agreed that I enter the monastery just as I was: a Messianic Jew.

"I told my parents. My mother was beside herself with joy at the fact that I was going to be a religious. For her, that meant that I was returning to the Catholic Church, so all was well. It was more difficult for my father who thought that I would forget my Judaism.

"In 2005, I entered the monastery at Bet Gemal. The Lord knew where He was calling me, and it was in His Presence, in His Love, that the door of my memory opened in order that the child that I was could live. That child had never stopped loving Him and never desired anything other than to consecrate her life to Him."

At the end of our conversation, I was stupefied by her story. I saw, attached to her rosary, not a medal of the Virgin (all the other sisters have one attached to their rosaries), but a medal with an inscription in Hebrew. I asked her to translate it for me: "If I forget you, O Jerusalem, let my right hand wither!"[1]

1. Psalm 136

8

There's no unity without love

On a personal level, the monastic sister's story struck me deeply, and she opened horizons for me that I had barely considered before. I knew almost nothing about Messianic Jews, and I was intrigued by the Protestant pastor who had helped a female Messianic Jew bring to fruition her vocation in a Catholic monastery! I had the good fortune to meet with him and his wife.

Ulf and Birgitta Ekman were at the end of a pilgrimage in the Holy Land with a group when I arrived at Bet Gemal. They very kindly agreed to come to Bet Gemal for the evening before leaving for Sweden the next day. We ate dinner together, and afterwards I remained with the memory of their warmth and openness. They answered all my questions with great simplicity and straightforwardness. It was a moment more than ecumenical.

Ulf was originally a layperson. He hadn't been at all interested in God, "just enough to know that He exists," was how he put it. When he was twenty, one of his close friends converted him. While he was studying ethnology, history and religion, Ulf delved deeply in the Bible and did some evangelizing work. He came into contact with the charismatic movement and decided to become a Lutheran minister. It was at that time that he met the woman who would become his wife.

Birgitta's father was a Methodist pastor. She grew up in India where her parents were missionaries. She returned to Sweden and had a few difficult years before she met Ulf. They have been married for thirty-seven years, they have four sons and they live in Uppsala, Sweden, when they aren't traveling around the world.

They both explained to me the foundations of the Lutheran church. It's a very liberal theology based on a strong rationalism and humanism. They observed a serious deficiency of biblical knowledge, especially among young people, during their evangelizing missions. They decided to study in a biblical school in the U.S. before founding a biblical school themselves in Sweden. "There was an incredible thirst" in the 1980s, and immediately young people came in droves to study the Bible for one year or longer. Ulf was also the student chaplain at the University of Uppsala. He was overextended, and he left the Lutheran church to be able to travel more freely and to preach, in particular, in Stockholm once per week. It was then that he felt the need to found not only a biblical school, but also a church called "Word of Life." It wasn't at all his intention in the beginning. "I didn't want to found a church, because it's a controversial subject. But there comes a time when one realizes that teaching isn't enough, that it's necessary to watch over and care for the people who come for instruction. The pastor of the church in Stockholm encouraged me to found a church. And that's what we did. It's a church built on three pillars: a personal experience of faith, evangelical preaching and missions. We have a lot of missions in Russia, Moscow, Saint Petersburg, Albania, and also in Singapore, Taiwan and Indonesia."

Birgitta added: "When the Soviet Union collapsed in 1989-1990, there were innumerable atheists who didn't know God. They ran to Jesus. They came by the thousands. They were very thirsty."

Ulf: "Today, we have the most important Protestant church in Moscow and also a large biblical school where the Orthodox also teach with the agreement of our pastor who meets with them regularly."

In 2002, Ulf and Birgitta felt called to spend one year or more in Israel in order to begin a biblical school there, but also to reflect on several questions. "The Lord had begun to make us face the question of unity in the Church. I was involved in some activities in the Church, I tried to work in the Spirit of the Church, but we weren't at all sure that we had understood the essence of the Church. What is the Church? Where are we in the Church? Of course, we could have remained content with what we had done in our church 'Word of Life,' but in our hearts, we felt that we had a deep connection with the body of Christ, the universal Church."

During their stay in Jerusalem, a little statue led Ulf and Birgitta to the sisters of Bethlehem's gift shop at Bet Gemal! Birgitta recounted the story. "One day, when we were walking in the old city, we saw a statue of the Virgin and of the child Jesus which we thought was beautiful. I bought it. On the back, it was written: sisters of Bethlehem. The statue made me want to know more about these sisters and their artwork. We didn't know where they were, and we thought that they were Arabic sisters of Bethlehem."

Ulf added: "Inès, you should know that there are two things that frighten Protestants: the pope and Mary. Authority and the mystical life. When we in Jerusalem, we were struck by all that concerned Mary."

Birgitta: "I had really fallen in love with the statue. I thought it was marvelous, but I didn't know how to find the sisters. One year later, in the Jerusalem Post, I saw a photo of the same statue and of the monastery at Bet Gemal. The article said that it's a beautiful place to walk on the day of Shabbat. We decided to go there and to bring with us a young woman who was a Messianic Jew and who worked for us."

And that's how the monastic sisters found themselves at the crossroads of two stories: that of the young woman who became one of them and that of the Protestant couple that grew very close to the community. Ulf has a very clear memory of their first visit with Judith: "We went to the chapel. As soon as we arrived, she stood still as a statue before the Blessed Sacrament. We saw the tears in her eyes and we left. Something important was occurring between the two of them. She came later to join us when we were talking to the sisters. There was fire in their eyes. I'm serious. And, above all, there was a presence in the room, which couldn't have been anything other than God. Judith was seated on the floor and she was crying."

Birgitta: "We understood that God was calling her, but I asked myself if that life was really for her. You know the end of the story."

Ulf: "That opened the door of this monastery for us, and we have returned very often. There's a very strong presence of God here."

I was, of course, touched by their story. And it was clear that the encounters which they had had were not haphazard. There I was with Protestants in a Catholic monastery where the Virgin is omnipresent, and they weren't at all troubled by her presence. Quite the contrary. "For me," Ulf added, "there was a visible sign, that of Love. It is by Love that we recognize the apostles of Christ. Adoration, joy and the simplicity of their life are also clear signs. Contemplative life reveals God's love, Christ's love and Mary's. The fact that Mary has such a central place in the sisters' charism was a real revelation."

But contemplative life might appear useless to some people.

Ulf: "That's what we ourselves thought! Being of Lutheran origin, the most important things for us were the family, work, laypeople and missions. We pray in our homes. What's important is to go and preach the Gospel to all the nations. For us, to close oneself in a monastery had no meaning. But now that the Lord has led us here, we know that prayer works powerfully for the salvation of the world. It's like a spiritual motor. I think that the Protestant charismatic renewal led to a deeper understanding of consecrated life. Before, there was a strong reaction. Now, in many places, people are rediscovering contemplative life and they understand it better."

Birgitta: "I think that the youth in Sweden understand it better and better, and they have a deep thirst for a life lived more deeply in God. They go on retreats in the Lutheran church and in other big churches. They even sometimes go on pilgrimage. The need is there. There's too much noise in the world, and people seek silence and God's voice."

Ulf: "Contemplative life is the salt of the earth, the light of the world. When we remain in God's presence, we can intercede for the world in a particularly powerful way. The Presence of the Trinity: that's the first thing that I sense when I arrive here."

Birgitta: "When we came here, I went to the office of Vespers. What we saw, and what really touched us is the fact that the monastic sisters prostrate themselves, with their faces to the floor, before God in adoration. It's beautiful and pure. We had never seen anything like that. How could we not feel that God is here? And together we adore Him."

Ulf: "For me, a person is created in order to prostrate himself in adoration of the Trinity. This gesture reveals the most central, the most beautiful and the most important element of their life. And when I see that, I say to myself: that's the meaning of life, to adore God before the Blessed Sacrament, before the presence of Jesus. To remain constantly before God gives an intensity of life to the body. Their prayer for the world and for the salvation of the world is like a powerhouse. It's the only place in the world where I can remain for hours without understanding one single word. The presence is there even before I arrive, and I just have to enter the presence. It's incredible. It's like entering God's heart, the heart of the Church, that's why I love coming back here. In no time, I'm led to live in my heart. I don't remain at the threshold, but I'm led instead into the holy of holies. I would also like to emphasize something that struck me even during our first visit: the joy. There's an incredible joy here."

I'm struck by the fact that this monastic family creates unity. I questioned Orthodox Christians, Jews, Muslims, and you today. Everyone speaks about love.

Ulf agreed with me: "Here, at Bethlehem, it's the contemplative life: love for God, for Christ and for Mary. It's a very pure love.

"There's no unity without love, and when there's love, unity is created. We all have the same thirst and desire."

Forgive me for insisting on this point, but I think that there's a reason for Mary's presence here.

Ulf: "Yes, the Mother wants to gather her children together. Unity is the only path of salvation."

9

Blessed are those who mourn

My stay in the Holy Land had almost come to an end, but I still had to meet with Benjamin Berger, the founder, with his brother, of the congregation of Messianic Jews who had welcomed the future sister of Bethlehem.

Benjamin lives in Ein Kerem, a village on the outskirts of Jerusalem. It is the place of the Visitation when Mary visited her cousin Elizabeth. I stopped at the fountain of Mary, which is now surmounted by a small mosque. A young woman who was all smiles was there and she offered me a small glass of cold water... How could one not think of the Samaritan woman in this place, in this land where even the most simple gestures are rich with meaning?

Benjamin's house, "Bet Avinu" (House of our Father), is on top of a small hill, above the sanctuary of the Visitation, in memory of the Virgin Mary's visit to her cousin Elizabeth. He came to the gate to welcome me and to lead me to his home. In silence, we walked through a garden in full bloom with beautiful olive trees. There was something mysterious about that place. We sat down in a large room on the ground floor, which was a bit dark, and we sipped pear juice. I was impressed by Benjamin's face. He is seventy, and he has a deep gaze and marked features. He knew that I had spoken with the monastic sister who had been a member of his congregation, and that I wanted to know more about Messianic Jews.

Benjamin and his brother Reuven grew up in New York in an Orthodox Jewish family of European origin. Influenced by American culture and raised in the purest Jewish tradition, they went to school in a *yeshiva*.[1] Afterwards, Benjamin studied architecture, and Reuven studied French literature and cinematography.

"After having received a very religious education, for several years I lived without faith. I became a humanist. For me, life consisted of a few simple principles: to live in peace with others and not hurt my neighbor. But I was hounded by two questions, and I wondered if one day I would find an answer: What is the meaning of my life? What is it to be Jewish? The question of faith was at work in me. I didn't believe in anything, and that disturbed me. I was ready to believe, but in what? I wanted to believe, but I had to find THE truth. Otherwise, what good is it to believe? I was alone with my reflections when something very surprising happened to me. It was 1967. At the time, I was working in Denmark in an architecture firm. It was a day like any other day, an evening like any other evening. I was at home reading the newspaper when I received a strange visit. Suddenly, I had the feeling that I wasn't alone in the room. Someone was there. I couldn't see him, but he was really there. It was a very pure presence. A wonderful presence... It was something that I had never experienced before. There was nothing magical. The presence was real, but mysterious, and it grew stronger and stronger. The "person" drew near to me, and it seemed to me as though he put a key into my heart and left it there. At that moment, my heart was flooded by a marvelous love, and I started to cry. I didn't understand why I was crying, but I continued to cry. I didn't understand what was happening, but I knew that it wasn't a delusion. I knew that it was real and that I wasn't going crazy. I heard a voice that said: "I am the God of Abraham, of Isaac and of Jacob. I am your God." It was a shock, but I didn't have any doubts. For the first time in my life, I heard the voice of God. He said to me, "Your life is like an open book before me. I see everything." And then there was an even bigger surprise: I heard the name of Jesus in Hebrew: Yeshua. I had never read the New Testament. I knew very little about Jesus. But when I heard his name in Hebrew, at the same time it was revealed to me that He was the Messiah, the Son

1. Yeshiva: A rabbinical school.

of God and God himself. The Messiah of Israel. I can't explain what I experienced. From that moment onward, something fundamental changed inside me: I realized that all the questions that I had about life, about existence and about being Jewish were answered in Him. He was THE answer. I knew very little about Christianity: I knew that Jesus was a Jew, that Jews don't believe in him and that they were persecuted because we bear the shame of his crucifixion. But I didn't know much more than that. What I experienced was different: it was truly the light of God and there was absolutely no doubt in my mind that what I had received was THE absolute truth for us Jews and for everyone. Since then and until today, I have never had the slightest doubt."

Have you talked to friends and to others who are close to you about what happened?

"I explained what happened to some of my non-believing friends. They thought that I had lost my mind, that I was crazy. Afterwards, I decided not to tell anyone, to keep it to myself. I didn't want to have discussions with people who thought I had gone insane.

"I read the New Testament for the first time in my life. What I read didn't seem strange or foreign to me. It seemed familiar, and I was even able to identify with what I was reading. I was raised in a very religious Jewish context and I know how the rabbis think. When I read, for example, a passage about Jesus and the Pharisees, it wasn't at all foreign to me. I know how the Pharisees think and I know what kinds of questions they raise. Since I had studied the Talmud, I was accustomed to the kinds of questions that they ask.

"Two or three years after the 'visit,' at the end of 1969, I came to Israel. I wanted to visit the places where Jesus had been. It was important to me. I made a pilgrimage alone: I visited what are called the 'holy places.' During that trip, I had a new experience. I realized in a very personal and deep way that Jesus had died for me on the cross. With an immense love, He died on the cross for me, for my sins. Until then, I had never thought about sin. From that moment on, I thought about sin in my life and I asked God to show me my sins. Slowly, I received the light to understand that I wasn't living according to God's will. I then experienced a period of repentance, and I turned towards God. I left the country and, I think it was in 1970, God asked me a question: 'What are you going to do now?' I had to answer Him, and the only answer that I could give was: 'I will follow You. You revealed the truth to me. I'd be crazy if I continued to live as I did before.' In my heart, I consecrated myself to Him: "My life belongs to You." Of course, I thought that I was the only Jew who thought like that! But I knew that it was the truth, even if I was alone. Later, God showed me that I wasn't the only one, that there were others, and that we are living in a period when God is turning to the Jews and revealing Jesus to them. It was reassuring, even if I hadn't met any of those Jews."

Did you tell your family about any of that?

"No, but after my consecration to God, I decided to tell my parents. I left for the United States to tell them what had happened to me and to speak to them about my faith. As I had expected, it was a disaster. They were furious that their eldest son had become a Christian. I tried to explain to them that Jesus is the Messiah of Israel even if they don't believe in Him. I told them that He is the Messiah of all the nations, but they couldn't understand.

"My younger brother was also at home when I returned. We hadn't seen each other for a very long time. I talked to him alone. Surprisingly, after he heard my story, he became a believer. He had also been searching for a while, and he understood that I what I told him was the truth. He had 'heard' that Jesus is the Messiah, that He is God. He became a believer and, shortly afterwards, he felt called to come and live in the land of Israel. I joined him one year later, in 1971, and we have stayed here ever since.

"That's how my life began... you can see that it's also a love story."

Today, forty years later, you are the "shepherds" of a congregation.

"My brother and I have lived in Israel for forty years, but we have been 'leading' the congregation for twenty-four years. It is a congregation of Jews and non-Jews who have joined us and who believe that Jesus is the Messiah and that He is God.

"I travel, I teach, I preach in different countries. My brother also. In this house, we are a small community of three people. There's a young Israeli who has been with us for ten years. There's also an elderly woman who is ninety-seven years old, and who has been living with us for a long time. Our work is in our congregation, but our hearts are in unity with all those who believe in Jesus. We don't put barriers between Catholics, the Orthodox or Protestants if they love Jesus. In various ways, we work for unity and reconciliation. I taught in Germany for several years on the subject of repentance, forgiveness and reconciliation. I also teach here in different communities and congregations."

You are a Messianic Jew and I'm a Catholic. Can you explain to me what the difference is between us?

"There's no difference between you and me concerning the fact that we both belong to God. There's no difference in Jesus' 'heritage.' The calls are different, but salvation is the same. There's only one salvation for everyone: for Jews and non-Jews. Jesus died for all of us. He died for Israel and He died for all of mankind because he is the representative of all of humanity. There's no difference, as St. Paul explains, between Jews and Gentiles when it comes to salvation.

"The calls are different: nobody has the same call. The Jews have their own call and the nations have their call. Together, they make a whole. The nations are incomplete without the Jews and the Jews are incomplete without the nations. Reread St. Paul's Epistle to the Romans (chapters 11, 16 and what follows). He speaks of the cultivated olive tree: that's the believing part of Israel. He explains that some branches will fall because they don't believe. And other branches from a wild olive tree will be grafted onto the branches of the cultivated olive tree. There's only one olive tree, composed of cultivated and wild branches, which are the Jews and the nations. That's all I can say: we are equal before God. I'm not better than you and you're not better than I am. We have different calls. All Christians, all people who believe in Jesus, have the responsibility to bear witness to the truth. We do it as soon as we have an opportunity. I testify to a lot of Jews. At first, when I tell them that I believe in Jesus, they don't understand and they think that I have become a Christian. If I tell them that Jesus is the son of David, the Messiah...it's different. Jews believe in the Messiah, and they believe in the resurrection of the dead. He is the Messiah. So if I believe that Jesus is the Messiah that God sent to Israel, why would I abandon Judaism?

"We must be witnesses to the Truth whenever we have the opportunity. Because we live in a world that is in darkness. Deep darkness. And Jesus is the light. He is the only light. We have a responsibility to bear witness to the light. Not only by our words, but by our lives. Even if our lives are and should be different."

Benjamin, why aren't you married?

"We asked ourselves the question of marriage, my brother and I. We didn't know what God wanted for us. We prayed, and in prayer, we understood that God was asking us not to get married, to remain single and to devote ourselves entirely to Jesus. That's what we have done."

How did you meet the sisters of Bethlehem?

"You heard about the young woman who was a member of our congregation and who worked for Ulf Ekman. After she had a very powerful experience in the chapel at Bet Gemal, she told us about it. She was a little anxious about how we would react in our congregation. We were respectfully silent, and she entered the monastery. We were there for her first and second consecration in her monastic family. That's how we got to know the community of Bet Gemal and we became friends. A very deep and precious friendship has developed between us, and we experienced the sisters' openness and their love for

Jesus in an intense way. For us, that's the most important thing. Our friendship has continued to deepen. I regularly go there to teach the sisters. We study the Scriptures together. We started with the book of Moses, and we're going to study all the books."

What do you think is the sisters' charism?

"The sisters have a solitary life. Each sister is alone with God and, as I told you, we see that there is a deep love of God, a deep love for Jesus in their community. I think that they have a special charism of love and a charism of openness that one doesn't see very often among Catholics. It's a profoundly 'consecrated' community. They are before God, and the world is in need of people who pray and who are concentrated on God. There aren't many communities that unite so many people. When one sees what's happening in our churches...in Europe and even in the United States, it's not surprising that people distance themselves from God.

"In this community, one can draw close to God: it's a grace and a gift. Only God can do that, no one else. We see that the hand of God is upon them. I can deeply identify with this community."

At the end of our interview, Benjamin wanted to offer a prayer:

"I thank God for the friendship of our hearts and I ask Him to bless the sisters here in this land of Israel and throughout the world. May Sister Isabelle have the strength, in the Holy Spirit, to guide all the different communities. I thank God for His wonderful 'plans' which are hidden from us.

"Lord, we know that You have a 'plan' and that You'll complete what You have begun, even if the devil fights against it. You are greater, and You always defeat Satan. Thank you for this time in which we live. Your return is drawing near. It is no longer a matter of thousands of years. It is much nearer. We pray that we may all be ready. We pray that the child of the Book of Revelation will be born and that this birth will bring a fullness of blessings to You and to the entire world."

Benjamin, forgive me, I have one last question. In your prayer, you spoke of God's "plans." What does that mean for you? Which plans?

"We don't need to know what God's 'plans' are. We only need to believe. That's very important. We need to stand strong in the faith, even if we don't know, even if we don't understand. We don't need to know; God knows. We must believe that God knows, that He is able to do it, and that He will do it. That's all we have to do. I work for unity, for the Bride: that's what is in my heart, but I don't know how God will accomplish it. It's very important to have faith that the Bride will be gathered and to pray for this. This is in line with the second coming of Christ. He will not come first to condemn the world but He will come first for his Bride. He won't come before the Bride is ready. When the Bride is ready, he will come for her. If we have an ardent desire for His second coming, we must have the same desire that his Bride be ready. It starts with us, and we must be prepared. The two main parts of the Church that I have spoken about to you, the Jews and the Nations, they must be gathered in unity. That is very important to God. It is thus that we also open the way for all other 'parts' that they also may enter into unity."

10

A revelation

> And a great sign appeared in heaven, a woman clothed with the sun, with the moon under her feet, and on her head a crown of twelve stars; she was with child and she cried out in her pangs of birth, in anguish for delivery. And another sign appeared in heaven; behold, a red dragon, with seven heads and ten horns, and seven diadems upon his heads. His tail swept down a third of the stars of heaven, and cast them to the earth. And the dragon stood before the woman who was about to bear a child, that he might devour her child when she brought it forth; she brought forth a male child, one who is to rule all the nations with a rod of iron, but her child was caught up to God and to his throne, and the woman fled into the wilderness, where she has a place prepared by God, in which to be nourished for one thousand two hundred and sixty days.[1]

When I was with Benjamin, something was revealed that still remains a mystery to me. I had come a long way since the beginning of my "investigation." My questions were disappearing before the faith of the men and women whom I had met. The love of God, which they never doubt, and the fear of God, which is nothing other than respect for God, spared them intellectual contortions. And yet, I had in my head, ever since the beginning, chapter 12 of the Apocalypse of St. John. During the eschatological weekend, several sisters had tried to explain to me that this text is central to the understanding of their vocation. I had heard it several times; I had read it. Sister Z offered me the following commentary:

---

1. Rv 12, 1-6

"It is the Virgin, assumed into heaven, who gives birth to the Church. It's also the Church herself who brings multitudes to birth in the kingdom of God and implicates us in her life in the desert. She gives us all that she lives in glory…an ineffable happiness. And at the same time, she makes us participate in the great battle that she is living. The woman is attacked by the devil because she is about to give birth to her male child, Jesus, and to each one of us who form His body. It is the battle against the devil who dominates the world. She is sheltered from the devil because she is without sin, but she is attacked because God has entrusted to her, with Christ, the salvation of the world and each one of us. It is the battle between Her and Satan who wants to destroy the world, who wants to destroy Humanity, who wants to destroy the Church. She prays incessantly. She has chosen those who are insignificant and poor for her army, and she has won the victory."

I knew that Benjamin Berger was a sort of Apocalypse "specialist." I questioned him about the subject. He began by reassuring me that "it's a very mysterious chapter" before offering me a true and passionate exegesis. I'm not sure that I understood everything, but it seemed to me that his explanation was somewhat "prophetic," and even alarming. It was an exhortation to remain vigilant.

Who is the Woman?

"You aren't obliged to adhere to my interpretation, but for me, I see her as a woman who represents a multitude. She's not only a woman, but 'the' Woman in whom one can see all churches and all believers. And she's pregnant. She gives birth to an infant, a son, who is like Jesus. One finds this infant in chapters 14 and 17 of Apocalypse, and he is depicted as the "144,000," because it is said that they are virgins and without blemish and that they sing a new song, which they alone can sing. This is a very special group, these "144,000." In chapter 7, they come from the twelve tribes of Israel. In chapter 14, they are the first fruits. For me they represent, through this infant, the salvation, which is to come for Israel. But it's a very difficult birth.

"In fact, I believe that there will be a birth in Israel. And this Woman, once again, represents the believers, the Christians who pray – because they have it in their heart to do so – for a birth in Israel, and this cannot happen except in Israel. In Israel, there are people, like myself, who end up believing in Jesus. There are numerous, and they are the first fruits. And after the first fruits, there will be many others. That's how I see the Woman and the male infant who is about to be born. And, of course, the Woman is persecuted: because the Woman is part of the Church (she isn't the entire Church, but she's a holy segment of the Church), she will be persecuted. There's no doubt about that. But God will protect the Woman. She will be persecuted because those who are consecrated to God always suffer persecution from the devil. The devil persecutes...one sees that throughout the Bible and in history, and we too will see it.

"The book of Micah (5, 2) speaks of the birth of the Messiah and therefore of Bethlehem. 'But you, O Bethlehem Ephrathah, who are too little to be among the clans of Judah, from you shall come forth for me one who is to be ruler in Israel, whose origin is from of old, from ancient days.' The book of Micah therefore speaks of the birth of Christ.

"The following verse is very interesting: 'Therefore he shall give them up...' Whom is he going to give up or abandon? What does it mean that 'he will give them up'? The answer is in the next verse: 'Until the time when she who has labor pains has brought forth.' He speaks of another birth after that of Jesus. 'He will give them up': I think that that means that God will spiritually abandon Israel, because Israel is spiritually blind. They can't see Jesus 'until the time when she who has labor pains has brought forth': the woman who is pregnant has given birth to a child and that is what is spoken of in Apocalypse 12.

"Then it says: 'then the rest of his brethren shall return to the sons of Israel.' Who are 'the rest of his brethren'? These brothers are the Messiah's brothers: they are the nations. When Israel will be born spiritually, the nations (those who believe in Jesus) and Israel shall become one.

'He shall stand' (that is, Jesus) 'and feed his flock in the strength of the Lord, in the majesty of the name of the Lord his God. And they shall dwell secure, for now he shall be great' (Jesus will be great) 'to the ends of the earth. And this shall be peace.' Christ is our peace.

"These verses from the book of Micah are to be read in connection with chapter twelve. It's a mystery, but chapter twelve is marvellous."

Benjamin, what connection do you see between chapter twelve and the Sisters of Bethlehem?

"There is a definite connection. The sisters are women of prayer; they are there to receive everything from God. Their prayers are very powerful before God because they are totally consecrated to Him. One very important thing that only the Holy Spirit can give us is to let ourselves be inhabited by Him and rendered fertile so as to bring forth a birth in this country, so that a male infant can be born in this country. And only God can bring about a birth in this country."

The following day, after that interview, I left the Holy Land.

It was my last evening in the monastery. Sister Isabelle came and knocked at my door. I was packing my suitcase, and she wanted to slip into my luggage a few gifts, which she had chosen for my husband and children. We spoke, seated on the edge of my bed. Before leaving, she read this text to me written by one of the sisters who reposes in God in the cemetery of Bet Gemal:

> What do you have, O Beloved, more than all others
> To draw us by the very scent of Your Name
> And from the four corners of the world to gather us before You?
> Where are You ascending, striving with all Your being?
> Towards the hill of incense?
> Towards the mountain where God eternally provides?
> O You whose forward course ravishes our hearts
> Tell us, where will You finally let yourself be found?
> Always waiting in openness for something, our arms no longer
> need anything but to open in eternal Praise.

In Your shadow, so desired, we wish to find rest
At the feet of Your divine Majesty
to taste the sweet bitterness of the fruit of Your Word.
O Beloved King, bring us into Your dwelling place
In the cleft of the steep rock, where You alone can lead us.
Tell us, O You whose Name fills all our vigils
When will You come and knock at the door of our hearts
To bring us to your Wedding Banquet?
Keep us from falling asleep on the smoking lamps of our chimeras…
With what haste have you removed the tunic of the ineffable Mystery?
And Your feet, are you really going to dirty them with the mud and blood of our sins?
Do You not know that Your hand is extended to the cleft of our indifference?
The hand upon which You have engraved each one of our names.
Do You not know that it will soon be seized by the torment of our passions
and transfixed for eternity as an offering…?
In the arms of His Mother, the Child was silent...
In the Father's kind gaze
with whom He is eternally pleased.

I returned to France. Somewhat like the Little Prince, I returned to my planet. In the plane, I had in my head one of the Beatitudes: "Blessed are those who mourn, for they shall be comforted." I needed to be comforted, as I always do every time I leave the monastery where my sister lives.

But above all, I left a land sodden with tears that the war had provoked for so many years. I understood, through numerous testimonies, that God reveals himself in tears. "It's so mysterious the country of tears!" as Antoine de Saint-Exupéry says. The men and women whom I had met and who, for the most part, had met and found God in tears, had revealed something of this mystery. Consolation. Those men and women united in their lives to the offering that Jesus had made of His life, are already consoled. They are awaiting the Messiah, "the consolation of Israel" and the Holy Spirit, the Consoler, watches over them...

Finally, I was conscious of having lived at Bet Gemal something that puts a strong seal on this Family. Out of respect and obedience to the great Catholic monastic tradition, what the sisters live at Bet Gemal, because they are in the Holy Land, gains access to something universal because it is grafted onto Christ, in the land where He Himself lived.

To conclude my lengthy investigation in the Promised Land, I would like to give the last word to one of the sisters in solitude. It is a word of peace... a message of love...

> "When I arrived at Bet Bet Gemal five years ago, I immediately asked if I could live in the solitude of a hermitage. And when I entered my cell, I exclaimed: It's Paradise with the Cross!
>
> Paradise is to live in the gaze of God, in the gaze of the *Father who sees you in secret.*
>
> To taste the tenderness of the Father, which surpasses all love.
>
> Solitude is never to be alone!
>
> It is Jesus who said to me: 'Love one another as I have loved you.'
>
> Solitude is the 'as' of this commandment.
>
> 'As the Father has loved me, so I also have loved you.'
>
> It's a life of radical obedience, otherwise it would quickly become an infernal life of oneself! Absurdity!
>
> It's Mary's silence.
>
> This is a cry: Father, Abba.
>
> 'And a sword will pierce your soul so that the thoughts of many hearts may be revealed.'
>
> 'But one of the soldiers pierced his side with a spear, and at once there came out Blood and Water.'
>
> It is to follow Mary who follows the Lamb wherever He goes, to bring to birth multitudes .
>
> It is to be a mother who cries to the Father.
>
> It is to give everything in order to receive everything, in preference of the One who gives everything because in Him is perfect Joy.
>
> It is God Himself who wants that we resemble Him.
>
> It is the love of the Father for the Son, who gives everything to the Son.
>
> Solitude is silence and silence is communion.

Solitude is a state of unceasing mendicity; it is thirst and a fathomless desire.

When I am in God, I am in solitude.

'Lord Jesus Christ, Son of the living God, have mercy on me a sinner.'

It is an act of Faith to always begin anew.

It is prostration before the mad love of God.

It is God Himself who gives Himself.

O Father, I adore You. I believe in You. *O Bonitas*!

It is the bride who keeps vigil while singing: Marana tha! Come, Lord Jesus!"

VI

COME AND SEE

Introduction

In the heart of Paris, the sisters of the Monastery of Notre-Dame de la Présence de Dieu live under exceptional conditions. It is not easy to go in search of the desert in the din of Victor Hugo Square and of the main shopping avenues. There is a fire station adjacent to the monastery whose sirens are a regular reminder that the fire of the Spirit is not the only fire here.

There is a certain music to the monastery's bells in this hectic world. They seem to be far away and they labor to be heard. But when they succeed, it is as if God is giving a little wink: "I too am here!"

Thanks to Sister Marie's initiative and the energy of the prioress of this monastery, the former church Saint Honoré d'Eylau was beautifully transformed and now resembles a church of the East. Sister Marie had just come from Damascus, when she visited this church for the first time. It was icy cold, and everything was black and dirty. But she loved the big nave, and imagined it covered with carpets, because she wanted everyone to feel at ease here... And in the tribune, there would be cells hidden behind partitions where the monastic sisters could live a true life of solitude. A few years after sister Marie's death, her dream was realized: the interior of the church was completely restored and it now sings something of the *Orientale Lumen*. While I often pitied the sisters for having to live in the heart of the noisy chaos, they explained to me that there was a "particular grace" in Paris. Upon entering the church, there is no doubt that one is in Bethlehem! As Didier Decoin so aptly expressed it, "God's silence is more deafening in the hushed silence of convents than in the tumult of the world." In Paris, the silence is all the more striking since it is engendered amid so much tumult. The semantron resonated in the church to call the sisters to gather at the time of the liturgical offices.

Lamps from the Middle East cast a gentle light upon the iconostasis, which surrounds the entire choir of the church. Before the altar, there is a seven-branched candelabrum. And there are stalls for the sisters. There is adoration every afternoon of "the Big Jesus," as the sisters say. There is a magnificent monstrance for both the Body and the Blood of Christ.

The liturgical offices and daily adoration of the Blessed Sacrament are open to all. There are the regulars, but there are also those who are just visiting. Some days, a lot of people come for adoration and to meditate and pray with the sisters...

In 1977, Cardinal Marty offered this church to the monastic sisters of Bethlehem. A few years later, in a homily for the profession of a sister in this church, Cardinal Lustiger emphasized that the sisters' life is at the heart of the mission that God has entrusted to the Church:

"As Bishop of Paris, I want to tell you that the life and presence of your community in this diocese is of great value. It was not on a whim or because of personal preference that you were invited to this city. It was because we – all those who are baptized – share the same mission; and that is why my predecessor, Cardinal Marty, offered you this site, provided by the parish of Saint Honoré d'Eylau.

"The Church's mission is fundamentally a mission of holiness and sanctification. All the Church's tasks – bearing testimony to the love of God, proclaiming the Good News, sharing the Word, salvation brought to all people, openness to what is universal – man cannot perform these tasks, unless he relies on the power of God. In fact, they are a manifestation of the grace that has its source in the mystery of Christ.

"Having said that, my sisters, I remind you of the mutual promise that we made to one another a long time ago, not only to pray for one another, but to pray also for this city's apostolate. It is an apostolate of supplication, mercy, redemption of sins, true charity and compassion, which Christ makes visible through the mystery of his Church. You are responsible for bringing before God this apostolic and ecclesiastical work in your austere and solitary prayer.

"As the heart communicates life to the whole body, so your contemplative experience communicates life to the entire Body of Christ. It is the 'heart of the heart' of the mission that God entrusts to the entire Church. The Church is the Body of Christ and all vocations are rooted in its history where everyone finds his place and where all are begotten to a new life. Saint Paul forcefully asserts in the Epistle to the Romans: "We know that in everything God works for good with those who love him, who are called according to his purpose.[1]"

1. Rm 8:28

1

Profession

Can you consent to content yourself
with nothing other than to welcome Me,
in all the circumstances of your life on earth,
in the depths of your free will and of your heart?
So that I can be the light of love that shines in you?
So that all that I am can live in you and sing in your life,
so that everything, absolutely everything in you
will gradually be made simple and rendered unified by My mad love,
making you (if you let go)
exclusively transparent of Me, gentle, simple, and rigorous,
wherever My love decides to put you,
wherever my love leads you.
You will go only where I will be in you.
You will want only what the good pleasure of My love will manifest clearly to you.
You will dream of nothing else.
You will accomplish absolutely all that your deepest and most exacting intuition, inspired by my Spirit in your heart of hearts, will lead you to do.
Perhaps, in the beginning, it will be terrible?
But one day, at last, you will be re-born.
And then the jubilation of a life illuminated by love will be your secret, your bread, your dynamism and the pearl for which you will sell everything.

Sister Marie

Inscribed in the Heart of God

In Paris I attended the first profession of a monastic sister. Almost immediately, I put away my paper and pencil…it was impossible to take notes. My gaze was fixed on the sister who was stretched out face down on the floor, her arms in the form of a cross, at the foot of the altar, while the community and the assembly invoked the consecrating Spirit. It was an intense moment of emotion, deep humility and total surrender to God's grace.

"In the strength of the Holy Spirit, yes I do."

The monastic sister replied five times to the bishop with these words during her profession.

"What do you ask for?

—The mercy of God and of the monastic family of Bethlehem, of the Assumption of the Virgin and of Saint Bruno.

—Rise up."

The first profession is celebrated during the course of a Mass to manifest the fact that the Church responds to this act of the monk or of the monastic sister who commits himself or herself to God and to the community for a period of five years by the vows of chastity, poverty, conversion, obedience, stability, continual growth in love and the continual prayer of adoration. Family and friends are invited to share in the joy of this consecration.

There was a good crowd on that day of the feast of Our Lady of Lourdes. The monastic sister who took her vows is Egyptian, from a Coptic Orthodox family, and it was with great emotion that the East and the West came together to celebrate the completion of a life, but also in a certain way, of Bethlehem's charism. It was a great moment for the representatives of both Churches that were brought together in the choir to participate in the Profession of "their" monastic sister.

Surrounding the bishop were ten priests, including a brother of Bethlehem and two deacons. From the Church of the East, there was a Lebanese Basilian monk, a Lebanese priest of the Syrian Church, an Iraqi Dominican priest, a Coptic

Orthodox priest, two "abounas" who were Orthodox monks, a Syrian Catholic deacon from Baghdad and two Coptic Orthodox deacons.

After the Mass readings chosen by the monastic sister, and then after the homily, the ceremony of the profession proceeded in an atmosphere of intense recollection. The Gospel of the Annunciation was read in French, Arabic and Aramaic. The monastic sister then went forward to kneel before the celebrant to listen to the monastic catechesis. The catechesis is a reminder of her freedom and of her vocation, a warning against the dangers that lie in wait for her, and an encouragement to always persevere in prayer, trust and wisdom. The bishop blessed the veil and the *cuculle*[1] with which the monastic sister would be clothed. The bishop then took from her hand the scissors with which he then cut her hair. He said to her, "It is from the hand of Christ Himself that you take these scissors. See to whom I join you, toward whom you go, whom you renounce, in the name of the Father, of the Son, and of the Holy Spirit." The bishop cut her hair with four snips to signify her renunciation of natural attractiveness and her preference for Christ's beauty. "May the Lord, after having stripped you of the old self and of his deeds, now clothe you with the new self created in justice, in holiness and in truth. "

After having been clothed with the wimple, the veil and the *cuculle*, she then received a Bible, a breviary of the Divine Office, the Constitutions of the family of Bethlehem, a rosary and a candle lit from the Paschal candle, "as on the day of your Baptism, for your consecration renews in you your baptismal innocence."

Then came the solemn moment of the profession of her vows. The brothers and sisters of Bethlehem who were present during the ceremony committed themselves to be "responsible for better and worse" for their sister.

Then, on behalf of the general prioress and of the family of Bethlehem, the prioress received the profession of the monastic sister, which she pronounced in Arabic, her mother tongue. The prioress also replied in Arabic.

---

1. The monastic habit.

The bishop then invited her parents to come forward. He warmly thanked them for the gift of their child to the Church: "You have been her father and mother in her faith as a baptised person, you are now her father and mother in her monastic profession and an even stronger and more tender bond unites you to her. If she belongs to God, and to God alone, she is not any less yours. You know that you can always count on her prayer, her intercession for you and your family, and upon her tenderness. Your signature on the text of her profession expresses all of that. May the joy of the Lord be your stronghold!"

The newly professed sister then signed the text of her profession, which was on the altar. The bishop, the prioress, her parents and other sisters also signed the text of her profession.

The Mass then continued. At the moment of the final blessing, the sister went and knelt before the bishop to receive his blessing, and she then knelt before each of the priests present to receive their blessing. Among the priests present was one of her brothers. After having blessed her, he helped her to her feet with great tenderness.

In this family of five children, three of them are now consecrated to God.

As the young professed sister greeted each one of her sisters with a kiss, the Coptic choir sang songs of praise punctuated by responses sung by the sisters: there was a unison of hearts, on that particular day more than any other, in that church illuminated by the light of the East...

Who is rich in love?

I had spoken with the sister a few days before her profession. To be honest, I had a kind of vertigo when speaking with her... Her commitment seemed unimaginable to me, and yet the reality was before me: a young woman eager to finally surrender herself entirely to God forever. As with my own sister, I saw in her eyes that unmistakable spark...the spark of love.

I asked her about her youth, and I enumerated all the small pleasures of life that her contemporaries enjoyed and that she would no longer enjoy, all their ambitions which she had renounced: success, wealth. At her age, everything still seemed possible...

"Rich? In love? Who is rich in love? It's just a matter of appearances...When we look at our hearts, we discover how poor we are in love. The desire to do everything for love of others, to see others as God sees them, to love them as God loves them...that's what it means to be rich in love."

When everything is done out of love, is there necessarily an element of sacrifice?

"Yes, it's a life of sacrifice...it's not an ideal. I'm not seeking myself. We are here for others, to give life to the world by our sacrifices. If I stay in the monastery, I can't push the Cross aside. The Cross is the most secret center of the heart, a mystery of extreme love.

"Who are we that He came to us and carried his Cross, charged with our sins?"

The transition from her Orthodox Coptic family to her Catholic monastic community, which has received a lot from the monasticism of the Church of Egypt, was relatively smooth. "I feel that I'm in a big family," she said. "It's Jesus' family. In my family, the one where I grew up with my brothers and sisters, I received a family spirit that mattered more than anything else. And Bethlehem is also a family that is very human – we feel it in the bond of love that unites us as sisters – and divine, because we are all immersed in the Trinitarian family…a huge fire that burns between all the members. Our monastic family is very human because divine."

You didn't have to renounce your family roots when you entered Bethlehem, because it is rooted in the tradition of the monasticism of the East.

"That was vital for me. I wouldn't have been able to live in a Coptic community, or in a more 'typical' or 'normal' Catholic community. In Bethlehem, I discovered the East and the West in a unified way. This 'unified way' gives a kind of 'truth in love' or an 'authenticity in relationships.' It's difficult to explain because it's a gift that we receive… it's a family spirit.

"Perhaps it's also because Bethlehem is 'effaced' before God: there is a kind of abandonment of the structure in order that the encounter with God be all. This community has also inherited from the East the role of the *staretz* (the prioress) who helps each sister personally on her path. Each person is unique, received from God and accompanied by a *staretz* so that she can grow in freedom before God."

What kind of freedom can we speak about in a monastery?

"I'm here because I want to be here. I want to encounter God, and let myself be encountered by Him. It's also God's will, which I welcome with joy. It's a gift from God."

What is difficult in your life?

"What's difficult is to know that there are people who don't know Jesus and that I can't encounter them to tell them about Him, to say to them: 'Come and see.'"

2
Foundations

Con mucho gusto

Foundations of the monasteries of Bethlehem, of the Assumption of the Virgin and of Saint Bruno are currently beginning in Mexico, Jordan and Africa.

Since 2011, according to the desire of Our Lady of Guadalupe, a small community of monastic sisters was welcomed in the parish of Santo Domingo de Guzman, Tlaquiltenango, in Mexico. In the heart of parish life, in the simplicity of the site, the sisters live a life of silence and solitude, and fraternal and liturgical communion. The community is preparing in prayer the construction of the future monastery that will be located in the region of Valle de Vazquez, which is hidden among mountains and valleys.

In Paris, I met Beto and Ceci, an enthusiastic Mexican couple whom I was able to question about the recent foundation. Before being sponsors, Beto and Ceci love their country, the Virgin of Guadalupe, and, truth be told, the Sisters of Bethlehem. Beto and Ceci are also great travellers and very involved in the Mexican Catholic Church. It was during a trip to the Holy Land in 2004 with the Apostolic Nuncio in Mexico, that they became acquainted with the family of Bethlehem. Like so many others, it was in the tribune of the chapel of Bet Gemal that they received a shock and the intuition to begin a foundation in Mexico. "You can't imagine what we felt," Ceci told me. "After a few minutes, we asked ourselves where we were. We couldn't believe our eyes... I was in tears when I received communion. I know very many religious, but I've never seen anything like what I saw there."

I turned my gaze to her husband, Beto. He has a very imposing presence and he is a veterinarian by trade. He is also a businessman and a politician, and he confided in me saying: I have always believed in angels, but I never thought that I would ever see any, and yet there, during Mass, there were angels before me...the sisters are angels!"

Ceci and Beto explained to me that Mexico is still a country that is very devout and Marian. "Everyone loves the Virgin of Guadalupe. There's an emotional and loving dependency on her. You can't imagine the Mexicans' fervour: they can walk two hundred kilometres, and arrive on their knees before the Virgin and pray for hours. On Sundays the churches are packed. But a lot of sects that come mostly from the United States are seeping in, and it worries us a lot. They take advantage of the simplicity and poverty of a fringe of the population, which lacks the culture necessary to discern what to avoid. They are very poor, and the sects offer them presents. We must also acknowledge that the Church has been negligent *vis-a-vis* these populations."

In this context, where religious communities are also very present, Beto explained: "The monastic sisters will give new meaning and presence to the religious orders, because they attract those who can approach them. They have great humility, simplicity, spirituality and intelligence. People who encounter them really love them. It's striking. All orders are respectable, but I think that the sisters' presence will bring about deep change. The first time that we went to Teposlan, people came and they wanted to meet them! Their spirituality and their incredible joy touch the hearts of those who meet them. First of all, Mexicans had to learn how to know them before helping for them for the construction of the foundation. When they arrived, at first there was a lot of curiosity. Their habit is very different from the other religious of Mexico who are always in black. Their joy is contagious. It's very impressive to see the impact of their presence since they are only four sisters in a rural area of Mexico where people are very simple and very poor. It presupposes a spiritual and social change. Farmers are very rough and uncouth, and yet they are touched by the sisters' gentleness. They are humble. When they go somewhere they go by foot, and when they visit a house, they help the family and they do the dishes. Men are impressed by the sisters' work; they use tools, and shovels when they need to dig a hole. I think that the sisters' example will change the image of women and hence the fate of many young Mexican girls. Peasant women suffer a lot because of machismo. Mexican women need to be recognized. The sisters' solitary life also inspires respect. They are impressed when they see them praying so long. We Mexicans, we pray three minutes and then we are tired!"

We left each other in the Mexican way, with a hug and a warm *Con mucho gusto!*

God...the only hope

There are seven Mexican monastic sisters in Bethlehem. One of them is at the monastery in Paris. After my meeting with Beto and Ceci, I spent some time with her.

This sister grew up in a family of eighteen children. A tough life made her immigrate early to the United States, to Chicago, to work a lot and to help her mother raise her younger brothers and sisters. From her tough youth, she kept a sense of effort and sacrifice without any *miserabilism*, but with the joy of giving "the little things." She was very happy to talk to me about the Virgin of Guadalupe. "It's the Virgin who educates us, she is the Bible for those who are illiterate, for those who don't know the Scriptures well and who don't understand them. When the Virgin appeared in Tepeyac, there weren't many believers. On that mountain, we originally adored a goddess whom we called our mother... she was the mother of all the gods. When the Virgin appeared, in place of this goddess we continued to adore her as the real Mother of God. It's a big gift that the Lord gave us to awaken Mexico.

"In my family, that is the first image of the Virgin that I had. My mother was very devoted to her and made us pray the rosary every day – even my brothers. She turned off the television and if we fell asleep during the rosary, she would give us a little slap!

"When I left Mexico to work in the United States, my mother was worried. I didn't have any documents and my mother said to me: 'If you get there, it means that the Lord has prepared something good for you.' She was right...huh?

"I kept my mother's words in my heart and everything went well. I knew that I had nothing to fear."

How did you get from Chicago to the sisters of Bethlehem?

"God does strange things! When I found my sister in Chicago, she was very pious, but I wanted to party. She didn't want me to get lost in all of that, and so she brought me to church. I was interested and more and more I wanted to really find God. Not to be a religious...but I wanted to go to Heaven! And at the same time, I wanted to help my mother. Life was very hard at home. My Father didn't work. I worked day and night with my sister to send money to my mother so that she could feed my younger brothers and sisters and send them to school.

"Finally, I came to realize that money alone wasn't enough: my family still had a lot of problems. In fact, what they lacked was love and above all the love of God. I wanted to give God to my family and I asked Him for a sign, I asked him to send me someone to help me.

"I was in a church. I said the Our Father, and I lifted up my hands for the first time saying to God 'If you want me to serve You, put someone's hands in my hands, and I'll know that that is the person who will guide me.' I closed my eyes with the very strong hope that someone would take hold of my hands. She came. It was a girl the same age as me... an angel who prayed a lot and who taught me *Lectio*, the Rosary and many other things. I started looking for a community, and I had a friend who knew the Sisters of Bethlehem. She had been invited to attend the evangelical month and she wanted me to accompany her because she didn't know much about them and she was a little afraid. Everything went very quickly. Two weeks later, we left."

You must have had a shock when you arrived at Les Montsvoirons?

"Yes, I was somewhat in a turmoil. I found it bizarre that everyone was silent and that monastery seemed very mysterious to me. I had trouble understanding the teachings even if everything was translated. But I saw Love. The love of the sisters: love in every look, in every smile. And silent joy."

Did you make your decision at the end of the month?

"No, I decided after only two weeks! I wanted to enter Bethlehem, but I was agitated because I didn't know how to do it. I heard the words of Jesus: Don't worry about things that are fleeting. I went home to Mexico to inform my family.

"My father wasn't happy. He told me that I had to work, but it's because he doesn't understand the mystery of God. My mother was very happy and supported me. She understood that it was the fruit of her prayer. My brothers and sisters also thought that it was a gift for my mother."

Was it also a big sacrifice for them and for you?

"Yes, of course, but my family understands that if my love for God is first, I love them too. And for me, yes, it's a big sacrifice; the separation is very difficult. But if I didn't miss my family there wouldn't be any sacrifices! I like the fact that it's difficult, because I know that my life is really in God. I don't want life to be easy: I've never wanted that. The Lord asks of us little sacrifices: to eat everything on our plate, or to eat the things that we don't like, to ask for forgiveness, to sacrifice our pride."

You now live in Paris, in a rich country, and often the richer one is, the more one forgets God. Would you say that the poorer we are, the more we seek God?

"The poor seek God because the poor are in need. They are always begging; every day they live from their begging. In Mexico, I saw that the poor draw close to God to beg from Him all that they need. The rich don't have time for God because they are always busy buying things. They accumulate material goods, but they too are in need. Nobody can avoid suffering: it marks all human beings. The poor seek God because He is their only hope."

3

A love that never left me

I met some wonderful people in Paris and I experienced, as François Sureau had said, the generous hospitality of the Sisters of Bethlehem in this monastery. Since they are in the heart of the city and since their offices are open to all, many people stop in. There are those who know the sisters, those who live in the same neighborhood, those who are lost, those who thirsting for something more and those who are seeking something: by chance they opened the door of the church. It is sometimes said that fate is "the name of God when He travels incognito..."

That is how I met Stéphane. "Right now, as I speak to you Inès, I have to admit that I'm absolutely nothing! I'm not a monk, I'm not a priest, I'm not a religious, I'm not married, I have no status, but I belong to God! I don't really know anymore what I want, but I trust. We all have a mission...I just haven't found mine yet."

Stéphane is thirty-seven years old, with striking blue eyes. His life was marked in his childhood by the death of his mother. She was a courageous woman who raised her five children alone. Her husband was always absent. Barely forty years of age, she died from exhaustion. "I was four years old," Stéphan said to me. "I have very few memories except for the day of her death – that I remember as if it were yesterday. When she died, she left me something enormous, but I wasn't able to name it until much later. She left me her incredible presence... even when I was playing ball I felt it! Always. Always. Even at night. I always felt someone next to me who loved me, whom I could trust and with whom I could talk." And yet... After the death of their mother, the five children were separated, tossed from one family to another and Stéphane finally wound up in the home of such a nasty woman that "thanks to her, I never forgot my real mother. There was so much hatred in that house that my love for mother developed even more."

After graduating from high school and completing his military service, Stéphane found refuge in his sister's home in Paris. "After such a painful childhood, I had such a deep thirst for freedom that I began to do everything that is prohibited. "It was the beginning of a real life of debauchery. As a salesman in a Kenzo boutique, Stéphane was quickly spotted to be a model in a fashion show. It was that first fashion show that opened doors for modelling, with fast and easy money, drugs, sex, alcohol and parties.

"I was a model for seven years: it was a life of total depravity until a model friend invited me one day to go and see one of her friends...Saint Anthony of Padua! I knew nothing about the Church, and I thought that he was a living person! She took me to a parish of the fifteenth arrondissement, and I found myself in front of a huge statue! Before disappearing, my friend told me: "Talk to him...I often come to see him!" In that church where I was seated before a saint about whom I knew nothing, I received a real blow because I felt that the 'presence' was there, the 'presence' which had never left me since my mother's death and which never ceased to love me even during all those years of debauchery. It was God and nobody else: it was perfectly obvious. I didn't know anything about Him. I had been baptized when I was nine and I studied the catechism, but my father was firmly opposed to all of that. I learned much later that my mother was very religious. I found her book of prayers of Saint Therese of the Child Jesus. Without a doubt it was she who entrusted me to that 'presence.'

"Before Saint Anthony, I realized that God had been there since my mother died and that He had given me the grace of consolation that I needed when I was a child. The Lord gives to each one of us what we need.

"From that moment on my life changed. I started detaching myself from my work and from all that is superficial. At the time, I had a lot of contracts. I had been in a competition in Turkey which opened many doors for me, but I didn't hesitate a second, I rejected all of it. There was no conflict between my conversion and my professional life. I made choices. I'm a person who lives so much 'to the full' that when I do something, I do it right to the end. My motivation completely disappeared; I didn't see the point anymore of being in magazines and on posters. The Lord granted me another grace: I didn't even desire any of that anymore. Before, I used to run after auditions, wherever they were. I tried to secure as many contracts as possible. And then it all appeared to me so stupid!

"Every day I went to see St. Anthony. I had become very attached to him and I asked him for a lot of material things, and I received what I asked for...it was great, but it's no longer like that! Then one day, I noticed a small cross on the wall behind the statue of my 'very close friend' who whispered in my ear: 'Don't look at me, but at Him.' I looked at the cross, and then I heard the Lord say to me: 'I'm here...Pull yourself together! Get to know me. Why is it, do you think, that I am here, nailed to the cross?'"

Then a very difficult period began for Stéphane. No work. Fewer and fewer messages on his answering machine. And then one day there was nothing. No more messages, no more friends and not much money. "I couldn't pay the rent for my apartment. I got a maid's room in the sixteenth arrondissement, because I still had a few friendships there. I kept a few contracts in order to live, but I refused all jobs that had to do with swimsuits and underwear. I came to realize that my work was in contradiction with what I was discovering. We are created in God's image. We are created gratuitously, by love and for God. And I used to sell that image. I was filled with guilt at the beginning of my conversion, but then I was freed from the guilt."

How did you meet the Sisters of Bethlehem?

"I lived behind Victor Hugo Square, and one evening, exiting the subway, I saw that the gates of the church, which is in the Square, were open. At the time, I entered all churches, because I was searching, and I was trying to learn more about Jesus as He had asked me to do.

"That evening, it was midnight, and as I was intrigued by the fact that the church was still open. I decided to enter. It was dark: there were no lights, no candles, but I saw a huge wooden cross in the back of the church. At the foot of the cross there was a shroud. Jesus, dead, was in the arms of Mary. And I saw some white hoods, and even some navy blue hoods. They were prostrate in adoration. It was Good Friday. There was hardly anyone besides the sisters. It's hard to express what I felt at that moment. I realized what God has done for us. He gave us his Son. I started to cry. I felt a great closeness to Christ. I, too, wanted to give my life... that was the least that I could do for Him. I drew closer, and I stood there and I prayed. I felt so good that I even wanted to lie down. I was overwhelmed, but at the same time I had peace and joy. I returned the next day, and I spent the Easter Vigil at the monastery...it was almost the whole night! It was a very important stage...it was like a new birth, but I find it difficult to talk about it.

"During the week after Easter, I returned to the church in the daytime. The sisters were cleaning the church. I took a broom, and I helped them and we began to talk to one another. I told them my story. Immediately, they proposed that I join a prayer group with young people, but they were very respectful of my freedom. For a year and a half, I came to the prayer group every week. I made new friends and at the same time I learned a lot. I also made retreats. And then one day, I spilled the beans!

That is to say?

"I wanted to be a monk! There was a fire in me that kept burning, that lived in me, that never ceased to grow; a fire of love that I had known as a child. Everything was clear, obvious. I had such a thirst, such a desire to be with Him...always. I was seized by that desire. The fidelity of God is a love that doesn't leave us. The Lord always wants to lead us further. The joy and peace that the Lord gave me in the beginning of my conversion never left me despite the hardships.

"The sister who met with me and helped me was very cautious concerning my desire to be a monk. She told me to be patient, and she urged me to wait. But since I kept telling her about my desire, she suggested that I go to evangelical month. And I did. Then, I went to Israel to enter the brothers' monastery in Tel Gamaliel. I was thirty."

Did you notify your family? Your father? Your brothers and sisters?

"I had very little contact with my father, I saw him every three years. But I went to Normandy to tell him. My grandmother was there too and one of my brothers. They were all excited because when I told them that I had something to announce to them they thought I had won the lottery! It was terrible. My father, who is a non-believer, began to cry and said, 'Your God took my wife, and now He is taking my son...' I didn't think that he would react like that...there is so little love between us. My brother didn't judge me, and my grandmother made a funny face!

"I left and my father was so enraged that he went to a lawyer to ensure in his will that nothing would go to the Catholic Church. And I set off for the Holy Land. I entered the school of life with the brothers. Everything went very well. I was very happy, but it didn't last long. After three or four months, I began to suffer. Humanly speaking, I couldn't cope, I couldn't comply with all the rules. I had been carted around in my childhood... I didn't say anything to anyone because, in my heart, I really wanted to give my life to God. I persevered. I really wanted to receive the habit. But the struggle increased. During the day, we used to work. I had to chop wood. It's not easy to go from fashion shows to chopping wood...I prayed, I besought Jesus: 'You know me, I trust in You and I know You'll make it possible.' At the time, Bethlehem was my life. I had finally found my place after having wandered for so long... But the time came when I couldn't hide my struggle anymore. I spoke with the brother prior. I wanted to try a little longer. But faced with the impossible, I decided to leave. The sisters welcomed me for a time. My heart was torn apart because I felt like I was leaving my family. I made a ten-day pilgrimage in Galilee, in the footsteps of Jesus. And then I decided to try elsewhere, in other congregations. For five years, I spent my time in monasteries. I went everywhere, as far as Italy, with the brothers of Mother Teresa in Rome. I wanted to enter the seminary. I tried different communities. Nothing worked. I returned to Paris shattered by grief."

Did you feel rejected?

"No, never. I didn't understand, because I really felt called by the Lord. My 'thirst' grew deeper and deeper. But no, I never blamed the Church. I wanted to be a religious, but I can't live in an enclosure. I wanted to share everything, to be a sign of Jesus' love.

"I suffered a lot over the years, but I have no regrets. Today, my life is difficult. I live in great poverty, but I'm always at peace. I returned to 'the world' a year ago, but I don't feel that I belong to the world. I'm seeking, continually seeking. It's a very narrow path. I don't understand, but I haven't lost my faith. That's a grace that the Lord gives me. I realized that I am very weak and that the Lord doesn't ask of us acts of heroism. What matters to Him is love, that's all that He wants. I think that I've consented to listen to Him. The one thing that I've decided is to give myself to God without any 'status.' I'm not a 'consecrated lay person.' I haven't taken any vows. All that matters is the Lord. And Bethlehem is really my family. If I die tomorrow, I won't have any regrets."

4

Love never fails

The hardest war is the war against oneself.
We must disarm ourselves.
For years, I have waged this war. It has been terrible.
But now I am disarmed.
I am no longer afraid of anything, because Love casts out fear.
I am disarmed of the will to be right,
to justify myself in discrediting others.
I am no longer on the defensive, jealously clinging to my wealth.
I welcome and I share.
I am not particularly attached to my ideas or to my projects.
If you present to me something better, or not even better, but good,
I accept it without regret. I refuse to make comparisons.
For me, what is good, true and real is always the best.
That is why I am no longer afraid.
When one has nothing, there is no longer any fear.
When we are disarmed and dispossessed of self,
if we open to the God-Man who makes all things new,
the bad past disappears and a new period begins
where everything is possible."

—Patriarch Athenagoras

In life, no one can avoid the war against oneself that Patriarch Athenagoras speaks about. In a monastery, perhaps more than elsewhere, the struggle is hard...inevitable: a war between the call received, which the monk or monastic sister accepts as best they can, and the "inner self" that struggles between the four walls of the cell. There is an interior labor both spiritual and psychological, which one cannot escape when living in solitude. A labor that may be the necessary price to attain a greater freedom that some of the sisters spoke about. A labor which puts one at the risk also of loosing oneself: in wanting to lose oneself in God, one can lose oneself altogether.

"Life is harsh and the sisters' life is no different. I lived their life it for many years. I gave my life. I professed my vows to belong to Christ, and then I left the monastery fourteen years ago. I was forty-eight. I returned to my work as a nurse. I had some anger, but I've never been bitter. I rebuilt myself, and I was able to put things into perspective. The important thing is to move forward in life. Life isn't clear or linear for anyone. I'm always *en route*. I don't know what I'll become when I retire in two years. I belong to the family of Bethlehem: I feel like I'm 'clothed in my heart with the habit'... more than when I was really clothed with the habit..." Before leaving me, Victoria wished to read a short text by Maurice Zundel: "The Christian vocation is to be the face of God. Men cannot be saved by discourses, but only by a Presence, and normally, this Presence appears to them only through a human face. Let us be a stained-glass window where the sun sings."

Psy and spi

I was inhabited by a contradictory feeling. I had experienced gentleness in the monasteries: the silence and the apparent "ease." When I was in the tribune of the monasteries I watched the sisters and I had met several of them in the guest areas: they seemed happy. But how could I not think of those who were in deep silence? How could I forget those who have returned to "our world?" In some of the the interviews and in the testimonies of some of those who left the monastery after several months or even several years of monastic life, I was able to understand something of the suffering, of the trial that is specific to their life of silence and solitude. It is the confrontation with oneself day in and day out throughout the years, which no monk or monastic sister can avoid. That was confirmed by

Marie-Claire, a clinical psychologist and psychoanalyst. She had exercised her profession prior to her entry to the monastery where she spent four years. A decade or so ago she left the monastery and returned to her job.

It is through her parents, responsible for religious education, that she got to know the sisters when she was a young girl. Regularly, they went to Mery for retreats. Marie-Claire was attached to that community without having the slightest inclination to enter it. With friends, she participated in various projects of the monasteries, including Hautecour. In her busy professional life, she took periods of silence and solitude at the monastery of Poligny. Those "vital" periods of total solitude gave her the balance she needed. Her spiritual father suggested that she plunge her roots more deeply into the life of the Church, and so Mary-Claire decided to become a member of the Laity of Bethlehem and she got involved with them in various missions. That was how slowly, after two years, she felt "invited to give it a try." It was not a call, but an invitation. Since her desire deepened, Marie-Claire went to the evangelical month, and then afterwards, for six months, she terminated her commitments to her patients. Finally, she left everything and entered the monastery of les MontsVoirons.

Our interview was fascinating. She had had a hard life, and she analysed it in a way that was both very personal and very professional. She offered me an analysis of monastic life, which she lived from within. She now has the perspective needed to explain the psychological mechanisms involved in that life.

"My years at the monastery were both hard and happy. As the years passed, a state of frustration began to take hold of me. Because of my upbringing, I had a great sense of responsibility and I knew how to take initiatives. I also had a strong, even exaggerated sense of the other. Very quickly, I missed that dimension of the other, and I suffered because of it. I spoke to my prioress who initially reassured me: since I had entered the monastery late in life, it was perhaps even more important that I strongly renounce certain things. But over time, it didn't get any easier and my departure was organized in a very respectful way. The first thing that made an impression on me in their vocation of praise, prayer and contemplation is that the human person is immersed in an immense and unshakeable love. It was much greater than anything the humanities and psychology were able to offer me. It led me to a much greater depth that was more important than what I had experienced before. It was the love of God and human love lived in God. I also understood that the love of God helps us to look at others with something deeper than a human gaze."

Do you think that there is too much emotionalism in Bethlehem?

"That is a question for people who see Bethlehem from the outside and who see their overflowing joy. Seen from the inside, I don't believe that there's an excess of love. Contemplative life permits us to face and to deal with our inner resistances, and with our shortcomings and those of others. I didn't experience monastic life as an excess of love nor did I feel that I was living in an overly emotional world. When one observes this life from outside, one tends to forget the harshness of solitary life, and I believe that the bonds of love lived in the monastery are counterpoints to the life of solitary prayer. Since there aren't many relationships quantitatively speaking, a vocation of solitude demands that the relationships be strong qualitatively. It's perhaps surprising that life in God and community life go together: if I'm not well in one, I'm not well in the other. When they start to get to know the community, some of the sisters are touched by the freedom that they see; for me, it was their depth of love. It's a love that goes unto the end. It is the 'unto the end' that drew me and finally tipped the scales. Their love is based on the evangelical counsels of poverty, chastity and obedience. The radicalness with which they live the three evangelical counsels gives their vocation its grandeur and beauty."

Not long ago, someone said to me that "the obedience in Bethlehem is becoming excessive and even ridiculous!" Is there a limit to obedience?

"Monastic life requires a shifting of worldly values. It's very difficult for a person from the outside to judge obedience.

There's great beauty in the radicalness of their vocation. True obedience requires an incredible fortitude, and that fortitude is a virtue. I witnessed the radicalness of the oldest sisters' obedience, and as a result, I also saw their freedom. Obedience is a death to oneself, but that has nothing to do with infantilism. It is, in fact, the opposite. When one listens to the sisters speaking about obedience, it seems as though they have suffered a lot, but that's exactly where their vocation acquires its meaning. That is where it all comes together. They give up their human freedom, their ego, for something very beautiful. Freedom and joy are the fruits of their total abandonment.

"I remember that on All Saints' Day we used to draw at random a beatitude, and a cardinal virtue was applied to each one of them. For the beatitude "Blessed are the meek," the cardinal virtue applied to it was fortitude. He who is obedient is meek. The young sisters spoke very well about the strength that is necessary to be gentle and obedient. It demands an incredible strength – a strength that permits them to joyfully renounce everything."

When one visits the monastery, one has the impression that all that is achieved without violence and in gentleness.

"I wouldn't say that. What belongs to the sphere of spiritual warfare in personal prayer, in meditation and in solitude is unimaginable and inconceivable. I know because I lived with some sisters who weren't doing well, and I myself have lived through terrible periods. I was sometimes asked to help young sisters, and I was impressed to see that they were able to go through tunnels and painful realities while remaining 'straight' in their prayer before the Blessed Sacrament. That is something that I discovered at the monastery; it connects the spiritual life to the psychological life. All the incidents of our life, all that was disordered in our education, all traumas, all that we have undergone, all of that comes back in a very violent way. There are real storms and sometimes one doesn't even understand what is going on. The life of a monk or a monastic sister consists in accepting to be pierced in her heart in order to be readjusted and set right. One lets oneself be purified in God's crucible. That is something that I now understand with my gaze as a psychologist."

Would you say that God alone can "readjust" a person? Or would it be better to work on oneself before entering the monastery?

"It's difficult to speak in general. I believe that even if we have received help before entering the monastery, the fact remains that we are remade in the crucible of God's love and we must go through anew all that was disordered. All of that comes back when it has to come back, and it's unpredictable. The one thing that is important is that the prioress who helps her sisters never trivialise what is happening.

"She shouldn't say to her sister: 'Everything's fine, you're loved by God.' No, we must, on the contrary, help her to understand that everything that she passed through before entering the monastery will reappear one day. We must let her know that she will have very tough struggles, and that God will ask her to relive everything in His light.

"I would like to add that this is not the prerogative of the monasteries. I've seen in some therapies that life sometimes allows the re-emergence of an old trauma and only later do we understand why it was brought to the surface. The difference is that in a life of silence and solitude, it is impossible to avoid this in-depth work that God asks of us. It consists in undergoing again everything that was lived poorly or negatively in the past. What makes monastic life both great and difficult is that there is no escape. That is perhaps the Cross. When a sister leaves the office of vespers in the evening and enters her cell with an incredible distress and depression, there's no escape. In the world, there are numerous distractions and ways to entertain oneself and to dull one's senses. Life in the monastery is radical and there are no evasions."

With God's help?

"Yes, and with the help of the sisters and of the community that bears all of that and is aware of the suffering even without really knowing about it. I had the experience of seeing sisters turned upside down, sometimes for weeks. One feels it and one perceives it, and yet one knows nothing."

Was your return to 'the world' difficult?

"My reintegration wasn't difficult, but my experience can't be generalized. My departure from the monastery was smooth. Some sisters have to rebuild everything when they leave. For me, everything was already in place. The decision was hard. But once I made the decision, I felt a radical peace that didn't leave me. I had imagined that it would be very hard...but, in fact, it wasn't. My family was accepting, and I gradually reconnected with my friends. The sisters were very generous when I left. I took my time. I met many people. I let the plan to open my own practice mature, because I was determined to resume my work as a psychoanalyst. There was a decisive meeting with the head of the department of child psychopathology at la Salpêtrière. He knew that I was leaving the monastery. Knowing that many parents want to choose the therapist for their child, he encouraged me to settle into private practice."

Love casts out fear

Violaine is twenty-seven years old. She recently got married and is expecting her first child. "I spent a year in the school life at Bet Gemal," she said to me. "I was happy: the absoluteness of that life suited me – everything for God. I was so deeply thirsty, that I thought that my thirst couldn't be quenched anywhere except in an extremeness, in giving everything to God in a life of silence."

After a year, despite her apparent happiness, Violaine could not bring herself to request to receive the habit. Something held her back and pressed her to leave the monastery. "There were things that were not yet settled, and that I didn't want to see, because I wanted to be a monastic sister. I was twenty-two. Life with God didn't scare me, but I felt that there was a desire not only to live an absolute with God but also to run away. My prioress and I decided that I should leave for a few months to work on myself and to see if I had a call from God or if it was my own decision. A big facelift began!"

Violaine moved to Jerusalem, where she began to volunteer as a caregiver in the geriatric ward of a hospital. She then moved to Gaza with an NGO for nine months, and then, with two sisters, she went to Jordan, the land of a future foundation, to make a fresco. When she returned to Jerusalem, she was introduced to making mosaics, which is her current profession. It is a long and painstaking work that corresponds to the work that she was doing interiorly…putting every little part of her life in place. "My interior work has taken longer than expected," she explained. "As the months passed by, I discovered another Violaine whom I didn't know. I realized that I had constructed a part of myself in order to protect myself. Eventually, I realized that I'm always running away. First of all from my family, but also from my friends and from myself. I didn't listen to myself and, above all, I didn't want to become attached to someone. I closed off the access to my deep heart. Coming to this awareness has been very painful."

Wanting to take control of her life and having no work permit, Violaine found a small job as a waitress in a café-restaurant in the Old City where she used to go with friends. "I was coming out of a tough year. I wasn't doing well. I felt weak and I feared that I wouldn't make it in my new job. The owner, Elias, was forty years old, a Palestinian Christian, very discreet even a bit wild. His family, his parents, who were often there always had a very fraternal and respectful attitude. After a month, Elias' father congratulated me for my work, and when I looked at his son, he smiled – a smile that I will remember all my life."

Love at first sight or not... Violaine did not trust her eyes or her heart, and the struggle began all over again. "I was feeling better, and I wanted to enter the monastery. I was just waiting for Jesus to tell me: 'Go! Come back now. Now it's o.k.!' I turned to the Virgin Mary and told her concerning Elias: 'Don't do this to me...it's not at all amusing!'"

Violaine left the restaurant. That was her "Lenten effort!" When she returned at the end of forty days, Elias and Violaine declared their feelings for one other. There were still months of struggle, a return to France and then Violaine let go. "I now no longer feel that I have refused or betrayed a vocation. I wanted to live an absolute, something extreme with God and I thought I couldn't live it anywhere but at the monastery. But I'm now living that with Elias: having a Christian family in today's world is also a kind of absolute. I'm a daughter of Bethlehem, that I know. I will live the vocation of Bethlehem in marriage: our life as a couple is a fruit of Bethlehem."

"I will never be able to thank enough the community of Bet Gemal and the prioress who, by her discernment in the Holy Spirit, helped to lead me to my deepest self and even much further with the sole purpose of setting me free and fully developing my vocation, whatever it might be. Through her tireless support and her presence since I arrived in the Holy Land until now, I've come to experience a free and selfless love, a love that is patient and kind, that does not boast, does not seek its own advantage, a love that does not rejoice at wrongdoing but finds its joy in the truth (1Co 13), a Love that simply tells us of God."

A thread of life

Catherine lived for seventeen years in the monastery, which, when she entered, was not yet a monastery. "When I entered in 1969, we were Dominicans. A few years later, in 1980, Sister Marie proposed that we receive the rule of life of St. Bruno. It was a shift that I understand now, but that I failed to understand at the time. I tried it for a few years, but I think that I was afraid of a future that would lock me into something that I hadn't chosen. The path with Saint Bruno scared me."

It is not easy to enter a community when it is laying its first stones. At birth, Catherine was a premature child... perhaps her story with Bethlehem was also premature.

Catherine, the eldest of three children, was born in a non-practicing Christian family of little faith. Living in a small village in Anjou, she used to visit an old neighbor who spoke in a dialect and took her to church, to the great displeasure of her parents. "One day, in the church, I was about five years old, something very powerful happened: it seemed impossible that I could know Jesus and yet not dedicate my life to Him. My consciousness of God was suddenly connected with the thought of giving myself to Him. Since that day, my desire to become a religious has never left me. I grew up with it, or it grew up with me and when, at the age of eighteen, I announced to my parents that I wanted to enter the convent, my mother slapped me. For my father, it was very hard. I loved my parents…I waited until I was twenty-one to leave them."

Very committed in the Y.C.W. (Young Christian Workers), Catherine was twenty years old in May 1968. "There was a real turn. In June of 1967, I went to a large rally of the Y.C.W. at Le Parc des Princes. We were 80,000 and we listened to Pope Paul VI, who spoke to us via a large screen. One year later, on the same screen, it was the Communist leader Georges Marchais!"

It was in May of 1968, that Catherine discovered the Sisters of Bethlehem when she went for a retreat with her friends from the Y.C.W. at Mery sur Oise. "I had the shock of my life. There was a small church, which was a barn with straw on the floor. I spent a night of adoration with the sisters who were all very young, and I didn't recover from the experience. Afterwards, I came for several short stays, and a year later, I entered. The rupture with my parents was terrible."

Soon, Catherine left Mery to go to the Hautecour en Tarentaise monastery (which the sisters don't have anymore). At Hautecour, there was the "lower house" where about fifteen novices lived, prayed and welcomed the guests. A few kilometres away, at the top of the mountain, there was "the upper house," where several sisters lived a life of solitude and prayer.

"I arrived at Hautecour during a particularly harsh winter. We were very poor and I remember that, that year, we ate only carrots and cheese. We made pottery. It was then that I really discovered the liturgy, prayer and a 'family environment.' After a year, I left for Les MontsVoirons where I discovered another family environment that was about to undergo a big transition. We left the Dominican order and we were 'ourselves.' I really liked those years. The proximity of the Ecumenical Council of Geneva made ecumenism very present in our lives: we lived with Protestant brothers and sisters who came to spend a few months with us. It was also at that time that we began to receive the liturgy of the East, initiated by Michel Evdokimov and Father Bobrinskoï. It wasn't easy for everyone to move from the Dominican liturgy of Father Delalande to the liturgy of the East.

"For me, the small parcel of land where we lived was really the Church. I was deeply struck by the poverty, the attention and the love we had for each other and the prayer of the East which nourished us."

Was that first change difficult?

"No, because for me, monastic life goes together with the desert, the desert goes together with the Fathers of the desert and the Fathers of the desert are the East. That fascinated me, and I read a lot at that time. I devoured entire libraries to find texts from the East and to discover the recesses of the world of the Church of the East – the Coptic church, the Chaldean church, the Armenian church.... It was at Currière where I pursued my research."

And it was at that time also that the "years of Saint Bruno's" began?

"Yes. One of the sisters surely must have told you the story of the Carthusian brother's visit. Then the Church asked us to make choices, to be a graft on an ancient tree trunk. We went to see Lerins, because the Eastern tradition extended to Europe at Lerins. Having previously received the tradition of the East, Honorat and John Cassian lived at Lerins. It was a kind of eastern training ground for "how to live the monastic life." The East was a source of support, and the Carthusians helped us to plunge our roots in something very deep."

Was it then that you left?

"Not immediately. I went to our monastery in Mougères, in order to experience what it was like to live in a charterhouse.

I felt a dichotomy with the East, which had constructed me and educated me. I spent seven years at Mougères, and then I broke down. At that time there had been a deep rupture."

Has it been very hard for you?

"Very hard. Sister Marie cried when I left. I was torn apart, but I also tore apart a family. I had taken my final vows. I was part of a community, and I didn't want to be dispensed of my vows. I could have taken advantage of the fact that the Rule of life had changed between the time that I took my vows and the time that I left. But I never thought of that. One day, I committed myself in a vow of obedience, of poverty, of chastity: I now try to obey the Holy Spirit and to continue on that path."

And your return to the world?

"Awful. I imagine that people who leave prison have the same experience. I didn't get out of jail, but I saw the glances: what's wrong with this woman who doesn't even know how to write a check? I was twenty-one when I entered, and I left when I was thirty-eight. You can imagine all the changes in the world while I was in the monastery. I was very ill at ease. My parents didn't want anything to do with me. All that had been my life at the monastery – fraternal life, an environment of attentive respect and of listening – disappeared and then there was none of that anymore! I tried to take responsibility for my choice."

How did you manage to find a job?

"When I was at Les MontsVoirons, I met a Protestant sister in our ecumenical encounters. She helped me a lot when I left: she was the prioress of the Deaconesses of Reuilly. She helped me to get an apartment and she gave me a job, but more importantly, she was my spiritual mother for years. But she is dead now.

"I started all over again from zero. I began as a hospital attendant and I swept the corridors of the Deaconess Hospital. Then I was a nurse's aid and finally, a nurse. Thanks to that sister, and that is most important thing, I was never afflicted by acedia.

Acedia?

"I never lost the thread that bound me to God. My love for Jesus and the Church is the thread of my life, and I always try to remain faithful to that thread. The deaconess sister encouraged me in that direction. "Look at the landscape of your life before and after Bethlehem," she said to me. 'I am a witness to the faithfulness with which you respond to Jesus.' And it was true."

And now what is your relationship with the community of Bethlehem?

"I had no reason to blame them: I'm the one who left. However, I was very ill at ease with Saint Bruno for years. I held it against him that I had to leave my community because of him. I saw the film 'Into Great Silence' five times and it helped me to reconcile myself with Saint Bruno. After having made a real break with the sisters, and it is essential to do so, I'm once again very close to them. I'm at peace. Whenever I return to Bethlehem, I'm always welcomed with a lot of love. I now see the tree in its fruits. Bethlehem has changed. Some of the older sisters gave their blood. I wasn't loyal like them. Now there are a lot of young sisters who enter."

Are you still working?

"I've been on sick leave for three years. I have a serious health problem that no longer permits me to work. Just before I stopped working, I took advantage of those three years to do a research project on cathedrals because they are places that fascinate me. I'm especially drawn to Amiens and Chartres. Cathedrals are a place where the faith is transmitted. I take groups of young people to visit those cathedrals. There's always the thread of my life that I never let go of."

5

Unto the end

> "Put off your old self, which belongs to your former manner of life and is corrupt through deceitful desires, and be renewed in the spirit of your minds, and put on the new self, created after the likeness of God in true righteousness and holiness." (Ephesians 4: 22-24)

Diseases of the mind, diseases of the body. Those were the first questions I asked myself when my sister entered the monastery. How will she be cared for? Who will take care of her? An elder sister answered this question with common sense: before even treating the sisters who are ill, Sister Marie was careful to recommend a good balance for the health of each of her sisters. There is a wisdom of life not only for the soul but also for the body, a diet adapted to a simple life, a time for physical relaxation, a weekly fraternal walk and physical exercises everyday; all of that has been part of the charism from the beginning. A sedentary life on the one hand, a life marked by asceticism on the other hand: that requires a realism that keeps the body in a wise balance between prudence and self-offering.

The monastic sister who takes care of the sisters who are ill is Italian. A physician by training, a specialist in infectious diseases, she began her monastic life by the "intensive care of her 'old self'!"

"I entered the monastery for God," she told me with an Italian accent and a slightly hoarse voice, "not to be a doctor." For ten years, she began by making a clean break with medicine. She lived a life of solitude, prayer and service during the first stages of her monastic formation. "I've peeled tons of vegetables, worked on construction sites, handled a shovel, painted walls and window frames and I've done a lot of housework. That's my way to relax...that's what I prefer! And in all those little services, I learned to 'love unto the end.' It's all about living a continuous 'I love you.' An 'I love you' to God, to each of my sisters and now to each person that I am called to meet in hospitals or elsewhere. There's a real continuity between the two parts of my monastic life: I always try to go unto the end in all situations, even the most uncredible, to the end of love."

It was very late when we met. She had come from the hospital where she had visited a young monastic sister who was in a sterile room following a transplant. "When I treat a monastic sister, I look at the person in her uniqueness, in her ultimate finality, in her eternal election. She should never be considered only in her illness. If she were reduced to her illness, she would be cut off from the eternal dimension of love. Suffering is always the place where a sister can renew the 'yes' that she pronounced when she entered the monastery."

But why care for the sisters who are ill?

The sister looked at me with astonishment! "Because Christ became incarnate! The body is very important, and it must be given its rightful place. It is through the body that one can perform deeds of love, that we can manifest our love. Love is true when it is concrete. For example, each of us tries to be present to the sister whom I just visited, to express to her all our love. And I make sure that she receives the best care from very competent medical staff. But I also makes sure that her bed is prepared in the right way, that she doesn't lack pillows, that she eats what she needs to eat...all of that is also important.

Initially, in hospitals, they didn't believe that I was a doctor, and I was often asked to present my card of the College of Physicians. I didn't speak French very well and I was humiliated, but all of that did me a lot of good. I entered by the back door. I rediscovered medicine as a service to our family. I'm here, offering this service, as long as the Lord needs me. When He will no longer need me, I'll joyfully return to my cell!"

Do you also speak with the sisters' families?

"Yes, we discuss the sister's case, and it's often very beautiful. I'm always available to talk with the sisters' parents, and we always respect a sister who expresses her deep desire to her superiors, either to be in contact with her parents or about her treatment.

"Sacrifices are a source of joy.... One cannot bear the suffering for another who is ill. It's a moment when she is alone with God. But we can help her. I'm mandated by our family to help those who are sick."

It can't be easy to live as a monastic sister in that context.

"My years of 'intensive care' for my 'former self' have given me the freedom of mind necessary to adjust my life with God in this service that He asks of me. I try to privilege the important moments of community life for the sake of obedience. The moments of contemplative prayer that we have in our cell, I sometimes live them differently: at the bedside of a sister or in the chapel of a hospital between two appointments. I'm first a monastic sister devoted to God and the sister of my sister before being doctor."

6

Message from Father Guy Gilbert[1]

Father Guy Gilbert, you were right to warn me that "the forces of evil are cunningly hidden, but highly efficient."

I remember that little phrase taken from our interview. It was an interview that I had struggled to obtain. I wasn't one of the "good sisters" and, on the phone, I stammered when I asked for an appointment! Your agenda was packed, as usual, and your heart was heavy with the sudden death of one of your teachers at Falcon.

I remember how happy I was to have managed to arrange this appointment, thanks to Brigitte, your very kind assistant.

I remember that my computer was unusually slow that day, and I was a little worried that it might crash during the recording. It didn't, but an incorrect manipulation overwrote our conversation, as they say in computer jargon! Unrecoverable in spite of all the so-called recovery software! I entrusted it to a specialist; he couldn't do anything.

I seized my notes and here's what I still remember:

I remember that it was five o'clock when we met. You were beginning your lunch: lentils with carrots and a small piece of bread!

I remember that you welcomed the monastic sister who accompanied me with extreme gentleness: "And you, my little sister, where do you come from? From which desert?"

I remember that you asked discretion of us. Your desert days with the sisters are rare. Rare but precious. "Without my forty

1. A French priest who devotes his life to helping delinquent youth.

days in the desert, I'd be lost. If I don't close my mouth before Christ once a week, I can't manage."

I remember the seriousness with which you explained to us that "we find God only in silence."

I remember this little phrase: "The radicalism of the monasteries and of prayer is a joy for the Church. It's a sign of God."

I still remember your blessing when we parted. It was a challenging blessing for us, loving and encouraging for this book.

And I remember the final prayer:

"When we don't have time to say a prayer in its entirety, we can simply say: 'Holy Mary, pray for me now and at the hour of my death.' Now and the hour of our death: those are the two most important moments..."

Thank you, dear Father Guy Gilbert.

VII

RETURN TO THE ROOTS

Introduction

At the end of my investigation, I felt the need to go to Rome, to St Peter's Square. It was a return to the roots, to the birthplace of the Sisters of Bethlehem, in order to visit the heart of the universal Church to which they belong.

Let us return to the past. It is November 1st, 1950. Pope Pius XII has just declared the dogma of the Assumption. "We proclaim, declare and define as a divinely revealed dogma, that the Immaculate Mother of God, ever Virgin Mary, after her life on earth, was taken up body and soul, into the Glory of Heaven." Deep silence: one million people kneeling in silence before the mystery. With great rejoicing, the bells ring. There is singing, and the sky of Rome grows dark as thousands of white doves are released. Among the million people, there is a group of French pilgrims, including Sister Marie's parents. Her father recounted what he experienced at that moment: "I understood on that day that the Church's faith in the Assumption of the Virgin Mary was a decisive event in world history. I understood that a human being in the Glory of the Holy Trinity concerns all people in their life on earth, and in their eternal life to come. No one is excluded. And suddenly, your mother and I understood that something was being asked of us. The Lord asked us to give everything and to lose everything, so that the Virgin would not be left alone in the Trinity."

I met many friends and laypersons of Bethlehem. Like those who received from Mary the project of a new monastic family, they also made a commitment to the Virgin to "always try to begin again," without losing heart, to worship and contemplate the Most Holy Trinity. All of them faithfully respond to

Sister Marie's cry: "the Father seeks worshipers."[1] That is why today the sisters of Bethlehem never forget that the intuition of their foundation was born in the heart of laypersons.

I was in Rome on November 27, 2011, the first Sunday of Advent. The weather was glorious when Benedict XVI appeared at his window for the Angelus:

"Let us keep our spiritual dynamism. Our world needs those who keep watch and hope. Let us not wait passively, but let us actively and joyfully engage ourselves in this time of grace by opening our hearts and minds to the light of the Gospel. Following the Virgin Mary, let us watch and pray in awaiting the Lord's Return!"

Standing still beneath the imposing statue of Saint Bruno, I lifted up my gaze. What did he want to say to me in the immensity of St Peter's square? Surely that he loves his brothers and sisters of Bethlehem "more than everything else in the world after God," and he also surely wanted to encourage them to keep vigil in prayer and in hope, awaiting the Lord's Return. I remembered Hugues' words concerning Bethlehem's future: "I would be surprised if Bethlehem were to have one thousand years of security and solitude like the Carthusians. The Carthusians constructed a church, and today we are witnessing that it is in dereliction. The Church as we know it, the monumental church, is about to disappear. We will have to rebuild Christ's Church in a new way. On the one hand, monks will be the last witnesses of the time-honored Church. They will then appear in the fullness of their strength, and they will need a hospitality area for all the crowds who will come seeking meaning in their lives. It seems to me that it will be in the monasteries that this new Church will be born. Bethlehem will have an essential role to play in this resurrection; monks and monastic sisters will need the help of many friends so as not to be overwhelmed. A new sense of hospitality will appear and extend in the years to come, and maybe more rapidly than we might think."

---

1. Jn 4:23.

And there I was, in the heart of the monumental church, amidst a crowd of tourists, pilgrims, and those, perhaps, who are thirsting… In my visits to the monasteries, I had the feeling that I had caught a glimpse of something of the "new Church:" a Church with deep roots, like a beautiful tree, still young, and already solid, but not sheltered from the storms of this world.

Between 1950 and 2012, under the pontifical paternity of Pius XII, John XXIII, Paul VI, John Paul I, John Paul II, and now Benoit XVI, the monks and monastic sisters of Bethlehem have grown in obedience to the Church and in communion with each of those popes. Here, at St Peter's square, how can one not remember John Paul II? How could I not think of all those who spoke about him in our interviews, and of all of those who, near or far, have been touched or even transformed by his presence?

One year before his death, on Pentecost of 2004, the sisters of Bethlehem were united in Rome for their General Chapter. They met with him for the last time, and they received this message from him:

> "Through a humble and audacious fidelity in the silence that marks your hidden life, you are sustained by the prayer of the Virgin Mary. Through your contemplative life, you raise the world to God and remind the people of today to make time in life for silence and prayer. May St Bruno, tireless custodian of the Kingdom to come, obtain that you remain vigilant in prayer, keeping 'watch, holy and persevering, as you wait for the return of the Master, to open to him as soon as he knocks'[1] In particular, I invite your monastic Family, whose title bears the name of Bethlehem, the birthplace of the Emmanuel, to intensify its prayers for the Near East, imploring the Lord to grant the grace of peace and reconciliation to all the inhabitants of this region, battered by violence. With all my heart I willingly impart to you an affectionate Apostolic Blessing, which I extend to all the sisters of your Monastic Family, to the members of the male branch and to all those who are close to you."

1. Letter from Saint Bruno to Raoul, number 4.

1

Interview with Cardinal Antonelli

Cardinal Ennio Antonelli (president emeritus of the pontifical Council for families) was close to John Paul II. Bishop of Gubbio, and then Archbishop of the metropolitan diocese of Perouse, he met Sister Marie and the communities of the brothers and sisters of the monastic Family of Bethlehem in 1982.

In 1976, several men received the call to leave everything, and to form a community in the desert, according to the charism of the sisters of Bethlehem. On October 6, 1976, the feast of St Bruno, the first brothers received the monastic habit, in the oratory of Our Lady of Casalibus, place of the first monastery that St Bruno founded in the mountains of the Chartreuse. The newborn community of the brothers was first established in buildings, given by the sisters, next to their monastery of Currière-en-Chartreuse, in the diocese of Grenoble.

First established as a monastic "Pia Unio" by Monseigneur Matagrin, Bishop of Grenoble, Bishop Antonelli then granted the brothers recognition by diocesan right, and he became a real father for the community. Afterwards, the brothers went to the monastery of Monte Corona in the diocese of Perugia, Italy, and in 1986, Bishop Antonelli became their canonical superior. He explained:

"During the entire time that I was archbishop of Perouse, I participated several times in the brothers' liturgical celebrations. I also spent a few days with them to share in their life. It was an opportunity for me to have informal encounters with the community, and also to have more personal visits with each of the brothers.

"Right from the beginning, three things struck me: their poverty, their fraternal love and their joy. I had never met a community that lived so deeply in poverty, fraternal love and joy.

"Joy on earth comes from a joy that is born from the cross and from self-denial, and that's what I saw among the brothers and sisters of Bethlehem. When we experience sacrifices and poverty as a gift of ourselves, that doesn't engender sadness. We should understand that the deepest joy can be found in the biggest sacrifices. They aren't contradictory. St Paul says: 'With all our affliction, I am overjoyed.'[1]

"When we give ourselves, even if it costs a lot, it brings the joy of the gift of self, which is the joy of the Three Divine Persons. Jesus says in the Acts of the Apostles: 'It is more blessed to give than to receive.'[2] We are created for joy, for happiness, but on earth we won't ever find it in its purity and totality. Here below, it's always mixed with sacrifice, with death, with self-denial. But we can already see deep joy on earth, which is an anticipation of eternal life, and which is expressed in a mutual gift of self.

"I would also like to bear witness, because I saw it in the two dioceses, to the fact that their monasteries are like 'living Gospels' that touch people by their prayer, of course, but also simply by the fact that they exist, by their presence. The communities in Perugia and Gubbio make people think and they are impressed by their contemplative life."

In 1995, Bishop Antonelli became the General Secretary of the Italian Episcopal Conference, and regularly visited Rome, where he worked with the Congregation of Consecrated Life, to obtain approbation for the monastic family as an institute of pontifical right.

---

1. 2 Co 7:4
2. Ac 20:35

"There were no difficulties for the sisters, because they were already numerous. But it was more complicated for the brothers, because they were less numerous. I pleaded the case before Monseigneur Errazurriz, secretary of the Congregation of Institutes for Consecrated Life, that the brothers and sisters of Bethlehem might be recognized together, as one family, because they share the same spirituality, and their constitutions are almost identical. And so, on October 6, 1998, the monastic family of Bethlehem was recognized by pontifical right in a decree approved by His Holiness John Paul II."[1]

It was then that I discovered and studied the Constitutions of this Family, and to tell the truth, I had never read such beautiful Constitutions. There is a rare spiritual wealth, not only norms and rules. It is a beautiful Trinitarian and Marian spirituality, in the heart of the church: a calling to live with Mary in the heart of the Trinity. We must understand that it is something supernatural, but also very concrete. Mary, in her everyday life in Bethlehem, lived with one of the Persons of the Trinity: the Son of God made man. She was therefore living in the heart of the Trinity. What she lived by anticipation, she now lives in plenitude. Others, like the brothers and sisters of Bethlehem, can participate in Mary's experience, in spite of their human poverty. And it is extremely beautiful, when it is lived in harmony with and obedience to the Church. I was deeply struck by this monastic Family's obedience to the Church.

---

1. The government of the brothers and sisters is distinct, however, the general prior and prioress meet regularly. "The Family Council," composed of the two respective Councils, also comes together regularly to listen to the Holy Spirit and to seek how to incarnate more faithfully Bethlehem's charism. Their unity is constitutive of the vocation of the Family of Bethlehem in the Church. "The collaboration of male and female religious, with respect to their specific vocation, is very important in today's world" (Benedict XVI). There are approximately forty brothers with several postulants and they inhabit three monasteries: Currière-en-Chartreuse, in Italy and in the Holy Land. To earn their bread, they have various workshops where they try to express by their hands what their mouths do not preach: they work with leather, metal and ceramics, and they also make incense and candles.

Obedience, even in the heart of the Church, isn't always clear for certain communities.

"That's true, since some no longer see their superiors, those who command and those who have authority with a gaze of faith. It's not a question of obeying a man or a woman, but of obeying God. When we kiss a bishop's ring, we don't give homage to a person but to Christ the Pastor, the Bridegroom of the Church. Christ is present in the Church. If we lose the gaze of faith, obedience becomes impossible, and we can't understand why we should bow down before certain people. Many people have lost the gaze of faith upon the Church, and they see the Church as the work of society and of believers. It's a sociological perspective on the Church, which is partial and incomplete. It's false. The Church is the work of Christ in the Holy Spirit. The Church is a Sacrament. The Church is a visibility of the invisible; its center and model is the Eucharist. The Eucharist is the visible part of what is invisible. But I would like to return, for one minute, to the community of Bethlehem, to express another important point. When I visited the brothers and sisters in the Holy Land, and also in Jordan, I was moved by their icons, which speak to us about the other world. Through their art, the monks and monastic sisters express their experience of God and of the supernatural world. Paul VI said that "beauty is what now evangelizes." In Bethlehem's art, there is a force of questioning that is very beautiful… It's the beauty of art and the beauty of holiness. Not that the brothers and sisters are holy, in the sense of being perfect, but they willingly strive for holiness. In that sense, this community is a sign of God and of His Presence."

Monseigneur Ennio Antonelli was named archbishop of Florence in 2001. He was made cardinal in 2003, and was president of pontifical Council for the family from 2008 to 2012.

2

Who could leave the Virgin all alone?

After leaving Cardinal Antonelli, I walked about in Rome.

Earlier, I had met with a sister from Italy. She had been a student in architecture in the Italian capital, and she told me that she "tried to hear God's secret in stones." She pursued: "I entered all the churches and all the cathedrals. One day the light came: in the morning I was an architect, and in the evening I was a monastic sister in a cloister! In fact, the only architecture I was interested in was that of heaven."

This sister, who had grown up in the village of Como lake in a family of believers let the Lord gently guide her. Her path began at the age of fifteen, during a "decisive" night in a monastery in Umbria…it was an entire night of adoration of Jesus "hidden in the tabernacle." A few years later, in Lourdes, when she was still a student, she explained to me that she "could have passed through fire to go to the grotto." She spent the whole night there. "It was a night as decisive as when she was fifteen. There I heard the call; Jesus said to me: "do you want to give Me everything?"

"My parents were very moved when I shared my decision with them. They lived it in a very deep joy; it was a grace for our family to give a child to the Lord. I now live in the monastery of Monte Camporeggiano."

During our conversation, Cardinal Antonelli had spoken about the Constitutions of the monastic family of Bethlehem. The Italian sister had worked on the Rule of life with deep humility.

"Not long after my first profession, I spent two incredible years close to Sister Marie and a small team of sisters, writing the Rule of life. They were two very intense years, like a concentrated noviciate during which I received a lot. I spent my nights typing on the computer what the sisters had written during the day. The Rule of life is like a code of conduct or the rules of the road… It isn't a constraint. Quite the contrary. It's a Rule that protects us and that amplifies the choice of love that we have made. It's a Rule of love, and it appeals to our freedom in the deepest way. It helps us to understand and to enter into the plan of love that God has for each one of us. During those two years, I discovered the charism in its depth. And I discovered our call to live intensely in adoration and prayer in relationship with the glorified Virgin."

Like an echo of what the Cardinal had said, she ended our conversation by saying in confidence: "We can't leave the Virgin Mary all alone in the Trinity."

Bethlehem-Jerusalem, from the desert to the city

While there are many who wonder about the link between the three names of the family of Bethlehem, one can easily guess that the Virgin Mary is the mysterious link between Bethlehem and the Assumption and we could try to look at "the birth" on earth as in heaven. Birth on earth of the Child Jesus in Bethlehem, birth into Heaven of the Virgin Mary in her glorious Assumption.
Father Daniel Ange, who is always in a very visionary movement, has spoken of the "Bethlehem of Mary":
"The co-existence of the two words, Bethlehem and the Assumption, is surprising on the surface and at the same time it is essentially the same mystery, although there appears to be no direct link. Jesus receives His Mother into heaven with her body, because His Mother in Bethlehem received God in her body. She gave her body to God. And the Assumption is "the Bethlehem" of Mary, her birth in Heaven, her birth in the Kingdom, she who gave birth to God in Bethlehem. We always speak about the heavenly Jerusalem, but perhaps we could speak as well about the heavenly Bethlehem because, like Mary, in the footsteps of Her son, we will be in a state of continual birth after our period of gestation on earth.
As for St. Bruno, the third name of the Family, he gives his wisdom of life to enable the Family of Bethlehem to be born and reborn with Jesus, with Mary, 'on earth as in heaven'."

"Earthly Bethlehem, celestial Bethlehem", this audacious expression of Daniel Ange finds a startling resonance in the 2011 Christmas homily of Sister Isabelle to her sisters, a homily that speaks also to the Little Prince we all have inside...

And so, who are they, and from whence do they come, the billions of creatures who have been dancing since the beginning of time in created spaces and no longer in infinity, to the rhythm of time and no longer to the rhythm of eternity? Angels and human beings shaped from the clay of incorruptibility, crowned with royalty, servants and princes of a cosmos clothed with beauty. Living beings, images bearing the imprint of their origin from divine hands, inchoative resemblance on the verge of vibrating to the life of the uncreated Light of Love, so small and finite, yet immense in the end to which they are called.

If you want to know more, let the gaze of your faith pierce what is a night of mysterious incoherence for your limited intelligence. Enter, penetrate the secret, and you will see the divine Goodness open its perfect immensity in an enormous rupture from which flows a river of stars impossible to count, of mountains, hills, seas, streams and the entire procession of the created world which would be too long to list.

Yes, it is true, you will see the divine Goodness offer itself in an enormous opening of the heart, in an outpouring of an immense crowd burning with thirst to love and to be loved. Remember that in the infinite deserts of divine gratuitousness, multitudes of free wills are chosen and then created in the only Beloved – free wills incorporeal and human, angels and archangels, men and women, young people and elderly, blacks and Caucasians, gold and copper, humanity surrendered to the nobility of its will, of its choice of Love always in necessity of being born and reborn.

It is true that the mystery of evil came to wound this angelic and human beauty, but immediately the divine Affability stooped down to its creature. And God still stoops down to the *chef-d'œuvre* of his Goodness without ever growing weary. He "looks down from heaven upon the children of men to see if there are any that act wisely" (psalm 13). He listens to the stifled cries of thirst. He hears the clamor that is enclosed in the noise of lies and illusions. He sees the misery of his people who are so beautiful. His gaze searches the tears of his beloved people who have been wounded, though never deprived of beauty.

Have we taken notice of the succession of deserts that we have crossed? We have crossed one desert after another. From the desert of eternity to the desert of Judah. And behold: Someone is coming to cross the breadth of your thirsty heart and to make of it a desert: a desert of endless love. It is You, Jesus.

Today You say to me: "Do you know that you are vaster than the heavens! My littleness made yours burst open. Today, I, the Little Child, I make you a little less than a god."

Today, as on the day of the Nativity in Bethlehem, you can let Love speak to you, because He speaks to you with the language of a Newborn. John Paul II the blessed wrote in a poem when he was still Karol: "One day, love explained everything to me." But no, it is not the day to ask oneself what Love is, it is rather the day to let Love teach us. It is the day to let the Newborn speak to us in the silence of his infancy, from the horizons without disturbance of his eternal Love. Like Mary, it is the day to keep it in the secret of her maternal innocence. Yes, He is going to explain everything to us: what and who.

A Newborn, without speech, comes to tell us of the eternal Fatherhood, because only a Little Child can speak of Another who is infinitely powerful, tenderly loving and tenderly loved – He is a Father! Yes, He had to become "infans" to show us the Father in the silence of his transparency. Who sees Me sees the Father. To see who Jesus is is to see the invisible and hidden Father. It is to see Love as a spring of water and to drink at this spring and to burn with this Love, like those who are thirsty.

Today, Jesus comes to reveal to me the "measurelessness" of the Father, of his inexhaustible Goodness, of his Fatherhood without interruption, of his forgotten Love that is once again revealed. Jesus comes today to expand the dimensions of my being. An immensity where I lose myself because He dwells there. My littleness and his immensity meet in an ineffable encounter of Love; and in this encounter, they will make of me what I really am because He will be what He really is. He comes to make of my limited being, of my calculating heart a great and bottomless opening filled with his gratuitousness.

And Jesus says to you: "To follow Me, to renounce everything, to lose everything, that does not mean that you have to deprive yourself of your beautiful humanity, and you certainly do not need to be frustrated. It means that you have to lose yourself in the Love of a forgotten and rediscovered Father who makes you stand upright on the solid ground of the Life of Light and of Love of the divine Fatherhood.

Let us remind ourselves that this Love beyond all, for which God chose you and created you, is revealed today in the little Child who is vaster than the heavens. This Love cannot be explained if you yourself do not dare to commit yourself and remain in the succession of deserts, from the desert of eternity to the desert of my heart which is inhabited, burst open and burned in passing by the desert of the heart of Mary, who gives birth in the desert of Judah.

Hide yourself in the silence of solitude of infinite love. Dare "to go out of yourself by the hidden door" (Saint John of the Cross), without being seen by yourself. Go out, go straight ahead into the desert, to the cleft in the rock, to encounter and to be filled by the immeasurable Fatherhood, because Jesus and his Spirit have set you ablaze.

We have understood that one lives this adventure from Bethlehem to Golgotha. It is a struggle against oneself where the Beloved Son, today a Newborn, a pyromaniac of Love on this frozen earth, precedes us in the solitude of the One who was abandoned, to offer us to the Father in pure gratuitousness.

And if it is said that a new Jerusalem is being prepared, a city that comes from Heaven, why not imagine that its coming will be preceded by a new Bethlehem, the city of monks? A new Bethlehem, city of monks in the desert, of poor creatures seeking deeper resemblance to the greatest Love, city of Love in the desert that prepares a new era with all the giants of Love hidden in the innumerable deserts of humanity: the deserts of suffering, of hunger, of violence, of exclusion, of shame, deserts of isolation, injustice, deserts where the humble prepare to reign over the world, where the meek already possess the earth, where the poor appropriate the Kingdom.

Today, why not construct the new Bethlehem of tomorrow and of yesterday, the Bethlehem of forever, the Bethlehem which, from the beginning of time, populated these regions which resemble the infinity of God, even though they are limited? And why shouldn't this Bethlehem be the Woman of the Book of Revelation who flees to the desert, as at the time of the grotto in Bethlehem of Judah, to give birth, in the end times, to the male Child who will be taken up to the Father and to his throne? By giving birth, and at the cost of a gratuitous Love, of a Love totally surrendered, she makes the New Jerusalem descend, the whole Christ, the mystical Body containing the entire universe.

Bethlehem preceded Jerusalem in the history of the New Covenant of the Incarnation, but is it a question only of history, of a thread that unravels in time and which we celebrate today? Bethlehem preceded Jerusalem in the history of the New

Covenant, but why not – since Bethlehem continues in the present and touches eternity – once again, at the end of time, now? For the desert precedes the city to become one with it in the New Heavens of the New Earth.

With Mary, the new Eve and Mother of God, come, let us adore Him.

Jerusalem, Christmas 2011.
Sister Isabelle, Monastic Sister of Bethlehem.

Acknowledgements

A phrase by André Chouraqui, which his wife Annette shared with me during our conversation in Jerusalem, stayed with me while I wrote this book: "We say that we are waiting for the Messiah, but it is the Messiah who is waiting for us." That's the real question: whoever we may be, do we respond to his waiting?

He is waiting for us to recognize Him and to love Him as He loves us. Monks and monastic sisters respond to his waiting with all their heart, their soul and their strength. They remain ready; they keep vigil with the world and for the world for "you know neither the day nor the hour."[1] And what if tomorrow were the great day of his return?

Dostoevsky says that "monks are not apart from us, but only what every man should be." In the end, I'm not sure that there's a lot to understand of the lives of monks and monastic sisters. It's more a matter of consenting to recognize and accept their lives, which exceed ours. It is, with them, to take seriously this question: "Will He find us when He returns?"

I cannot complete this book without thanking Sister Isabelle who trusted me and who, with great respect, helped me in my work, my doubts and my discouragement.

I would also like to thank my sister and, with her, all the sisters of Bethlehem. Those whom I met with and who had the kindness to tell me their stories and the patience to listen to my questions. Those who, in silence, accompanied me in my work by their prayer. I know that without them, I wouldn't have written a single sentence.

1. Mt 25:13

I would like to thank all the people whom I met with during my research. They helped me to find the hidden Treasure…the Love forgotten by the world.

I would like to thank Chantal Delsol in particular who, by her exactingness, helped me a great deal in my manner to reflect on my questions.

I would like to thank my editor, Christophe Rémond, who welcomed my work and enriched it by his advice.

I would like to thank Marie-Claire, Ivana, Nathalie, Hedwige and Genevieve for their precious criticism.

And finally, I cannot forget Richard and our children, Alexis, Clément, Pia, Yvanna and Juliette who, for one year, allowed me to live the life of a monastic sister…or almost!

ANNEXE

CONGREGAZIONE
PER GLI ISTITUTI DI VITA CONSACRATA
E LE SOCIETÀ DI VITA APOSTOLICA
DECREE

The "Monastic Family of Bethlehem, of the Assumption of the Virgin and of Saint Bruno" is composed of a branch of monks and a branch of monastic sisters. Both mother houses are in Currière-en-Chartreuse, in the diocese of Grenoble, France. This Monastic Family came into existence on November 1, 1950 thanks to several pilgrims who listened attentively to the voice of Pope Pius XII as he proclaimed the Church's faith in the Assumption of the Mother of God, taken up body and soul into the communion of the infinite Light and Love of the Most Holy Trinity.

The members of this Monastic Family receive the call to let their whole lives be drawn by Christ, ascended from the earth into the Glory of the Father. With Mary, who gave birth to Emmanuel at Bethlehem, stood by the Cross, and is now glorified forevermore, these monks and monastic sisters are called to live "hidden with Christ in God." Following the monastic tradition they strive to stand, "holy and immaculate in Love," overshadowed by the Holy Spirit, with the crucified and glorified Lord Jesus, in the presence of the Father. Choosing to follow the example of the Virgin Mary who was progressively drawn by her Son into the Glory of the Father's Love, they seek to fulfil in their humble human condition day after day the Father's Will on earth as in heaven. On receiving this call, the members of the nascent community committed themselves to reserving for the glorified Virgin Mary the title and function of Prioress and of Foundress of their Monastic Family. Thus they would exercise governance only by constantly and humbly begging the grace to fulfil, with Jesus and Mary, every Will of the Father.

They devote themselves to listening assiduously to the Word of God and to prayer of the heart in a life of solitude, silence, liturgical and fraternal communion, obedience and humble manual work. In order to be faithful to this vocation they receive the twofold monastic tradition of East and West. They are disciples of Saint Bruno, receiving his spiritual fatherhood and wisdom of life. With him they are trained in the school

CONGREGAZIONE
PER GLI ISTITUTI DI VITA CONSACRATA
E LE SOCIETÀ DI VITA APOSTOLICA

Prot. n. G. 115-1/89
Prot. n. P. 209-1/97

DÉCRET

La *"Famille monastique de Bethléem, de l'Assomption de la Vierge et de Saint Bruno"* est composée d'une branche de moines et d'une branche de moniales. Les deux maisons généralices se trouvent respectivement dans l'archidiocèse de Pérouse et dans le diocèse de Gubbio, et les deux maisons-mères se trouvent à Currière-en-Chartreuse, dans le diocèse de Grenoble. Cette Famille monastique est née le 1er Novembre 1950 de l'écoute spirituelle attentive offerte par quelques pèlerins à la voix du Pape Pie XII à l'heure où il proclamait la Foi de l'Eglise en l'élévation de la Mère de Dieu, en son corps et en son âme, dans la Communion de Lumière et d'Amour infinis de la Très Sainte Trinité.

Les membres de cette Famille monastique reçoivent l'appel à se laisser attirer en toute leur vie par le Christ élevé de terre dans la gloire du Père. Avec Marie enfantant l'Emmanuel à Bethléem, se tenant auprès de la Croix, puis glorifiée à jamais, ces moines et ces moniales sont appelés à demeurer "cachés avec le Christ en Dieu". Selon la tradition du monachisme, ils s'efforcent de se tenir, sous l'ombre de l'Esprit-Saint, avec Jésus crucifié glorifié, en présence du Père, "saints et immaculés dans l'Amour". À l'exemple de la Vierge Marie qui est progressivement attirée par son Fils dans la Gloire d'Amour du Père, ils veulent, selon l'humble condition des hommes, vivre en accomplissant jour après jour la Volonté du Père sur la terre comme au ciel.

En recevant cette vocation, les membres de la communauté naissante se sont engagés dès l'origine à toujours réserver à la Vierge Marie glorifiée le titre et la fonction de Prieure et de Fondatrice de leur Famille monastique, et à n'exercer le gouvernement qu'en humble mendicité et accomplissement, avec le Christ et avec elle, de toute Volonté du Père.

Ils s'adonnent à l'écoute assidue de la Parole de Dieu et à l'oraison du coeur en une vie de solitude, de silence, de communion liturgique et fraternelle, d'obéissance et d'humble travail. Pour être fidèles à cet appel, ils reçoivent la double tradition du monachisme oriental et occidental. Ils sont disciples de saint Bruno. Ils reçoivent sa paternité et sa sagesse de vie. Avec lui ils sont à l'école de la "Divine Philosophie", c'est-à-dire de Jésus, Sagesse éternelle du Père. Ils montent une garde sainte en attente du retour du Seigneur.

Leur vie est donc entièrement ordonnée à la divine contemplation, dans le plus grand amour des Personnes Divines et des personnes humaines. De toutes leurs forces ils coopèrent à l'accomplissement du Projet de Dieu posé sur chaque personne humaine libre: Que chacune soit image de Dieu. Que sa vie soit ressemblante à la Vie de Lumière et d'Amour infinis des Personnes Divines.

La branche des moniales fut érigée de droit diocésain le 24 juin 1986 et celle des moines le 25 mars 1992.

Cette Famille monastique s'étant aujourd'hui beaucoup agrandi et répandue dans plusieurs diocèses, sa Sainteté Jean-Paul II, après avis favorable de la Congrégation pour les Instituts de vie consacrée et les Sociétés de vie apostolique, a bien voulu donner son assentiment à la demande du Prieur des moines: Frère Patrick Gilbert, et de la Prieure des moniales: Soeur Marie Dupont, pour que cette Famille monastique soit reconnue de droit pontifical.

Par le présent Décret, cette même Congrégation déclare donc que la *Famille monastique de Bethléem, de l'Assomption de la Vierge et de Saint Bruno* est un Institut religieux de droit pontifical *en ses deux branches de moines et de moniales*, et qu'elle doit être reconnue ainsi par tous. La branche des moines est cléricale.

Le Dicastère, en outre, *approuve en forme spécifique et confirme "pour dix ans, ad experimentum"*, les articles du texte français des Constitutions rédigés "en grosses lettres", dont un exemplaire est conservé dans ses archives. Les autres articles du texte sont approuvés en forme générique.

Nonobstant toutes choses contraires.

Du Vatican, le 6 octobre 1998, fête de Saint Bruno

Eduardo Cardinal Martínez Somalo
Préfet

+ Piergiorgio Silvano Nesti, C.P.
Secrétaire

of "Divine Philosophy," which is Jesus Himself, the eternal Wisdom of the Father. They keep a holy watch awaiting the return of their Lord. Their life, then, is entirely ordered to divine contemplation and the greatest possible love for the Divine Persons and for all human persons.

Since this Monastic Family has grown considerably and is now present in several dioceses, His Holiness John Paul II, after having received a favorable notice from the Congregation for Institutes of Consecrated Life and Societies of Apostolic Life, was pleased to consent to the request made by the Prior of the monks, Brother Patrick Gilbert, and by the Prioress of the monastic sisters, Sister Marie Dupont, that this Monastic Family be recognized as being of pontifical right.

By the present Decree, this same Congregation declares, therefore, that The Monastic Family of Bethlehem, of the Assumption of the Virgin and of Saint Bruno is a religious Institute of pontifical right in its two branches of monks and monastic sisters and that it must be recognized as such by all. The branch of monks is clerical.

Furthermore, the Dicastery, approves in specific form and confirms "for 10 years ad experimentum" the sections of the French text of the Constitution written "in large letters" a copy of which is retained in its archives. The other articles of the text are approved in generic form.

Notwithstanding anything to the contrary.

From the Vatican, October 6, 1998, Feast of Saint Bruno.

Piergiorgio Silvano Nesti, C.P. – Secretary
Eduardo Cardinal Martinez Somalo – Prefect

Bibliography

Philippe Barbarin et Luc Ferry, *Quel avenir pour le christianisme*, Salvator, 2009.
Bertrand de Boissière, *Maurice Zundel*, Presses de la renaissance, 2009.
Christian Chabanis, *Obsession de Dieu*, DDB, 1990.
André Chouraqui, *L'amour fort comme la mort. Une autobiographie*, Le Rocher, 1998.
–, *Chercherai-je un autre Dieu que Dieu*, DDB, 2011.
Didier Decoin, *Les sentinelles de lumière*, DDB, 2009.
Chantal Delsol, *L'Âge du renoncement*, Cerf, 2011.
Guy Gilbert, *Éveilleur d'espérance*, Philippe Rey, 2011.
Les Frères Jaccard, *Mission impossible sans Lui*, Le Livre ouvert, 2011.
Isabelle Jarry, *L'archange perdu*, Folio Gallimard, 1996.
Patrick de Laubier, *Quand l'histoire a un sens – À la lumière de l'Apocalypse*, Salvator, 2009.
–, *L'eschatologie,* PUF « Que sais-je », 1998.
–, *Le temps de la fin des temps. Essai sur l'eschatologie chrétienne*, F.X.de Guibert, 1979.
Brigitte Peltier, *Père Bernard Quinquet. La tendresse de Dieu*, Éditions Pippa, 2006.
Bernard Peyrous, *Des saints au XXe siècle. Pourquoi ?*, Ed. Emmanuel, 2005.
Premiers Frères chartreux, *Des étincelles sur la neige,* Cerf, 1999.
André Ravier, *Saint Bruno le Chartreux*, Lethielleux, 2003.
Dominique Rey et Fabrice Hadjadj, *L'héritage et la promesse,* Ed. RCF Méditerranée, 2011.
François Sureau, *Inigo*, Gallimard, 2010.
–, *Sans bruit sans trace*, Gallimard, 2011.
Une moniale, *Le petit cyprès*, illustrations par Agathe FSM.

Table of contents

IV
THE MOST BEAUTIFUL OF THE CHILDREN OF MEN

V
RENDEZ-VOUS IN THE PROMISED LAND

VI
COME AND SEE

VII
RETURN TO THE ROOTS